ASSURING FREEDOM TO THE FREE

A Century of Emancipation in the USA

ARNOLD M. ROSE, editor
University of Minnesota

with an introduction by the honorable
LYNDON B. JOHNSON
president of the United States

Detroit, 1964 • Wayne State University Press

For permission to quote from copyrighted material, acknowledgment is made to the publishers of The Crisis, in which John Hope Franklin's essay, "The Emancipation Proclamation, 1863-1963," originally appeared; to W.E.B. Du Bois, author of "Litany of Atlanta," in Darkwater (1920); and to Viking Press, Inc., publishers of James Weldon Johnson, Along This Way (1933).

Grateful acknowledgment is made to the MC GREGOR FUND of Detroit for financial assistance in the publication of this book.

CONTENTS

PREFACE

The Emancipation Proclamation
in Historical Perspective

THE EMANCIPATION PROCLAMATION was formally issued on January 1, 1863, three-quarters of a century too late to save the United States from the problems of race relations which have beset its entire history as a nation. In the first draft of the Declaration of Independence, Thomas Jefferson included a provision to abolish slavery immediately in the rebellious colonies. Had this point of view prevailed, the new-born country would have saved itself, not only a tragic civil war, but many not-less-tragic political and social problems before and since. In 1776 Georgia and the Carolinas were jealous of Virginia's eminence and wealth, which they attributed to slavery; and they insisted on the deletion of this early emancipation proclamation so that they might also benefit economically from slavery. The other states did not care enough about the issue to overcome their narrow perspective.

As a matter of fact, if there had been no American

1

Revolution, slavery would probably have ceased to exist in what became the United States, for in 1833 the British Parliament passed an act which wiped out slavery throughout its territories and possessions. This act probably saved the British Empire for a century, for the adjustments attending required manumission were minor compared to what the United States later had to face. The United States had a second chance to eliminate slavery peacefully when Congress passed a law in 1808 outlawing further importation of slaves. The southern states ignored the law, and with the aid of New England sea captains, smuggled slaves into the country at an ever-increasing rate. It is estimated that as many Negroes were illegally imported into the country between 1809 and 1861 as had been legally brought in during the two preceding centuries. Slavery would have gradually died out if that law had been enforced, but again the nation could not gain an historical perspective, and allowed the smuggling of human cargo. The South had by then attached itself to a cotton economy more dependent on slavery than had been earlier types of production. This brought it great wealth, but also moral and political problems and eventual holocaust.

Even when the nation was beset by the Civil War, it still did not move toward emancipation with a single mind. Aside from the South, for which the maintenance of slavery was one of the war's goals, the rest of the nation still could not clearly see that its future could not tolerate a continuation of slavery. By then, most of the civilized nations of the world—the few exceptions being some of the South American nations—had abolished slavery. The leaders of the Democratic party in the early 1860's did not favor emancipation, and President Lincoln led a minority faction within his Republican party seeking to gradualize the end of the primitive institution. While Lincoln procrastinated, some of his generals issued their own local emancipation proclamations. Military and economic considerations, as well as political pressures, finally forced Lincoln to issue the Proclamation, which abolished slavery in the rebellious states; and the loyal slave states soon thereafter adopted plans for compensated manumission.

Even after military defeat, much of the South did not acquiesce in the end of slavery, and reinstituted it on a *de facto* basis when the North turned its attentions elsewhere after 1876. By the 1890's the condition of the Negro in the South was, for the most part, worse than it had been under eighteenth-century slavery. Emancipation was the law, but in no sense—legal, political, economic, or social—was it enforced. The South systematically violated it, and the North ignored what was going on in the South.

A minority of Negroes began pulling themselves up by their own efforts in the early part of the twentieth century; and they were aided by impersonal social forces, such as the demand for cheap industrial labor in the North beginning with the First World War. But there was no emancipation of the masses of southern Negroes until the 1940's; in fact, there was a considerable amount of peonage in the South not greatly different from slavery right into the 1930's, and in the North a majority of Negro adult males were unemployed.

Then a complex combination of events recommenced the work, that had been laid aside in the 1870's, of truly emancipating the ex-slaves. The granting of political and legal rights, and economic and social opportunities, began to be forced on the South—not by the North but by events. Some of the southerners resisted, motivated now by race prejudice rather than by economic advantage, and the struggle is by no means over. But it can truly be reported, in this year of the one hundredth anniversary celebration of Emancipation Proclamation, that emancipation is increasingly a reality. The United States is almost ready to treat its citizens with legal equality, the South is almost ready to rejoin the Union, and racial discrimination throughout the nation is markedly diminishing. Even if Lincoln's Proclamation was reluctantly promulgated and scarcely enforced, the Supreme Court, the Presidency, and the Congress of today are finally enunciating an effective Emancipation Proclamation.

Thus, we do more than celebrate a centenary: We mark the beginning of a new era in which emancipation will be a fact. We announce that Negroes are finally full citizens of the United States, and that this nation, finally divested of its primitive institution, has about solved the most serious social problem of its history.

Many organizations and institutions throughout the United States have recognized and celebrated the centenary of the Emancipation Proclamation, but none I believe has taken the celebration so seriously as has Wayne State University. Located in the large northern industrial city of Detroit, which has had a great influx of southern whites and Negroes over several decades, Wayne State University represents in its student body and faculty the integration of the races in the American future. With the aid of a grant from the McGregor Fund of Detroit, University officials conceived of the celebration of the Emancipation Proclamation as a year-long event, having international as well as national implications.

A faculty-staff committee, chaired by President Clarence B. Hilberry and staffed by Hubert G. Locke, was set up early in 1962. This included Harold A. Basilius, Mark N. Beach, Lee Benson, Broadus N. Butler, Juanita Collier, John Dorsey, Winfred A. Harbison, Ronald W. Haughton, Alfred H. Kelly, Charles W. Quick, Victor A. Rapport, and Hamilton G. Stillwell. They asked Gunnar Myrdal to be Honorary Chairman. John Hope Franklin and I were asked to be functioning co-chairmen of the events. Further, I was asked to edit a selection of the scholarly contributions for publication.

4

Needless to say, only a portion of the centennial program could be included in the paper of the present volume. The selection had to be made by the editor and by the publisher mainly in terms of relevance to a single theme. That theme was expressed in the title chosen for the book, a phrase of Abraham Lincoln's, "assuring freedom to the free." It was essentially the social science aspect—defined broadly—of the year-long celebration which was to be preserved in this centennial celebration volume. It was essential that the contributions be sufficiently scholarly, innovative, and mutually coherent for the volume to make its own mark.

I am grateful to all those named in this Preface and in the following calendar of events for indicated help which made the volume possible, singling out for special appreciation President Clarence B. Hilberry, Secretary Hubert G. Locke, and Publisher Harold A. Basilius for the guidance and aid necessary for the presentation of this volume and of the extensive public program which underlies it. Finally, it must be said that it is to the everlasting credit of Wayne State University that it could host such a creditable program and of the citizens of the Detroit area that they could attend and absorb it.

May 1963   ARNOLD M. ROSE
                                           University of Minnesota

THE EMANCIPATION
CENTENNIAL
1863-1963

Anniversary Celebration of
The Emancipation Proclamation
Presented by Wayne State University

Theme: The Development of the American Negro and of
   a Free Society

Preliminary Inauguration of the Emancipation Centennial
                                           September 24, 1962
   Presentations by Clarence B. Hilberry, *President,*
   Wayne State University; Governor John M. Swainson,
   Dr. Broadus N. Butler; and Professor Arnold M. Rose

Inaugural Centennial Convocation   *January 6, 1963*
   Address by Lyndon B. Johnson, *President of the United*
   States

An Evening with Langston Hughes   *January 9, 1963*

"The New Scene in American Literature"   Professor
   Nathan A. Scott, Jr., *University of Chicago*
                                           January 28, 1963

Symposium: Strategies of Stimulating Change
February 13-14, 1963
"Civil Rights Action and the National Association for the Advancement of Colored People"—Roy Wilkins, *Executive Secretary, NAACP*
"Civil Rights Action and the Urban League"—Whitney Young, Jr., *Executive Director, National Urban League*
"Civil Rights Action and the Congress on Racial Equality"—James Farmer, *National Director, Congress on Racial Equality*
"Race Relations in the United States: The Next Hundred Years"—Mr. Wilkins, Mr. Young, Mr. Farmer, Professors Charles Quick and Leonard Moss, *Wayne State University*

Conference: The Negro in a Changing Society
May 2-8, 1963
"The Worldwide Emancipation of Underdeveloped Nations"—Professor Gunnar Myrdal, *University of Stockholm*
"Legal Status of American Negroes: One Hundred Years After"—Nicholas deB. Katzenbach, *Deputy Attorney General of the United States*
"Distortion in the History of American Race Relations" —Professor Arnold M. Rose, *University of Minnesota*
"Changes in Occupation as they Affect the Negro"— Professor G. Franklin Edwards, *Howard University*
"The Changing Structure of the American City and the Negro"—Dr. Robert C. Weaver, *Administrator, U. S. Housing and Home Finance Agency*
"The Changing Legal Position of the Negro"—Professor Alfred H. Kelly, *Wayne State University*
"American Negroes and National Economic Development"—Professor William Haber, *University of Michigan*
"The Changing Political Position of the Negro"—Dr. James Q. Wilson, *Harvard University*

Discussion: The Role of Government in the Economy
May 3 and 4, 1963
Professor Gunnar Myrdal, in discussion with Detroit area business and trade union leaders

Symposium: The Negro and Religion in America
November 4-6, 1963
"The Negro and Religion in America"—Dr. Liston Pope, *Yale University Divinity School*
"The Black Muslims as a Protest Movement"—Professor C. Eric Lincoln, *Clark College*
"Black Gods of the Metropolis"—Dr. Arthur Huff Fauset, *New York City*
"Religious Roots of the Negro Protest"—Professor Carleton L. Lee, *Central State College*

The Negro in the Cultural and Intellectual Life of America
November 12 and 20, 1963
"American Negroes and the Changing Character of Education"—Professor Rayford Logan, *Howard University*
"The American Negro: Image and Identity"—Professor Sterling A. Brown, *Howard University*
"The Transformation of the Negro Intellectual"—Professor John Hope Franklin, *Brooklyn College*

Festival of Negro Art and Music   *November 18-27, 1963*
Exhibition of American Negro Art and Sculpture
November 18-27, 1963
Alvin Ailey Dance Recital   *November 18, 1963*
Philippa Schuyler Piano Recital   *November 19, 1963*
Symposium: The Negro and the Changing Arts
November 20, 1963
Professor Juanita Collier, *Chairman*; Philippa Schuyler, *Concert Pianist*; Valter Poole, *Detroit Symphony*; Ruth Murray, *Wayne State University*; Richard Kinney, *Wayne State University*
The Detroit Symphony Orchestra Presents "Afro-

American Symphony," with William Grant Still,
Composer-Conductor   *November 24, 1963*
Guest Recital: William Warfield, *Baritone*
          November 25, 1963

INTRODUCTION

LYNDON B. JOHNSON,
President of the United States

On January 1, 1863, one hundred years ago, the President of the United States issued an executive order which has been described as "an immortal blow for human freedom." Time has proved the immortality of that Emancipation Proclamation by President Lincoln. If that proclamation—like its author—now "belongs to the ages," the fulfillment of the spirit and true purpose of that proclamation is a responsibility which belongs to those of us who live today.

In his message to Congress regarding the Emancipation Proclamation, President Lincoln said eloquently: "In giving freedom to the slave, we assure freedom to the free —honorable alike in what we give, and in what we preserve."

His words were true. But, as Wendell Phillips said of

*An address delivered at the Inaugural Centennial Convocation, January 6, 1963 by the then Vice-President of the U.S.A.

it, "that proclamation frees the slave, but ignores the Negro." Those words also were true. Today, one hundred years later, it is the challenge, the duty, and the opportunity of our generation to direct our efforts toward overcoming the vestiges of what the Emancipation Proclamation of 1863 ignores.

To strike the chains of a slave is noble. To leave him the captive of the color of his skin is hypocrisy. While we in America have freed the slave of his chains, we have not freed his heirs of their color. Until justice is blind to color, until education is unaware of race, until opportunity ceases to squint its eyes at pigmentation of human complexions, emancipation will be a proclamation—but it will not be a fact. To the extent that the proclamation of emancipation is not fulfilled in fact, to that extent we shall have fallen short of assuring freedom to the free.

In these times, it is appropriate to recall at this observance that the Emancipation Proclamation itself was issued in the midst of a great struggle which divided our country one hundred years ago, as the world in which we live now is divided by an even greater struggle.

President Lincoln was counselled on many sides not to proclaim the freedom of the slaves until that struggle was won and the peace was made stable. To do so, he was told, would invite the danger of further secessions from the Union and impair the chances for success in the struggle to preserve the Union. But we today know the consequences. The Emancipation Proclamation was a turning point in the success of the Union's cause.

Directly and specifically as a result of President Lincoln's fidelity to the principles and ideals of our country's conception, world opinion and sympathy shifted to the support of the Union cause—and the ultimate success of that cause was assured.

Today as then, we are engaged in a great struggle. We too hear counsel urging restraint and urging delay. We too are counselled that for the Government of the United States to concern itself with the equality of its citizens invites the risk of impairing the chance for success in our struggle to uphold the cause of freedom in the world.

The counsel of delay is not the counsel of courage. A government conceived and dedicated to the purpose that all men are born free and equal cannot pervert its mission by rephrasing the purpose to suggest that men shall be free today—but shall be equal a little later.

We are spending billions of dollars—tens of billions each year—to preserve freedom on this earth. Yet the annual economic cost of inequality among Americans—of discrimination by Americans against fellow Americans— costs more each year than the total of our budget for the exploration of outer space. To preserve freedom costs billions. To make progress toward equality costs mainly time, effort, and perseverance. If we can afford the billions, we can certainly afford the time, effort, and perseverance.

In speaking today as I do, I am personally aware that I speak as a grandson of Confederates to grandsons and great-grandsons of Union soldiers. I am aware, as an heir of Appomattox, that the barriers of bias and prejudice within our society are not all barriers of race and color— or of religion and creed. In our land, as in many lands, men know discrimination for the geography of their birth as well as the genetics of their birth.

But the point of our times is not that discrimination has existed—or that vestiges of it remain. But rather, the point is twofold: first, that we are making an effort in America to eradicate this cancer from our national life— and, second, that we must proceed with dispatch in these efforts.

We may be white or Negro, northerner or southerner, Catholic, Protestant or Jew—but the description is neither dual nor hyphenated, for the challenges before us require our unity as Americans. In the years of the twentieth cen-

tury which remain before us, our country cannot meet
what is expected and what is required of it unless and until
we overcome those biases which exclude any from full participation in citizenship and productive effort on the basis
of race, religion or region of their birth.

We are in the midst of the greatest technical revolution
in history. Of all the scientists who have ever lived, ninety
percent of them are alive today. More mathematics has
been created since the beginning of the twentieth century
than in all the rest of history combined. Ten years from
now three-fourths of the people working in industry will
be producing products not yet invented or discovered.

In this period, we in the United States face a problem
which we have not as yet fully acknowledged—the pressing problem of our shortage of highly trained, fully educated manpower.

In 1955, the number of earned degrees in the physical
sciences conferred in the United States at the bachelor's
level number 10,516; at the master's level, 2,544; and at
the doctor's level, 1,713. In 1961—despite the known need
and increased demand from space, defense and industrial
research—the number of men and women receiving degrees in physical sciences had only climbed to 15,500
bachelors, 3,799 masters, and 1,991 doctors. This is progress, but not the progress we need to meet our needs. And
to make the outlook worse, enrollment in the biological
sciences, in engineering, and in other such fields has been
declining rather than increasing during the last ten years.

The situation in medicine is grave. In 1955, 6,718 men
and 338 women earned their M.D.'s and in 1961 the graduates of medical schools numbered 6,648 men and again
338 women. That was a loss of 70 men entering one of our
top-paying professions.

At the public school level, the United States is today
losing one million students a year who quit high school
before graduation. In the higher levels of education, forty

per cent of those who enter college drop out before completing the work for their degrees. By the 1970's, we must graduate fifty per cent more doctors than we are graduating now. We will need 7,500 Ph.D.'s in engineering, mathematics and the physical sciences—compared to our total of such Ph.D.'s in 1960 of only 3,000. By 1970, we will need 80,000 graduate students in these subjects—and in 1960, we had only 34,000.

Time is already running out. Practically every student who could obtain a Ph.D. by 1970 is already enrolled in college now.

It is true that there are some who say that nothing more need be done, should be done, or can be done in this realm of support for education in America—but such views are not realistic. America's commitment to education as "the Guardian Genius of Democracy" is a commitment which has not yet been made and is not now being kept. We cannot long afford to continue on this course, for as Thomas Jefferson once wrote, "If you expect a nation to be ignorant and free, you will expect what never was and never will be."

To deal with this subject—and to recite these statistics —is to give attention to the principal sector of unfinished business for America since the Emancipation Proclamation of January 1, 1863. If America is to have the manpower resources which these later years of the twentieth century require, the diplomas of our high schools and the degrees of our colleges must not be "white" diplomas or "white" degrees.

America needs the resources of all its young minds without regard to color or heritage or religion or region.

In that Emancipation Proclamation, one hundred years ago, Abraham Lincoln said: "I hereby enjoin upon the people so declared to be free to abstain from all violence, unless in necessary self-defense; and I recommend to them that, in all cases when allowed, they labor faithfully for reasonable wages."

In our times today, our national self-interest requires that we go much beyond that language. It is not enough to recommend to any among the American family that they "labor faithfully for reasonable wages—in all cases when allowed." A determined national effort must continue to be made for the purpose—and with the objective of being certain:

That the talents of all are sought out and put to their highest use.

That opportunity and promotion come on the basis of ability.

That the highest rung on the ladder of our society be as accessible to all of talent and genius as are the lowest rungs.

It is our responsibility and our trust in this year of our Lord 1963, to strike the chains of bias and prejudice from minds and practices as Lincoln, a century ago, struck down slavery.

I

THE NEGRO
IN THE CONTEXT
OF HISTORY

Few other aspects of American life are so dominated by history as has been the Negro problem. Whereas other social problems arising out of an historical concatenation of events undergo great changes and even disappear—like women's suffrage, the central banking system, the income tax, the assimilation of the immigrants, corruption in the cities—the Negro problem is much as it was in the 1870's or even, if the legal institution of slavery be excepted, in the 1820's. Yet, the Negro problem is not like those universal problems afflicting all societies in all periods of history—crime, alcoholism, mental disorder, suicide. It is rather a distinctively American product, which grew up at the turn of the nineteenth century as a result of peculiarly American social forces.

The history of the Negro in America is a complicated one, and this is not the place to write it. But its diverse facets will be touched upon in this first portion of the book. The historian John Hope Franklin will examine the central stream of facts, of emancipation and subordination. My own chapter will consider how historians have generally contributed to that subordination. Carleton L. Lee will examine the sources of the Negro's protest against that subordination. Broadus N. Butler will take us back to the Emancipation Proclamation but now in the local setting of Detroit. Through these four diverse studies we learn some of the ways in which history has molded the position of the Negro in the United States. We learn that neither history nor historians have been kind to the American Negro, but that things have been changing as we move along in the second half of the twentieth century.

THE EMANCIPATION PROCLAMATION: 1863-1963

John Hope Franklin

When President Abraham Lincoln signed the Emancipation Proclamation on the afternoon of January 1, 1863, he remarked, "I never, in my life, felt more certain that I was doing right than I do in signing this paper." This statement on the momentous occasion represented even more clearly than the words in the Proclamation itself the strong convictions of the President regarding the evils of the institution of slavery. Despite his earlier doubts about the legality of a Presidential order to end slavery and despite his acceptance of prevailing contemporary views with respect to racial differences, Lincoln abhorred slavery. "Slavery is founded both on injustice and bad policy," he had said in 1837. On numerous other occasions during succeeding years he had denounced the institution. The signing of the Proclamation was, therefore, a source of great personal satisfaction to the President.

In 1863 there was much criticism of the Proclamation because it emancipated the slaves only in those states or parts of states that were in rebellion on January 1, 1863; and there has been much criticism of it over the years. Perhaps a purist could, with justification, carp over the wording of the Proclamation that lacked the eloquence of the Declaration of Independence; and perhaps a strict moralist could, with understanding, object to the fact that several hundred thousand slaves were untouched by the Proclamation. But the significance of the document and the possible impact of it were not lost by even some of the most uncompromising of Lincoln's contemporaries. That volatile spokeman for the abolitionists, William Lloyd Garrison, said, "The first day of January, 1863, has now taken rank with the fourth of July, 1776, in the history of this country. The Proclamation, though leaving much to be done in the future, clears our course from all doubt and our process from all uncertainty."

Lincoln could not have put the matter better, and he was the first to acknowledge that there was yet much to be done. He hoped that with the achievement of a Union victory all the slaves would be free. First, however, the victory would have to be won. Surely, that is one of the major reasons why President Lincoln extended, in the Proclamation itself, an invitation to Negroes to enlist in the "armed service of the United States, to garrison forts, positions, stations, and other places, and to man vessels of all sorts in said service." This would provide him and them with a lever by which both their complete freedom and their rights as citizens could be secured. He was delighted, therefore, to learn from his generals that "the emancipation policy, and the use of colored troops, constitute the heaviest blow yet dealt to the rebellion; and that, at least one of those important successes, could not have been achieved when it was, but for the aid of black soldiers."

Even before victory was won and all slaves were free Lincoln began to plan seriously for the establishment of a firm place for Negroes in American society. "Those who shall have tasted actual freedom I believe can never be slaves, or quasi slaves again," he remarked some months after signing the Proclamation. He hoped, therefore, that the states themselves would adopt some practical system "by which the two races could gradually live themselves out of their old relations to each other, and both come out better prepared for the new." In numerous remarks to advisors, in letters to federal and state officials, and in public utterances he addressed himself to this matter. As he advocated education for Negroes and the extension of the franchise to them in order that they could become first-class citizens, he doubtless had in mind his own words, uttered before the Civil War: "We feel that all legal distinctions between individuals of the same community, founded in any such circumstances as color, origin, and the like, are hostile to the genius of our institutions, and incompatible with the true history of American liberty."

The Thirteenth Amendment to the Constitution was proclaimed on December 18, 1865. It provided that "Neither slavery nor involuntary servitude, except as a punishment for crime whereof the party shall have been duly convicted, shall exist within the United States, or any place subject to their jurisdiction." This amendment was a clear fulfillment of the promise of freedom made by President Lincoln in his Proclamation. But Lincoln hoped for more than mere legal freedom. He hoped for real equality before the law and in the community; and he was working for it when he drew his last breath in April 1865. There were others who undertook the responsibility after he passed from the scene. Through the enactment of civil rights laws, the Fourteenth Amendment, and other means they sought to make secure the rights of Negroes as citizens.

In pleading for the enfranchisement of the Negro in 1866, Senator Charles Sumner of Massachusetts said that in the Proclamation Lincoln had promised to maintain freedom for the Negro, "not for any limited period, but for all time. But this cannot be done so long as you deny him the shield of impartial laws. Let him be heard in court and let him vote. Let these rights be guarded sacredly." Even when the promises of Lincoln and the pleas of Sumner were heeded, they were heeded begrudgingly, and thus stripped of the generous spirit of equality pervading them. Civil rights legislation during the Reconstruction period called for equality, but there were no teeth in the laws and no heart in those called upon to enforce the laws. Freedom became little more than a word; and equality was, for the moment, a pipe dream in which only the more idealistic indulged.

The process by which the hopes implicit in the Emancipation Proclamation were dashed is one of the really tragic chapters in the history of the United States. In the first seventy-five years of the Negro's freedom, it was not enough that he was stripped of the semblance of citizenship rights he enjoyed during the Reconstruction period and denied equal opportunities in education, employment, travel, housing, and virtually every phase of human endeavor. He was subjected to the most degrading treatment in the history of the New World. His new status seemed to inspire new forms of inhumanity. Lynchings and the parching of black flesh over open fires became a favorite pastime of rural mobs, while riots and lootings were favorite methods by which urban hoodlums checked the slightest efforts of Negroes to escape their past. Worse, in a way, because of their intellectual attainments, were the theories of white supremacy spawned by the more articulate element who encouraged the masses to exploit and degrade their black brothers in the name of the "master race."

This travesty of the Declaration of Independence and the Emancipation Proclamation was perpetrated in the presence of a federal government growing more powerful every day but daily protesting its helplessness in the matter of protecting the rights of citizens. Indeed, the government itself became a party to the process as it repealed significant provisions of civil rights legislation and as it rejected proposals to enact legislation to prevent lynching, to protect the rights of voters, and to provide for the efficient and fair administration of justice. Small wonder that during the administration of Woodrow Wilson a Negro cried out in despair, "We are given a stone instead of a loaf of bread; we are given a hissing serpent rather than a fish." Small wonder that in 1930 a member of the Black Man's Protective Organization of Macon, Georgia, wrote the Attorney General, "It strikes us that the time is just about at hand when we must cast aside our Bible, stop offering so many solemn addresses to the Supreme Being and fight for our rights. . . . We shall defend ourselves by fighting like hell for once. . . . We would prefer death in lieu of remaining here on earth and have our manhood trampled upon."

One of the reasons that Lincoln desired the franchise for Negroes was because he appreciated the power of the vote in the protection of basic rights. He could not have anticipated, however, that for so many years the federal government would have remained indifferent to the rights of Negroes or that virtually all the initiative for securing those rights would come from the private sector in which Negroes themselves would play a most significant role. But Negroes early realized that if they did not exert themselves in their own behalf, few if any of the promises implicit in the Emancipation Proclamation would ever be fulfilled. Thus, in 1865 and 1866 they organized societies and conventions dedicated to securing their rights. In Raleigh, Nashville, Charleston, Norfolk, Alexandria, and numerous other places they met, drew up their long list of grievances, and made their demands. Toward the end of the century, in places as widely separated as Boston, Philadelphia, and Atlanta, they organized equal rights leagues and protective associations. And in the midst of imminent danger to their property and their lives they made no compromise with equality and freedom. Early in the twentieth century, at Niagara Falls, Ontario, a group of young Negroes organized for aggressive action; and in the following year they excoriated American citizens for their treatment of Negroes through disfranchisement and lynchings. "Never before in the modern age has a great and civilized folk threatened to adopt so cowardly a creed in the treatment of its fellow-citizens, born and bred on its soil."

When the National Association for the Advancement of Colored People came into existence in 1909, with its interracial membership of some of the country's most distinguished citizens, it entered an arena where the struggle had been carried on for several decades by a considerable number of incredibly courageous Negro fighters. It proceeded to assume a major responsibility in the fight; and with its broader base and its resourceful membership, and in a slightly better climate, it was able to accomplish much more than any of its predecessors had accomplished. By constantly reminding the United States that real emancipation involves more than the granting of mere legal freedom and by forcing the recognition of this fact in the courts, the association has, during the last fifty years, pushed America a few steps closer toward realizing the promise of the Emancipation Proclamation.

In more recent years, the number of groups and organizations working to achieve full emancipation for the American Negro has increased mightily. Groups such as the sit-in demonstrators and the freedom riders, organizations such as the Congress on Racial Equality, the Southern Christian Leadership Conference, the Student Non-Violent Coordinating Committee, and numerous labor and religious organizations have, through direct action, dramatized both the lack of full emancipation and the efficacy of their own methods in bringing into being a more democratic society.

Happily, at long last, those who seek full emancipation have found new support in the actions and policies of the federal government and some state and local governments. New civil rights legislation, new executive orders, new Supreme Court decisions, and new positive actions by responsible government officials have not only created a better climate in which to secure equality, but have also contributed substantially to its achievement. It can hardly be gainsaid that while some of these new attitudes and policies result from strong and positive convictions, the growing power of the Negro voter and the delicate position of the United States in foreign affairs have had their effect in bringing about a substantial revision of governmental policy.

At the seventy-fifth anniversary celebration of the Emancipation Proclamation in 1938, J. Finley Wilson, the national leader of the Negro Elks, said, "Seventy-five years after emancipation we are still battling for our rights in the greatest republic of the world." Twenty-five years later the battle continues. In Louisiana a registrar disqualifies Negro voters with a test that she herself cannot pass. In Mississippi a lone Negro is able to enroll in his own state university only with the aid of an army numbering in the thousands of men. In Alabama an entire community of Negroes is disfranchised by the ancient canard of gerrymandering. In New Jersey a Negro child attends an all-Negro school despite efforts of the parents to have him transferred. In Illinois a group seeking to build a community in which interracial housing prevails is frustrated at every turn. The statement made by Mrs. Eleanor Roosevelt in her Emancipation Proclamation address twenty-five years ago is still true today, "We still do tolerate slavery in several ways."

The aptly worded motto, "Free by '63," remains an unfulfilled dream. One cannot know how long Lincoln thought it would take before real emancipation became a reality. One can be certain that his faith in the future was great and his faith in mankind was even greater. The inspiration of the Emancipation Proclamation and the man who wrote it lies in the fact that the great document of freedom was one that Lincoln was convinced could not be postponed one day longer. Surely, the time has come when complete emancipation cannot be postponed one moment longer. "Free by '63" remains a worthy goal.

DISTORTION IN THE HISTORY
OF AMERICAN RACE RELATIONS

Arnold M. Rose

I am not a professional historian. But I have read enough of the writings of many American historians to know that they have done an injustice to history itself and to their scholarly calling when they have dealt with matters affecting the American Negro. This was almost consistently the case until about 1950, and it is not yet completely remedied. The historians allowed bigots to invent —to invent, not to discover—the history of race relations in the United States, and now they have repeated these inventions as scientific truths in their summary text books and, presumably, their classroom teachings.

The consequences are most serious for the training of white youth throughout the United States. Sociologists and psychologists have discovered the major stimulus to prejudice and race-hatred arising out of the informal teachings of parents, clergymen, functionaries of community organizations, and public school teachers. It is to the credit of these last named categories of individuals that movements are now under way among them to expose the harmful consequences of false teachings. But a comparable movement for accurate scholarship and fair-minded writing and teaching among white history professors in our universities scarcely got under way until the 1950's. For generations, professors of American history tended to assume, because their discipline claimed to be scholarly, that the traditions they had learned and which they repeated to their students must have been accurate. Northern white historians did not call into question the pseudo-scholarship of the bigots who secured a near monopoly of research on the history of race relations between approximately 1875 and 1950.

This is a matter of great concern to the sociologist, who is interested in present-day relations between persons and groups. An important set of causes of *contemporary* interpersonal and intergroup relations is to be found in what people *believe* to have occurred in the past. The history that is an important influence on *present* human relations is not necessarily the history of *what occurred*. It is rather the history of what is *thought* to have occurred. Here the omissions from the reports of what occurred are as important as the deliberate distortions.

For example, the sociologist finds that a widespread belief that the post-Civil War period was one of "black domination" has a remarkable influence on present-day politics in the South. Elections are still fought on the issue of Reconstruction's "black domination." It does not make any difference whether or not there actually was Negro control over politics in Reconstruction days. It suffices that most white Americans believe that there was. And how does it happen that most white Americans believe this gross falsehood? It happens because their teachers teach it in the public schools, and the teachers learned it at teachers' colleges, and the teachers' colleges got it from the professors at the great universities. The professors got it, not out of scholarly researches, but out of the post-Reconstruction apologies for the South written by Negro-haters. It is not only in the southern white universities that these falsehoods have been taught, but also in the great universities and smaller colleges of the North.

To a considerable extent, then, the present is controlled by the myths of the past. George Orwell's brilliant novel, *Nineteen Eighty-four*, shocked many people into realizing what devastating things can be done to human beings by forcing them to accept false ideas about their past. The dictator in that novel had all history constantly rewritten to justify the day-to-day changes in his policies. People came to accept filth and squalor because they were told that it used to be worse before the dictator took power. People were convinced that they should support a never-ending war because they were told how dangerous and barbaric their enemies had always been. Through dramatic satire, Orwell makes us realize that the writing of history is not an ivory-towered pastime, but an essential function of the present distribution of power and a source of the meting out of justice and injustice.

My theme is that the manipulation and distortion of history is not a bugaboo to watch out for as we may approach 1984, but a constant and accepted part of the present. Probably no historians of the present are as evil-intentioned or as conscious of their role as the historians of *Nineteen Eighty-four*; but their influence has been, on occasion, almost as disastrous. This is partly because of the influence of the data of historians upon the interpretation of the data of the other social sciences.

The battle for human justice and against racial discrimination is currently being fought in our courts, in our educational institutions, before the controlling boards of our private associations, and in our legislatures and federal Congress. It is being fought with considerable success.

29

The changes may seem slow to those who labor under discrimination and to those who are victims of violence, but the changes are coming. Discrimination is being wiped out, slowly but certainly, from the laws of our country and from the practices of our industrialists, public servants, civic leaders, and even the people in general. As Americans we can continue to be proud of the strength of our national ideals. They help us to be ashamed of our malpractices and to make earnest and effective efforts to change them. Our own consciences and our desire to appear decent and strong before the world decree that the battles for "civil rights" are almost consistently being won.

But one battle has hardly been joined. That is the battle against the social psychological attitude of prejudice. It is true that changes in behavioral practices have a tendency to change mental attitudes, and changes in our laws are thus slowly reducing prejudices. This has been demonstrated by a dozen careful studies. But there is a lag: We are now in a period when people have learned that they cannot, and believe they should not, discriminate against Negroes as much as they used to; but, at the same time, they retain strong antipathies against Negroes and continue to hold many false beliefs about Negroes as people. This situation seems to be one that is highly productive of tension, frustration, over-sensitivity, and occasional eruptions of violence. There is just as much unhappiness and psychological harm to prejudiced whites in this situation as there is to Negroes, although the unhappiness and harm are of a different nature.

Out of many researches, sociologists and psychologists are turning up some valuable clues as to what can be done to remedy the situation. One is to increase the general level of satisfaction and psychological security in other aspects of life—especially in early childhood when life patterns are being formed. Another is to expose the covert symbolic meanings attached to group animosities.[1] By revealing to conscious scrutiny the unconscious and false beliefs that Negroes are symbols of rampant, uncontrollable sex impulses, and that Jews are symbols of mysterious and malevolent cosmic powers that manipulate us like puppets against our will, people will become more rational in their beliefs.

Without exhausting the findings of social science research, but coming to a halt so that we may proceed directly with our main thesis, we must mention a third important activity that could reduce prejudice and mutual distrust. This is to eliminate false reports and to disseminate true facts—both favorable and unfavorable, but true ones—about minorities and their relations with the majority.[2] Perhaps the most important single action along this line would be to have historians correct their writings and their teachings about the past, so that teachers and young people will not perceive the present with false perspective about the past.

Let me turn from the general to the concrete and indicate some of the specific errors of historians which—from the observation of the sociologist—do most to sustain the intergroup suspicion and hatred. My sources are the scholarly writings of John Hope Franklin, C. Vann Woodward, W. E. B. Du Bois, Bessie L. Pierce, Lawrence D.

---

[1] Children do not know about race or racial symbolism until they learn this in the home, in the school, and in the church. For example, in Detroit an interracial textbook was introduced and teachers were surprised that neither white children in the control group nor mixed children in the experimental group paid any attention to the interracial character of the book. (Communication from Broadus N. Butler, Wayne State University, Detroit, Michigan, April 1, 1963.)

[2] One of the facts is that *minority* and *majority* are fictions. E.g., Senator Ellender encourages white fears of Negro domination of southern politics on the basis that Negroes are in fact the *numerical* majority in Louisiana. This is not actually true, except for a few counties.

Reddick, and several others. I shall deal here only with American history pertinent to the position of Negroes and shall mention items in chronological order rather than in order of importance.

The first fact is that Negroes came to America long before the white colonists and they came as explorers and settlers.[3] When they were brought as chattels to North America, they were brought as indentured servants, rather than as slaves—as the historical myth would have it. They were free usually after seven years, and thereafter had opportunities to establish themselves to the same extent as did other citizens without means. It was not until Negroes had been residents in the English colonies in North America for some forty years that the first colony permitted some servants to be held in perpetuity as slaves. Other colonies did not make this legal transformation from indentured servitude to slavery for a hundred years. Even after slavery was instituted as a matter of economic interest and convenience, it was the custom for the wealthier and more generous slave-owners to free their slaves after a number of years' service. Moreover, a few wealthy Negroes participated in the slavery institution not as slaves, but as slave owners; and they were no less concerned to perpetuate slavery than whites.

One of the important implications of these facts is that the early poor Negroes had the same social status as did poor whites; but early wealthy Negroes were not unlike wealthy whites in respect to the institutions which characterized early America, particularly in the South. Many of the poor whites had also been brought to the colonies as indentured servants. There was relatively little feeling against social intercourse and biological amalgamation, and some of the offspring merged gradually into the "white race." Any southern white man who traces his an-

[3] Harold G. Lawrence, "African Explorers of the New World," *Crisis*, 69 (June-July, 1962), 321-32.

cestry back to the colonial period is not unlikely to discover a Negro forebear, and there was little or no stigma against such in those days. Moreover, there are American Negroes whose ancestors were never slaves, and Negroes who can trace their family lines directly to Thomas Jefferson and others of the colonial period. These facts are contrary to the myth that the Negro was always rejected because it is in the very biological nature of a superior race that it rejects an inferior race socially and sexually.

A related historical fact is that the complex of attitudes which we now call race prejudice, or racism, did not exist in colonial days. Most Negroes were looked down on by many middle- and upper-class whites and Negroes as being lower class, but so were lower-class whites looked down on. There was a certain curiosity about the physical features of Negroes; but racism and caste as we know it today did not arise until after the year 1800. The new profits to be made from slave labor in the South after the discovery of the cotton gin and sugar cane and the development of extensive world trade in cotton and sugar created a greatly increased demand for slaves. The importation of slaves expanded even after the statute of 1808 made it illegal, and the price of slaves rose several hundred per cent. The returns were political as well as economic.

The wealthy southern planters constituted an oligarchy that dominated the federal Congress, as well as the southern state governments, for many years. These accretions of wealth and power alone would not have created racism and caste. The other essential ingredient was a psychological sense of shame, the pangs of conscience which would not let people simply exploit their slaves rationally. The late eighteenth and early nineteenth centuries were a period of democratic awakening in which all western peoples were declaring their allegiance to liberty, equality, fraternity, humanitarianism, and progress. One by one the civilized nations were abolishing slavery, extending

33

the franchise, and humanizing the penal system. The southern oligarchy felt these world-currents, believed they should participate in them, and yet wanted to maintain their wealth and power based on slavery.

The only psychological solution was to adopt a series of rationalizations—beliefs which explained why Negro slavery must be an exception to the demand for democracy. These rationalizations included the religious ("the Bible sanctioned slavery"), the cultural ("a productive democracy—like ancient Athens—must be based on unpaid labor"), and the biological ("the Negroes were biologically inferior and must be helped like children or horses; they must also never be allowed to pollute the better blood of the whites"). These rationalizations were quite contrary to the findings of current and later scholars and scientists, but they served the function of justifying slavery. Their psychological power is demonstrated by the tenacity with which they are held and by their effectiveness as morale builders during the Civil War. The last-mentioned rationalization—called racism—proved ultimately to be the most powerful, and it had the most profound implications for later mistreatment of Negroes.

These historical facts are important for sociologists, as they explain how the caste-segregation system grew up, how recent it is—even though it is commonly believed to have existed for all ages—and on what flimsy bases it rests. If historians permitted, others could also know the facts. But the historians have perpetuated the popular southern myth that racism and caste have existed from the first interracial contacts and are endemic to race relations.

The complex historical misconceptions centering around the institution of slavery arose out of the southern oligarchy's need to justify that institution. The belief fostered by historians that there was no friction between masters and slaves serves to support the need to believe that slavery was productive of happiness to Negroes. Yet modern delving into the facts brings up 250 slave revolts between 1800 and 1860, as well as every evidence that whites in small isolated communities lived in almost constant fear of massacre in slave uprisings.

The tendency to equate Negroes with slaves, because the rationalizations for slavery did not square with a factual portrayal of them as independent workers and businessmen, is belied by the United States Census itself. That source shows that 12 per cent of those known to be Negroes in 1860 were free men. A population of these proportions today would be larger than all the Mexicans, Indians, Chinese and Japanese *combined* living within the United States now. Still another important fact about the pre-Civil War period that had to be concealed in order to maintain the myth of the Negro's inferiority was his control of all manual skills under slavery. When slave labor was cheaper than free labor, and the skilled workman was regarded as of low status compared with the farmer, practically all artisans and other skilled workmen in the South were Negroes. Even the famous iron grille work in New Orleans and Mobile was made by Negroes, and Negro masons and carpenters built most of the still-standing *ante bellum* homes of the South. The need to hide these facts from history coincided with the post-slavery need to obliterate it from factual existence, and Negroes were not allowed to exercise these skills after Reconstruction days.

The very word "Reconstruction"—referring to the decade immediately following the Civil War—almost epitomizes all that is false in American history books. The stories of what is alleged to have happened when the oligarchy was not in political control of the South are used to justify all the evil that has happened since. The "Reconstruction," implying a drastic change in what was assumed to be a perfect *ante bellum* society, has been distorted by historians to the point of agitating southerners by its mere mention. The factual distortions are many. In the first place, the length of the Reconstruction period is much exaggerated. Some say, in all seriousness, that it lasted from 1865 to the 1890's. Actually it began in 1867 and closed in some states as early as 1870; in all states it was over no later than 1877 (which means that it lasted a maximum of ten years). It was preceded—from 1865 to 1867—by a period in which the defeated southern states passed "Black Codes" to nullify Lincoln's Emancipation Proclamation in all but name. A Negro had no right even to change his place of work under the Black Codes. It was because of the South's failure to accept emancipation that the federal government moved in and started the period of "Reconstruction" in 1867.

The period is spoken of as one of "black domination" in referring to political control. Actually only *one* state legislature, for *one* two-year period, had a majority of Negro legislators. During the entire period from 1868 to 1901, all the southern states together sent only two Negro senators and nineteen Negro representatives to the national Congress.

But the southern historical apologists are not consistent here: with scarcely a sentence of transition from "black domination" they will say that the northern "carpetbaggers" controlled the Negroes for their own purposes. The "carpetbaggers" are depicted as conniving exploiters of the war-torn South. Actually, a significant proportion of northerners in the South at that time were soldiers of the United States Army, who—like military governors today—are perhaps not the ideal civil authority but who can be expected to follow some standards. "Carpetbaggers" did include a few self-seeking businessmen and fortune-hunters, exactly like those "romantic" adventurers who migrated to the "Golden West" in the 1850's, or like the "robber barons" who founded the great business empires of the North during the same 1870's. They were also civil servants, employees of the federal government sent out to staff the weak Freedmen's Bureau and carry out its strictly limited regulations. But most numerous of all, "carpetbaggers" were maiden ladies from the eastern states, whose potential mates had been decimated by Civil War and the western migration, and who found sublimated satisfactions in serving as teachers for an unschooled southern population. Organized by their churches and missionary associations, these unselfish women braved the strange land to teach children—white and Negro—to read, write, and do arithmetic.

This brings us to a major "horror" of the Reconstruction: money was bled from an impoverished South and "squandered." We are not told in our history books what the increased expenditures of the Reconstruction governments were for. Some reputable historians even repeat such silly canards as that the money was used to buy golden cuspidors for legislators to spit in. But an examination of budgets shows that most of the new funds were used for education. In 1867 the South was the only settled section of the country without a public school system. Few but the wealthy among the whites could secure even an elementary education. The Reconstruction governments instituted the first public schools of the South. The northern churches, northern philanthropists, and the Freedmen's Bureau provided some of the funds, but the Reconstruction state legislatures also helped. The raising of taxes for education was called "stealing" by the plantation owners, and the historians accepted their judgment. Who was to teach in a region where few could even read? Teachers had to be imported, and they were the northern spinsters called "carpetbaggers" by the partisans of the old days. The historians accepted their term also.

There were also the "scalawags"—the southern whites who were in favor of such things as freedom for Negroes and education for all children. What kind of people actually were these "scalawags," considered in the myth to be the local betrayers of their home region? There were some "little foxes" among them, middle-class men who dared to set up businesses and gain wealth without having the superior ancestry of the planters. The post-war period was one that favored the *nouveaux riches* in the North also. But most of the "scalawags" were poor backwoodsmen—followers of Andrew Jackson and Hinton Helper—who despised the blacks but reasoned that a greater enemy was the exploiter of their own white group. Later, in the 1880's, they dropped their uneasy alliance with the northerners, then returning home, and with the Negroes. In exchange for the abandonment of Reconstruction, the poor whites—including most of the "scalawags"—received a monopoly on skilled jobs which the aristocrats formerly accorded to Negroes. Few historians have reported accurately on either the provenance or the "disappearance" of the "scalawags."

A powerful myth of the Reconstruction was the story of Negroes raping white women. If any historian can find significant evidence for this outside the novels of Thomas Dixon, he has not yet reported it.

Almost all the facts about the end of Reconstruction are misreported by the historians of the South. It is admitted that the good Klansmen had to be a bit repressive for awhile, to correct the injustices of Reconstruction. But it is alleged that, after a few years, peace returned to the South and both races were happy in their respective places. The facts, on the other hand, show a steadily increasing repression of Negroes: The best available figures on lynching, for instance, reveal the high point in that activity to have occurred in the 1890's, not the 1870's. The deprivation of the Negroes' civil rights did not occur all at once, but increased steadily from the 1870's through the 1890's. The segregation policy was a product of this "Restoration" period, although historians before C. Vann Woodward implied its previous existence. The plantation owners and their followers did not legalize the Jim Crow system immediately after introducing it. Rather, it was not until the 1890's that the legalized Jim Crow system and the doctrine of "separate but equal" fastened themselves on the South. Under the sanction of law, the segregation system became much stronger and all-pervasive. Negroes were only gradually disfranchised after 1877; one Negro congressman was elected from the South as late as 1898. The new laws destroyed whatever minority efforts there were in the South to bring about a closer collaboration and harmony between the races. The historians of the South distorted all these facts, and generations of Americans have been brought up to believe their myths that good relations were restored between the races by 1900. In fact, the period 1890 to 1930 was the one of greatest conflict between the races, and the one in all American history in which the Negroes were most completely subjugated.

Reference has been made to only a few of the distortions in the history of American race relations. Their contemporary significance is not to be understood merely as part of "Negro history," but as part of general American history as it has been affected by Negro-white relations. The study of these matters is not the history of a particular group, but rather the history of important influences and currents in the United States as a whole. The distortions occur not only for Negro-white relations, but also for those of other minority groups making up this country. We have, for example, the myth that the Chinese meekly accepted the segregation into Chinatowns and minor service occupations, whereas the court records of the 1880's and 1890's reveal how they fought in the courts and were beaten down. Chinese-Americans have also had the myth fastened to them that they are given to crime and shady occupations. Actually, few groups in the United States have had such a consistently low crime rate as the Chinese, although practically no history texts record these facts.

Some distortions of history are perpetrated by historians of the minority groups themselves, although they do not have the degree of influence that our major historians have. For example, the picture of slavery they present is one of unmitigated horror and constant rebellion. Actually, the evidence is good that there were *some* considerate masters and *some* fairly contented slaves, and that the rebellions did not average over five-a year, mostly local in nature. In their antagonism to the very institution of slavery, some Negro historians fail to point out that it was a much more repressive institution after 1800—roughly the date when the ideology of racism developed to justify the purely economic institution—than it had been in the colonial period. Some of them, for the same reason, neglect the extreme harshness of the caste system that developed after 1880 when slavery was already abolished. There is also the recent tendency among some Negro—as well as white—historians to forget that Booker T. Washington toadied to Negro-hating whites, and took out his frustrations in meannesses toward his own people. He is now usually portrayed only as a wise leader and clever politician, who had to accommodate himself to the exigencies of his time.

The effort to explain distortions in the history of American race relations must rest on the basic truism that all historians must select their facts and that only a few can specialize on the history of any one particular time and area. These necessities, however, should lead historians to be especially wary of biases in their own selectivity and of the backgrounds and biases of those historians who specialize on such an emotionally laden subject as race relations. A second caution is to remember that all generalizations in science—including history—must be held as tentative. Many scientists tend to become overly impressed with the great weight of evidence in back of any given conclusion. A new finding can prove an "established" generalization to be wrong, but some scholars become so committed to a generalization that they do not examine a new finding with open minds. We should not neglect the possibility that science and history—like any aspect of culture—tend to become encrusted with mores. The scientists can *never* afford to become satisfied with established conclusions and must always retain some skepticism.

To shift the level of explanation from the general to the specific, it must be noted that the "cultural climate"—the *Zeitgeist*—of America, relative to race relations, has been conducive to distortion. From 1875 to about 1910, the North was fed up with the South and its problems and wished to forget about them. Educated northerners also found it convenient to forget about the earlier history of slavery in some of the northern states, and the earlier development of caste in that region. The desire to forget was shared by the leading northern historians, who became content to allow southern apologists to record the history of their region during the post-Civil War years without criticism. Historians of both the South and the North have shared the national bad conscience, which led them to derogate the Negro and to attribute social characteristics and events to biological inevitability. This permitted them to justify to themselves the harsh reality of race relations and still retain their faith in the national ideals of freedom and equality. ⌉

This psychology among historians has lingered into the present day, although it began to lose dominance after 1910. It was, however, partially and temporarily replaced, during the period 1910-40, by another kind of distorting ideology among historians. This was a pseudo-objectivity —exemplified in the writings of Charles Beard—which insisted that materialistic factors could alone account for historic change. Objectivity in history as a discipline was confused with interpretation of historical facts in terms of "objective" factors as opposed to "subjective" or psychological factors. That point of view eliminated any possibility of understanding race relations, where ideologies, subtle power politics, and symbolic meanings are the touchstones. Thus, the typical American historian prevented himself, at least until 1940, from beginning a thoroughgoing, insightful examination of the history of intergroup relations. In recent decades, historians have broken away from the limitations they set on themselves generally; but it was not until about 1950 that some of them began an objective study of aspects of the history of American race relations.

Still, there is a cultural lag in the re-examination of history. Not only have certain phases of the history of race relations not yet been reopened for study, but the findings of the newer studies have not been adequately disseminated to the textbook writers and to the school teachers. Thus the older injustices continue to be committed in the teaching of our youth. Historians need to be given greater encouragement to study the history of American race relations. The new findings need to be publicized, rather than allowed to sit on the library's back shelves. When teachers are found still relying on the old points of view dominant when they went to school, they need to have their attention directed to the newer scholarship. In recent years there has been a re-education of teachers of mathematics and physical science, to bring them up-to-date with the new findings in those fields. The same needs to be done for the teachers of history.

For the South there is a special need. For here is a great region, rich in natural resources, which has literally trapped itself in a morass of false history. It is hurting itself—economically, politically, and morally—because of the falsehoods its post-Civil War ideologists spun out and popularized. The progress of this great region will depend more on correcting its notion of its past than on anything else. To substantiate this statement satisfactorily would require an analysis longer than we have already given to our main thesis, but we may cite a single supporting example. John Temple Graves, an otherwise well-educated southern newspaperman, in a column on Abraham Lincoln, said: "February 12th is the birthday of the man who deprived more human beings of their social security than any other in history. They were secure against sickness, old age, unemployment, every moral vicissitude."[4] It is almost justifiable to speak of a social illness when a well-intentioned and prominent newspaperman can thus equate slavery and social security legislation. This regional social illness—which has its impact on the whole nation through the political influence of the South—has its roots largely in the false history taught in the schools.

Our review of the distortions in the history of American race relations has been necessarily superficial and selective. Much more could have been said from what is now supported by the new scholarship, and I would venture to predict that much that is important in American history has not yet been "discovered."

If continuing harm is not to be done to new generations of youngsters going through our schools and colleges, a thorough reinvestigation of American history, and of the teaching of American history with regard to race relations, must be made. If the historical falsehoods and half-truths are not to be repeated in legislative halls and in courtrooms to justify and buttress harmful policies, they must first be expunged from the classroom. Many governmental and economic leaders have been making heroic efforts in the last few years to gain understanding of intergroup relations and to erase the policies which have harmed this nation in many ways. The next major step is

[4] *The Shreveport Times,* February 12, 1950, p. 14.

to purge race hatred from our minds. The historians can perform a significant role in this effort without doing anything more than putting into practice their claimed ideals of good scholarship and science.]

RELIGIOUS ROOTS OF THE NEGRO PROTEST

Carleton L. Lee

This essay is a part of a more elaborate study of patterns of leadership among Negro Americans. Throughout the larger study, the role of organized religion in leadership was ever apparent. Often when the formal aspects of religion were not so clear—in some instances where religious ideology or faith was rigorously denied—the overtones of religion and religiously-oriented values seemed to be in evidence. The Montgomery story and other direct-action demonstrations in recent years bring into focus again the religious orientation of the Negro American community. The emergence of Martin Luther King, Jr., and his close associates in the nonviolent, civil-disobedience dimension of the civil rights struggle, may properly be regarded as a maturing or further developmental phase of the Negro protest. A similar appraisal may be made of the prominence of Elijah Muhammad and his followers. King and those associated with him in nonviolent agitation and demonstration, and Muhammad and his associates stand as distant opposites on a social continuum representing the religious roots of the Negro protest.

Our subject, "Religious Roots of the Negro Protest," is meant to apply to the whole gamut of experience of the Negro American community in the struggle to remove all obstructions to full participatory citizenship and freedom in American society. The term "roots" applies not only to "origins" but to a line of the "evolutionary development of a condition or trend" as well.

We undertake the task, then, of identifying these religious roots under the chastening rod and discipline of slavery in the process of the assimilation of the African to western society, in slave revolts, and in the spirituals. We point to the influence of the missionary education enterprise. We describe as prophetic the literary figures of note who have given expressive and imaginative formulation to felt and shared aspirations. Finally, we identify the role of institutional religion and the cults as peripheral forms of the conventional religious groups.

Leadership among Negro Americans, in the race relations structure, functions in the dynamics of the social forces of industrialization, migration, and urbanization. The ideological bases are the religious precepts and the political idealism inherent in the American creed. The religious orientation of the Negro American community in the United States provides the background for the persistence of appeals for equality in the name of justice and morality. Once it was believed that social competence comparable to that of the general population would remove the artificial barriers imposed by involuntary segregation. Now leadership tends to shift from this naïve faith in the automatic operation of the democratic process toward an understanding of the systematic use of the resources available in an urban secular society for promoting and accelerating social change. The Negro American community is being transformed from a southern, folk-like culture-complex with deeply rooted religious orientation, to an urban secular complex of a highly volatile character. It is important to the changes taking place in race relations today that these religious roots be understood as having particular relevance to the kind and quality of the pluralistic secular society.

The term "Negro American" describes persons who are identified as Negroes and are sufficiently conscious of the meaning of such identification to be engaged in the struggle to alter their subordinate status. The "Negro American" is distinguished from the abstraction "the Negro." The former is a self-conscious member of the Negro American community. He is not only "a person who has the status of a Negro," but one who is fighting to change the status of the group.

The chastening rod of slavery was considerably softened by the use of religion as a force to assimilate the African to American life. The Negro American community is conditioned positively and negatively by formal and informal religion. The Negro church is the major social institution; it has most influence; it is the oldest institution. Its leadership is called upon to support all good causes, religious and nonreligious, and is involved in fostering education and opportunity for youth. Negatively, the Negro American community knows that its church represents the most extreme racial segregation. In the development of the Negro American community, no significant leadership completely ignores the church. It does not seem far-fetched to conclude that the place of the church in the contemporary Negro community is rooted in the fact that the religious institution was the first in which the slave was permitted relatively free participation. The Negro church belongs to the Negro. The religious orientation of the slave to American life probably contributed more than any other single cultural force to his survival.[1] The eighth Atlanta Conference put the matter this way: ". . . we have in the history of the Negro Churches one of the most important examples of the meaning and working of Social Heredity as distinguished from Physical Heredity that the modern world affords."[2]

The church is of importance not only because of its historic relationship to the Negro American community, but also because of the historical relationship between religion and the development of the ideology of the American creed.[3] The church was an assimilative factor for the African and a channel of expression for the slave.[4] Lorenzo Greene has carefully pointed out that many colonists in New England felt compelled by religious scruples to give their slaves religious instruction; further, he notes that once it was established that conversion did not alter the status of slaves, they were instructed universally until other prohibitions were set. Charles II was interested in the conversion of slaves as a means of spreading Protestantism. Distinguished leaders like John Eliot and Cotton Mather devoted time to the teaching of Negroes.[5] Methodists and Baptists had the largest memberships among the slaves, but the Society for the Propagation of the Gospel in Foreign Parts sent the first missionaries.[6]

The most outstanding missionary to slaves in the South was probably Charles C. Jones, a Presbyterian, whose ministry was centered in Georgia. He believed that Ne-

[1] James Weldon Johnson, *The Book of American Negro Spirituals* (New York: Alfred A. Knopf, 1925), p. 20.

[2] W. E. B. Du Bois, *The Negro Church* (Atlanta: Atlanta University Press, 1903) p. 15.

[3] Ralph Barton Perry, *Puritanism and Democracy* (New York: The Vanguard Press, 1944).

[4] Cf. E. Franklin Frazier, *Negro in the United States* (New York: Macmillan Co., 1949) p. 17.

[5] Lorenzo J. Greene, *The Negro in Colonial New England* (New York: Columbia University Press, 1942) pp. 259-65.

[6] *Ibid.* p. 265.

groes would excel others in religion if given an opportunity; that the contempt in which they were held by whites would cause both to sink lower in the scale of religion and morality; that slave and master should worship together to prevent the deterioration that was certain, he felt, if Negroes had independent churches. He tried to show that slaves who received proper instruction had less tendency to insurrection, declaring that Nat Turner had been misguided by corrupt religious teachings.[7]

Jones has left an account of pioneer preachers who rose up among the slaves as leaders. One George Liele or George Sharp, taken from Virginia to Burke County, Georgia, sometime before the Revolution, was converted, baptized, manumitted, and set up churches in several places near Savannah. Later he went to Jamaica and had some influence in persuading the Jamaica Assembly to establish religious freedom there. Before he left Savannah he baptized Andrew Bryan and Bryan's wife. Bryan survived abuse, gained his freedom, and purchased members of his family. So impressive was his ministry and leadership that when he died the white Baptist Association of Savannah passed a resolution memorializing him for his distinguished service.[8]

Maurice R. Davie has written: "It was in his religious and church life that the Negro first gained freedom and first developed leadership, and he has to this day found fewer restrictions in this phase of his life than in any other."[9] The independent Negro denominations were initiated as protests against segregation of Negro communicants in "white" worship services in the free states. Richard Allen, who became the first bishop of the African Meth-

[7] Charles C. Jones, *The Religious Instruction of the Negroes in the United States* (Savannah: Thomas Purse, Publisher, 1842) pp. 50-51.
[8] *Ibid.* p. 51.
[9] Maurice R. Davie, *Negroes in American Society* (New York: Whittlesey House, 1949), p. 177.

odist Episcopal Church, made up his mind on the matter when he and Absalom Jones were disturbed as they knelt in their accustomed place, and were told that a special place had been provided for Negroes. Similar actions in New York by James Varick marked the beginnings of the African Methodist Episcopal Zion Church.[10]

Every protest made by slaves and by free Negroes was a part of the process in which new forms of life organization and leadership began to take place. In every instance we see more than mere protest or effort to mitigate the slave situation. We observe, too, the forces which make for the reshaping of personality and the creative modification of culture. The interaction between the individual and the environment is not mere mechanical process. It is process in which novelty occurs. This fact has a continuing relevance to leadership in the Negro American community. Insofar as the slave system permitted solidarity among its victims, that solidarity tended towards a religious community. It follows that the Negro American community is likely to interpret its problems in religious terms and seek religious solutions to social problems.[11]

That this has been the case is reflected in several of the more dramatic slave revolts. Using a "more severe" definition of insurrection or conspiracy among slaves, Herbert Aptheker has "found records of approximately two hundred and fifty revolts."[12] One of these, led by Gabriel in Richmond, Virginia, is said to have been inspired by the impression made upon slaves that, like the Israelites, they could throw off the yoke of slavery and God would come to their aid.[13] Denmark Vesey, leader of a revolt in South

[10] E. Franklin Frazier, *The Negro in the United States* (New York: Macmillian Co., 1949), 99, 74-75.

[11] See, W. Stuart Nelson (ed.), *The Christian Way in Race Relations* (New York: Harper & Brothers, 1948), pp. vii-viii.

[12] Aptheker, *American Negro Slave Revolts* (New York: Columbia University Press, 1943), pp. 162-63.

[13] Frazier, *The Negro in the United States*, p. 87.

Carolina, is described as "constantly quoting Holy Writ to prove that slavery was wrong,"[14] James Weldon Johnson says,

> Nat Turner gathered his followers and inspired them to act by "command of God." On the eve of action he is recorded as saying to them: "Friends and brothers, we are to commence a great work tonight. Our race is to be delivered from bondage, and God has appointed us as the men to do his bidding; and let us be worthy of this calling . . . we do not go forth for the sake of blood and carnage, but it is necessary that in the commencement of this revolution all the whites we meet must die; until we have an army strong enough to carry on the war upon a Christian basis.[15]

When the religious roots of the Negro American community are discussed, the tradition of the folk as it is reflected in the spirituals emerges. The spirituals have been regarded as a way of meeting the impossible demands of slavery; a form of sacred literature socially relevant to the slave regime; forms of protest in the slave situation, and art forms serving as collective symbols.

Students of folklore and folk music are agreed that the spirituals represent the creative religious literature of an illiterate, oppressed group. Higginson, one of the first collectors of the spirituals, writes of the religious quality in the singing of the Negroes he knew in army camps.[16] Kerlin compared them with the Psalms and the "chanted prayers of primitive Christianity."[17] Krehbiel, appraising them for both musical and historical purposes says:

[14] Joseph C. Carroll, *Slave Insurrections in the United States 1800-1865* (Boston: Chapman and Grimes, 1938), pp. 85-86.

[15] James Weldon Johnson, *Black Manhattan* (New York: Alfred A. Knopf), 1930, pp. 36-37.

[16] Thomas Wentworth Higginson, "The Negro Spirituals," *The Atlantic Monthly*, XIX (1867), 693-94.

[17] Robert Kerlin, *Negro Poets and Their Poems* (Washington: The Associated Publishers, 1923), pp. 9-10.

Here the most striking fact that presents itself is the predominance of hymns, or religious songs. The reasons for this will readily be found by those who are willing to accept Herbert Spencer's theory of the origin of music and my definition of the folksong. Slavery was the sorrow of Southern blacks; religion was their comfort and refuge. That religion was not a dogmatic, philosophical or even ethical system as much as it was an emotional experience.[18]

Du Bois refers to this same quality as "a faith in life, sometimes a faith in death."[19] Thurman asserts that the "clue to the meaning of the Spirituals is to be found in religious experience and spiritual discernment."[20] James Weldon Johnson put the matter of the religious quality of the spirituals more forcibly when he insisted that they were the vehicles through which the slaves made Christianity their own and thereby assured their own survival as a people.[21] The vitality of the spirituals and their subtle infusion into American musical literature suggest their force and power. This quality is a universal characteristic of the folksong. Religion gave validation to the slaves as "children of God," thereby making it "impossible for all the brutality of their environment to destroy them."[22]

But the spirituals were not only a religious literature. They were, according to John Lovell, a means of communication among the slaves, which their masters were not intended to understand. When the character of the power relations between master and slave are examined, it

[18] Henry E. Krehbiel, *Afro-American Folksongs* (New York: G. Schirmer, 1914), p. 29.

[19] Du Bois, *The Souls of Black Folk* (Chicago: A. C. McClurg and Co., 1903), p. 261.

[20] Howard Thurman, *The Negro Spiritual Speaks of Life and Death* (New York: Harper and Bros., 1947), pp. 11-12.

[21] James Weldon Johnson, *The Book of American Negro Spirituals*, pp. 20-22.

[22] Thurman, "Religious Ideas in Negro Spirituals," *Christendom*, IV (1939), 515-16.

follows that at least some of the spirituals were songs of protest. At least they were *used* as a means of protest:

> The Spiritual, then, is the key to the slave's descrip-
> tion of his environment. It is the key to his revolutionary
> sentiments and to his desire to fly to free territory. With
> it we can smash the old romantic molds, which are still
> turning out ready-made Negroes. . . . Most important of
> all, the Negro Spiritual is a positive thing, a folk group's
> answer to life.[23]

Miles Mark Fisher asserts that the "slave songs are history." And the history they recount is the protest of the
slaves against bondage, sustained by the survival of African cults in American life. The cults were secretly held and
the slaves were signaled as to time and place by a song like
"Steal Away."[24] Others have pressed the issue of the spirituals as protests, especially those spirituals which are
Biblical in origin.[25]

When the Union armies marched into the stronghold
of slavery, they were followed by bands of Christian missionaries committed to the cause of the slaves and freedmen.[26] No single movement—among the many that can be
mentioned in this connection—has been as decisive for
laying the foundations of leadership as the missionary
education enterprise. Jointly with the Freedmen's Bureau,
the major Protestant church bodies sought to prepare the
freedmen for their new role as citizens. From the outset,
they repudiated the "iron law" of separation. Until recently, most collegiate education among Negroes was carried

[23] John Lovell, Jr., "The Social Implications of the Negro Spirituals," *Journal of Negro Education*, VIII (1939), 638.

[24] Miles Mark Fisher, "The Evolution of the Slave Songs of the
United States," unpublished Ph.D. dissertation, University of Chicago Divinity School, 1948.

[25] See Earl Conrad, "General Tubman, Composer of Spirituals,"
Etude, LX (1942), 305.

[26] Cf. Dwight Oliver Wendell Holmes, *The Evolution of the Negro
College* (New York: Columbia University Press, 1934), Pt. II.

largely by these church groups. Almost always, they faced aggressive hostility from their southern white neighbors.[27]

The hostility and indifference of the South was itself a powerful force in motivating freedmen to learning. The aggressive friendliness of the missionaries, who identified themselves completely with the freedmen, contributed to race consciousness and group morale. The South, which had enslaved the African in an agricultural economy, had assimilated him at a high cost to his humanity. In spite of the brutal aspects of the system, Negroes emerged with a fair store of the culture prevailing at the time. They had received religious instruction, sometimes in violation of the law; and the missionaries came bringing reality to the good news of the Gospel in everyday contacts. The South denied the humanity of the slaves; the northern missionaries affirmed it. The South had justified slavery on the basis of Biblical teachings of servility and obedience to masters. The missionaries affirmed brotherhood with all mankind and denounced, sometimes at great personal sacrifice, the active opposition to the "sins of caste." In this seething cultural cauldron of conflict began the Negro American community's awakening to the implications of freedom. Increasingly, the members of that community have sought to share in the full fruits of America's democratic faith.

Turning from the chastening rod of slavery to the latitudes and promises of freedom, the Negro protest continues. The growing sophistication of urban life has seen the rise of an intellectual elite. In the main, this group is regarded as indifferent to the religious bonds of community life. The acids of modernity appear to have eaten away their religious roots, which have been replaced by the secularization characteristic of urban living. The intellectual may be indifferent or hostile to religion; he may regard it as just another phenomenon of society to be taken

[27] E. Merton Coulter, *The South During Reconstruction* (Baton Rouge: Louisiana State University Press, 1947), p. 82.

into account; but it makes deeply personal demands upon him. In some instances he may have a vigorous religious life, both devotional and social. In any event, the nature of the common cause of the Negro American community has evoked prophetic voices in many areas. Moreover, an examination of the literature of this community suggests the persistence of the religious orientation in the Negro protest. This persistence is all the more impressive when the representative literary figures make no claim—indeed may deny any claim—to the relevance of religion—except in its purely institutional forms—to the common struggle.

Samuel Kincheloe has definitively dealt with the prophet and the prophetic. He writes:

> The term prophet is for many groups a value concept which they use to denote the person who reforms in the direction which agrees with their ideas of what reform should be. The term prophet, nevertheless, is more than a value concept. When we take the persons denoted prophet by various groups we find certain similarities among them. The term prophet is the name which applies to a moral leader who has for them an inspired message.[28]

Poets and other creative writers sometimes behave and reveal insights sufficiently like the prophets to be called prophetic. In many instances the poet and prophet merge into the same person, and the language of the real prophet almost always is a poetic one. Indeed, "the distinction of prophecy is not one of form, but of spirit."[29] When such figures as representatives of a movement speak the aspirations of their people and communicate inspiring ideas, their language is always that of poetry, broadly understood.

[28] Samuel C. Kincheloe, "The Prophet: A Study in the Sociology of Leadership," unpublished Ph.D. dissertation, Department of Anthropology and Sociology, University of Chicago, 1939, p. 27.
[29] *Ibid.*, p. 103.

Often in such moments the poems seem to write themselves. In these cases the poets and prophets give "impersonal expression" to the dominant mood of the community. Any literature which represents the life of the group and is not mere individual expression tends to be prophetic in its nature. The producers of it often have a sense of mission as they represent the culture of the particular locality from which they come. Poets as well as prophets have the sense of being more or less passive agents of forces outside themselves. A fundamental characteristic of the prophet, that of his "being moved to speak," is true also of poets.[30]

The framework of the prophetic is one of unrest. With the Negro American, it is that critical restiveness consequent to the condition of a group of people who have a sense of an historic wrong, still hemmed in and abused by the oppressive inequality of an involuntary biracialism; stirred and inspired by the precepts of political and religious idealisms. The conditions which evoke protest and agitation do not, however, make for absolute unanimity of opinion as to how crucial issues shall be met.

As representative "prophetic voices of protest" we shall look briefly at some of the writings of W. E. B. Du Bois, James Weldon Johnson, Langston Hughes, and Richard Wright. The combined productivity and creative span of these four figures stretches across almost the whole period of the Negro American's struggle under freedom.[31] Du Bois, Johnson, and Hughes are classified as poets although each of them has used other media of expression. The late Richard Wright wrote primarily in prose, largely fiction and critical essays. They are representative types, propagandists and partisans to the common cause who make use of literature to inform and influence public opinion.

[30] *Ibid.*, p. 105.
[31] Du Bois was born in 1868, Johnson in 1871, Hughes in 1902. Wright in 1908.

Du Bois' literary expression is at once disciplined and rhapsodic, regarding the Negro American's claim to freedom in the face of such brutalities as the lynching of Sam Rose or the Atlanta riots of 1906. He expresses the pain, anguish, anxieties, aspirations, and almost all the emotions deriving from sensitiveness to the violence and tragedy of such situations.

In his "Litany of Atlanta," written following the Atlanta riots, the prophetic element is seen in the social history of the status of the Negro American, in a description of the riot itself, and in the frustration of spirit ever present in the Negro American community in such crises:

We are not better than our fellows, Lord: we are but weak and human men. When our devils do deviltry curse Thou the doer and the deed, — curse them as we curse them, do to them all and more than ever they have done to innocence and weakness, to womanhood and home.

Have mercy upon us miserable sinners:

A city lay in travail, God our Lord, and from her loins sprang twin murder and Black Hate. Red was the midnight; clang, crack, and cry of death and fury filled the air and trembled underneath the stars where church spires pointed silently to Thee. And all this was to sate the greed of greedy men who hide behind the veil of vengeance.

Bend us thine ear, O Lord.[32]

This wail of the people encompasses the thoughts of those whose spirits have been wounded by the crass hostility and active evil of a segregated society. Were its form other than poetic, its inflammatory quality might be more apparent. But this is a genuine experience of the Negro American community, a cry bursting forth in response to one of the most extreme outcomes of the bipartite situation. Du

[32] Du Bois, *Darkwater* (New York: Harcourt, Brace & Co., 1920), pp. 25-26.

Bois reverts to the imagery most universal in the Negro American community, namely, that of religion. Style and form have undergone the discipline common to the intellectual. But the overtones are there; the poet utters the authentic life experience of a people. The "Litany" functions as a means of communicating to the entire group that of which it already has an awareness, but about which it is as yet something less than fully articulate.

In the last chapter of *The Souls of Black Folk,* Du Bois speaks of "the Sorrow Songs." His concluding paragraph is a defensive protest against the withholding of free participation in American life; a "proof test" denial that this is a white man's country; an affirmation of a truth deemed demonstrable, that makes black folk entitled to the full fruits of the American heritage, not as pariahs or beggars seeking sufferance, but as co-creators and "joint-heirs" with all other Americans. True to the prophetic mood, it symbolizes the entire range of experience. It moves towards despair, but always returns to some ray of hope, some notion that a saving remnant shall be left upon which a new future will be constructed. The black folk have brought three gifts: "the gift of story and song," "the gift of sweat and brawn," and "the gift of the Spirit."

> Our song, our toil, our cheer, and warning have been given to this nation in blood—brotherhood. . . . If somewhere in this whirl and chaos there dwells Eternal Good, then anon in his good time America shall rend the veil and the prisoned shall go free.[33]

Written in powerful and moving imagery, this prose restores and sustains morale and gives inspiration. It is both disciplined and spontaneous, its emotional timbre not lost on the printed page. This expressiveness is characteristic of Du Bois in his role as poet-leader. It sometimes breaks through his more deliberate works of research and scholar-

---

[33] Du Bois, *The Souls of Black Folk,* pp. 262-64.

ship, and is always discernible in his platform speaking as the "spirit of prophecy." Sometimes ecstatic, his writings are always expressive and generate a spirit.

The prophetic element in James Weldon Johnson is seen in the writing of the hymn-poem "Lift Every Voice and Sing." Over and above the content of the poem itself is the mood of its creation, a mood of ecstasy common among prophets. Johnson was principal of a school in Jacksonville, Florida. With his brother, Rosamond, he planned a song to be sung by five hundred school children at a Lincoln Day celebration at which he was to speak. He describes the creative act:

> I got my first line: —Lift every voice and sing. Not a startling line; but I worked along grinding out the next five. When, near the end of the first stanza, there came to me the lines:
> Sing a song full of the faith that the dark past has taught us.
> Sing a song full of the hope that the present has brought us.
> the spirit of the poem had taken hold of me. I finished the stanza and turned it over to Rosamond. In composing the two other stanzas I did not use pen and paper. While my brother worked at his musical setting I paced back and forth on the front porch, repeating the lines over and over to myself, going through all the agony and ecstasy of creating. And I worked through the opening middle lines of the last stanza. . . . I could not keep back the tears, and made no effort to do so. I was experiencing the transports of the poet's ecstasy. Feverish ecstasy was followed by that contentment—that sense of serene joy —which makes the artistic creation the most complete of all human experience.[34]

On a more critical level we would add that this description

---

[34] James Weldon Johnson, *Along This Way* (New York: Viking Press, 1933), pp. 154-55.

of a psychological state is similar to, if not identical with, that of the prophets.[35]

The reaction between "prophet and people" is described again by Johnson when he relates an incident connected with the recruitment of Negroes for overseas duty during the First World War. The passage cited here has so much of the setting and pattern of prophetic action and interaction that it is quoted at length:

> I addressed a mass meeting in Carnegie Hall and made the most effective speech of my whole career as a platform speaker. It was a great meeting; and the famous auditorium was packed to capacity. As I sat on the platform I felt depressed, almost listless. When I rose, every nerve in my brain and body was quickened by the intensity of feeling that came across the footlights from the audience to me. As I talked, I was lifted up and swept along by that sense of demi-omnipotence which comes to a speaker at those moments when he realizes that by an inflection of the voice or a gesture of the hand, he is able to sway a mass of people. It is a sensation that intoxicates; and it carries within itself all the perils of intoxication. Words surged to be uttered; and uttered, they were effective beyond their weight and meaning. One passage of my speech had an electrical effect; "I can never forget what I felt on the day I saw the 'Buffaloes,' New York's own black regiment swing out of Madison Square into the most magnificent street in the world. They were on their way to receive a stand of colors to be presented by the Union League Club. I followed them up Fifth Avenue as they marched with a vision in their eyes and a song on their lips, going to fight, perhaps to die, to secure for others what they themselves were yet denied. They halted in front of the club, and in a mighty chorus sang the STAR SPANGLED BANNER. Then from the balcony the Governor of the state came down and presented the colors. As he gave

---

[35] Kincheloe, *op. cit.*, pp. 71-76.

the flag into their keeping, he raised his voice, trembling with emotion, and cried out, 'Bring it back! Bring it back!' and the answer welled up in my heart: 'Never you fear, Mr. Governor, they will bring it back as they have always done whenever it has been committed to their hands, without once letting it trail in the dust, without putting a single stain of dishonor upon it. Then it is for you, Mr. Governor, for you, gentlemen of the Union League Club, for you, the people of America, to remove those stains that are upon it, upon it as these men carry it into battle, the stains of Disfranchisement, of Jim-Crowism, of Mob Violence, and of Lynching . . .'" The emotional tension of the audience snapped with an explosion of cheers and applause. I continued, finishing the passage: "The Record of black men on the fields of France gives us the greater right to point to that flag and say to the nation: those stains are still upon it; they dim its stars and soil its stripes; wash them out! wash them out!" But I do not think my voice reached farther than the length of my outstretched arms. I stood silent and waited for the tumult in the audience and the tumult within me to subside.[36]

The social situation which called the meeting; the total experience of the Negro American community; Johnson's wide knowledge and sensibility of the general conditions of the Negro across the nation; and his own spirit as vehicle and instrument through which his personal emotions and those more social aspects of his emotions—products of his experience as a Negro American and of his poetic broodings—combined in the interaction between prophet and people. (His role as prophetic leader of the militant protest did not reach its most telling point in this "non-rational" aspect, but rather in his efforts to persuade the Congress of the United States to pass an anti-lynching bill. But this is another story.)

Hughes is the people's poet. He is essentially prole-

[36] James Weldon Johnson, *Along This Way,* pp. 337-38.

tarian; not in a doctrinaire sense, nor in the sense of partisan political dogmatism, but he is sufficiently critical of contemporary society to be called Marxian in a purely descriptive connotation. There is a Marxian hostility toward the middle class among Negroes. His proletarian sympathies are expressed when he contrasts the style of life on Seventh Street with that of conventional "cultured colored Washington." He preferred Seventh Street because of its lack of pretentiousness:

> Their songs—those of Seventh Street—had the pulse beat of the people who keep on going . . . I liked the barrel houses of Seventh Street, the shouting churches, and the songs. They were warm and kind and didn't care whether you had an overcoat or not.[37]

Hughes is a race poet, capturing the warmth and spontaneity of the folk in transition. He combines his racial and proletarian themes in a manner suggesting that the two belong together.

When Hughes decided that a writer should be educated, he entered Lincoln University in Pennsylvania and was graduated in 1926. During his senior year two important events occurred: he completed his novel, and he made a survey which threw him into a decisive consideration of the race problem. Concerned with the impact of an entirely white faculty giving instruction to Negro youth who were to be leaders of the Negro people, the survey created something of a stir, which was climaxed when Hughes talked with an alumnus who thought its findings too blunt. This "old grad," who had built a "great institution" in a mid-western city, declared that he could not have done so if he had "told the truth to white folks." This experience made Hughes think about the nature of compromise:

[37] Langston Hughes, *The Big Sea* (New York: Alfred A. Knopf, 1940), p. 210.

I began to think back to Nat Turner, Harriet Tubman, Sojourner Truth, John Brown, Fred Douglass—folks who left no buildings behind them—only a wind of words fanning the bright fires of the spirit down the lanes of time. The old grad has his buildings, just as Booker T. Washington had Tuskegee. Yet how heavily the bricks of compromise settle into place.[38]

Hughes identified himself with the race "radicals" in leadership.

He has shown great versatility, publishing verses, short stories, novels, humorous essays, *libretti*, and other forms. He strikes a new key, different from that used by any previous Negro writer. Without Dunbar's use of dialect—yet true to the Negro idiom—he has caught the pathos of Negro life. Loving life and people, he is able to make the crudest of their experiences sing positively of the dignity of life, simply because it is human. His bitterness is turned into a subtle phrase of irony; his realism runs the gamut of human feelings; yet, he maintains an aesthetic warmth, a singing glow which is authentic.

We may classify Hughes's poetry into three categories; it is initially racial in temper and content; it is expressive; it is proletarian. By racial poetry we mean not only that race has been used as a theme, but also that race structures his style. One finds in his poems a style conforming to the spirit of the poetry. Whatever the literary critic may have to say of this structuring, the student of society understands it as reflection of the artist's capacity to incorporate into his work the sentiments of the people in whatever area of experience those sentiments occur. Hughes is always conscious of some beauty, some fragment of the heroic, wrested from American life by some black peasant or poor city-dweller not commonly regarded as being of aesthetic notice. He is racial, too, when he writes of the

[38] Langston Hughes, *The Big Sea* (New York: Alfred A. Knopf, 1940), pp. 309-310.

"tragic mulatto." He does for the Negro American community through poetry what James Weldon Johnson did as an interpreter of the spirituals and of Negro American literature.

Some of his poems are at once racial, expressive, and proletarian. The racial poems are descriptive, humorous with flashes of protest and pathos; expressive in the "blues" mood of some ordinary event that might occur in the life of anyone, but that has double significance when it happens in the framework of American race relations. Hughes has described how he came to write "The Negro Speaks of Rivers." He was enroute to Mexico for the second time. As he thought about his father, he wondered why his father disliked Negroes whom Hughes liked very much. He remembered how the new migrants to Cleveland had laughed and talked about their troubles, their complaints about Jim Crow and high rents. They seemed to him the "gayest, bravest people possible." As he thought, the train crossed the Mississippi River at sunset and he thought of the relationship of that river and of the fate and destiny of Africans in the United States. His mind turned to other rivers in the Negro past.[39] Then he wrote the poem. Of its writing he says:

> No doubt I changed a few words the next day, or maybe crossed out a line or two. But there are seldom many changes in my lines, once they're down. Generally, the first two or three lines come to me from something I'm thinking about, or looking at, or doing, and the rest of the poem (usually if there is to be a poem) flows from these first few lines, usually right away. If there is a chance to put the poem down, then I write it. If not, I try to remember it until I get to a pencil and paper; for poems are like rainbows: they escape you quickly.[40]

Here we see not only the poem, but also the manner in

[39] *Ibid.*, pp. 54-55.
[40] *Ibid.*, pp. 55-56.

which the poem is made. The poet as historian broods over the experiences of his people with the ancient rivers; the Negro people is an ancient race; it has lived long and thoughtfully even as the great world rivers are deep.[41] The expressive character of Hughes's poems lessens the rhapsodic; yet there is the quiet ecstasy common to the prophet; there is always a judgment on society.

Hughes is "not without laughter" in his service to the common cause, and he is the truly prophetic voice. He writes often for the sheer joy of expression, but he expresses himself more often as the creative mind setting forth the sentiments of the folk and the people. He has seen their problems first hand, felt their needs in his own spirit, brooded upon the meaning of the same injustices, and has discovered beauty, power, and worth in the most humble of their lives. His poetry returns to them in all the moods he has known.

If Hughes is "not without laughter," Richard Wright is a "pillar of fire." Rebecca Barton describes him in contrast with Du Bois and Johnson:

> ... this brilliant writer wields the surgeon's scalpel ruthlessly, and folds back layer after layer of motivation to reach the quivering reality beneath. . . . He does not utilize the detachment of a Du Bois or a Johnson in the midst of turmoil. . . . Wright has a strange capacity of immediacy. He is direct, specific, and of the earth. He flings himself into his analysis with an abandon which cannot be explained merely by his comparative youthfulness. He knows only what he knows and works from the bottom up, not from the top down.[42]

He lacks not only "the detachment of a Du Bois or a Johnson," but also their spontaneity, and he lacks the light-heartedness breaking through in Hughes; he does not have

[41] Cf. Kincheloe, *op. cit.*, p. 116.
[42] *Witnesses for Freedom* (New York: Harper & Bros., 1948) p. 255.

Hughes's gift of gaiety, sheer joy of life, the knack for subtle satire and clever irony. He is, rather, forceful, vivid, graphically shocking and realistic. His sabred phrases pierce the mind and sense with a painful sharpness. His writings give expression to their inarticulate awareness of the nature and character of their frustrations.

Wright belonged to that literary generation of American writers who budded and came to flower during the Great Depression. The motifs of that generation were the growing class-consciousness of American workers, and the self-conscious emergence of literary spokesmen for the dispossessed. He was caught in the vast sea of "debased feudal folk" and hurled from its flotsam and jetsam into literary eminence through a Federal Writers' Project. He was identified, too, with the source of the growing class consciousness, as a member of the Communist Party. He later withdrew or was expelled.[43] As he himself puts it:

> I did not feel so wounded by their rejection of me that I wanted to spend my days bleating about what they had done. Perhaps what I had already learned to feel in my childhood saved me from the futile path. I . . . said to myself: "I'll be for them, even though they are not for me."[44]

Wright is interested in depicting Negro life as he has seen and known it. He has explored and probed with great psychological understanding the depth of the Negro masses; made graphic their tragic existence; exploded the myth of the Negro as a happy, carefree, fun-loving, lovable creature, a little less than the rest of humanity.[45] He is struck by the "strange absence of kindness in Negroes," their passionless existence, their "hollow memories, their

[43] Richard Crossman (ed.), *The God that Failed* (New York: Harper & Bros., 1949), pp. 155-58.

[44] *Ibid.*, pp. 157-58.

[45] Cf. Richard Wright, *Black Boy* (New York: Harper & Bros., 1945), p. 33.

shallow despair." This voice is unlike the prophetic ones to which we have listened heretofore.

Two aspects of Wright's career as writer make his a prophetic voice. The first is that he vivifies and makes graphic the latent power for good or ill that resides in the masses. Secondly, he recognizes and appraises the Negro as a folk-peasant element in our population, in process of becoming an urban proletariat. This latter element appears in the closing passage of one of his short stories. In "Bright Morning Star," a Negro mother, whose son is a Communist, refuses to inform white officers of the law as to the whereabouts of her son and his white mistress. Under pretense of waiting to claim his body after he has been taken by a mob, the mother shoots one of the mob. It is a moving scene:

> She gave up as much of her life as she could before they took it from her. But the sound of the shot and the streak of fire that tore its way through her chest forced her to live again, intensely. She had not moved, save for the slight jarring impact of the bullet. She felt the heat of her own blood warming her cold, wet back. She yearned suddenly to talk. "Yuh didn't kill me; Ah come here by mahself. . . ." She felt rain falling into her wide open, dimming eyes and heard faint voices. Her lips moved soundlessly. . . . Focused and pointed she was, buried in the depths of her star, swallowed in its peace and strength; and not feeling her flesh growing cold, cold as the rain that fell from the invisible sky upon the doomed living and the dead that never dies.[46]

Wright is true to his thesis in *Uncle Tom's Children*: American society has brutalized white men beyond their power to save themselves. Their humanity stops at the color line. It has instilled a disruptive fear in Negroes, beyond their power to save themselves, even by heroic acts

[46] Wright, *Uncle Tom's Children* (New York: Penguin Books, 1947), p. 185.

of martyrdom as described above. But there is a "saving remnant" here, too. It is implicit in the titles of the stories from the first to the last. "Big Boy Leaves Home" is a symbol of the Negro's efforts to save himself by flight from his frustrations; "Bright Morning Star" is the secular symbol of redemption by blood, a symbol of far-off hope and promise that the little people shall one day rise above race and live with dignity, or at least die heroically. Against the background of the development of these themes Wright is prophetic and speaks on behalf of America's black masses.

Two other considerations which might be taken into full account may only be mentioned briefly here: the Negro churches as institutional forms and the several cults and sects which people the Negro American community. Because the church has been a major factor in the Negro American community, it has always been privy to the councils of the common cause. Ira Reid has summed it up well in another connection:

> The Negro churches . . . have long served as more than places of worship—they have been centers of the social and cultural life of the Negro community. Their pastors have long been more than ministers—they have been teachers and leaders in all "safe" programs for the improvement of the racial lot. The churches were the first places of free assemblage for Negroes. Here were championed the issues of slavery and of justice for the Scottsboro boys . . . In religion—the church, the denomination, and the minister—the Negro found a kind of peace and outlet for the expression of all his social interests and aspirations.[47]

Industrialization, migration, and urbanization have brought changes and challenges to the place of the church. The challenges have been the rise and sophistication of

[47] Ira De A. Reid, *In a Minor Key* (Washington: American Council on Education, 1940), p. 83.

secular leadership and the growth of sects and cults. Sophistication in secular leadership may be said to have been related to church groups which shared in mass demonstrations long before the Montgomery story began in New York, where Adam Clayton Powell and William Lloyd Imes with other clergymen took direct action against discrimination in Harlem.[48] Similar action took place in Texas and on the West Coast.[49]

Cults and unconventional religious behavior are as American as baseball. There is one important difference: baseball is universal in its American locus; cults are primarily products of urbanization, and their habitat is the city. In the main, the cults are not racially exclusive,[50] the exceptions being those groups which make race an article of their dogma. Related to the Negro American community, in this regard, are the Black Muslims.[51]

The Peace Mission of Father Divine is perhaps the most ubiquitous of the cults emerging on the frontier of race relations. The significance of such movements is that they project social, political, and economic goals calculated to remove or rise above the limitations imposed by segregation. They may be regarded as negative formulations of protest. All of them are designed to meet the needs of the emerging proletariat in process of transition from a folk-like background to the exigencies of city life. No little degree of their power and force is accounted for in terms of the charismatic leadership which most of them have. Herein is a phenomenon worthy of continued study: moving from the rural to the urban centers of population, many people experience the shock of the loss in interpersonal

[48] Adam C. Powell, Jr., *Marching Blacks* (New York: Dial Press, 1945), p. 96.

[49] *Ibid.*, pp. 106-11.

[50] Elmer T. Clark, *The Small Sect in America* (Nashville: Abingdon Cokesbury Press, 1949), p. 21.

[51] See C. Eric Lincoln, *The Black Muslims in America* (Boston: Beacon Press, 1962).

relations. These losses occur on the level of primary contact at which values and meanings are sustained. The anonymity of city life may provide all the material needs required—though this is rarely the case—but the interpersonal relations between leaders—symbols of meaning—have frequently been destroyed. The charismatic leader of a sect or a cult apparently provides the necessary bridge in this transition. There is, in other words, a kind of social-psychological interim from rural to urban life. A religious charismatic may provide not only a temporary stabilizing force for the religious and other folk demands, but also a channel for economic and political expression. This is a challenge to old-line patterns of religious leadership.

If, as we have suggested, Negro protest is religiously oriented and rooted, an understanding of this fact should throw some light on the contemporary focus on race relations in the United States. Positively, it suggests that the Negro American community, for a long time to come, will continue its protest against racial segregation and discrimination as "devoutly" as the Roman Catholic attends Mass, or as faithfully as the Moslem turns toward Mecca to pray, or as surely as the Jew observes his high Holy Days. Moreover, one cannot understand the ease with which the Negro American community responded to the leadership of Martin Luther King, Jr., or the sit-ins without an appreciation for the religious orientation of the Negro American community. However one interprets the cults and sects that have grown in our great metropolitan areas, they, too, are part of this basic orientation and complex. This is why no appeal to "go slow" or any other counsel of moderation—whether it come from the Attorney General of the United States, or belatedly from the late "oracle" of Oxford, Mississippi, can be accepted without the Negro American community becoming reacreant to its trust or sharing in a contemporary apostasy.

Recently, Louis Lomax has written a book describing

the "Negro Revolt."[52] Such a description of the civil rights struggle is a distortion—if not a misrepresentation—of that struggle. Revolt is usually an attack upon the established legal order when all efforts for redress have been exhausted. The Negro American community has for the most part carefully avoided extremes. Conciliation, negotiation, appeals to justice and morality, and legal remedies have characterized the Negro protest. These protests are persistent demands in the stride toward freedom[53] in the Montgomery story, or in the black nationalism expressing extreme reaction to white supremacy. In one form or another we may expect such protest to continue rather than abate. So long as Negro Americans have faith in the fulfillment of the rich promise of American life, they will "beat against the bars with a strange insistency" until "all God's Children" can "walk in Jerusalem, just like John."

[52] Louis Lomax, *The Negro Revolt* (New York: Harper & Bros., 1962).

[53] Martin Luther King, Jr., *Stride Toward Freedom* (New York: Ballentine Books, 1958).

THE CITY OF DETROIT AND THE EMANCIPATION PROCLAMATIONS*

Broadus N. Butler

It is little known that the city of Detroit has had a unique relationship to the Emancipation proclamations of September 22, 1862, and January 1, 1863, issued by President Abraham Lincoln. Specific events and circumstances in the history of Detroit, and the consequences of them emanating from the city to the nation, contributed directly to the crystallization of almost every major process making for a definition of the issues of slavery and for the enunciation of programs and principles for the realization of freedom for everyone, even beyond the full emancipation of slaves.

*I am grateful to the late Mr. Fred Hart Williams whose unpublished manuscript, "Detroit Heritage," provided inspiration; to Mr. Henry D. Brown, director of the Detroit Historical Museum; to Dr. James M. Babcock and the staff of the Burton Historical Collection of the Detroit City Library; to Dr. Philip P. Mason of the Wayne State University Archives Collection; and to the staff of the Wayne State University Library for courtesies, resources, and assistance.

The history of the city of Detroit—of her neighboring Canadian communities of Windsor, Sandwich, Chatham; and of her sister Michigan cities of Ann Arbor, Jackson, Battle Creek, Cassopolis, Marshall, Shelby, and Adrian—provides a microscopic, but exceptionally accurate, kaleidoscope of all the nuances of struggle, of conflict of values, of exercise of extremes of political and economic power, of enunciation of high principle, of testing of purpose, and of final achievement of emancipation's goal, achieved in part despite strong internal and external opposition. This was the goal which defined the national quest for full freedom for all Americans during the period 1833 to 1870.

When the full story of the role and meaning of Detroit in the emancipation process is known, the fact of the Underground Railroad and the anti-slavery societies, and the names of Shubael Conant, Erotius Parmalee Hastings, Laura Haviland, Mary Margaret Chandler, the Rev. William C. Monroe, William Lambert, Seymour Finney, William Webb, George DeBaptiste, Mother Martha Cook, Henry Bibb, Elijah Willis, Harriet Tubman, Sojourner Truth, Frederick Douglass, and John Brown—not all Detroiters—who played significant roles in Detroit anti-slavery and abolition activity, will come alive in their full historical significance. Theirs was a supreme moral contribution to the city and the nation. These men and women from different places, and of different races and faiths, dedicated their lives and devoted their whole beings to the succession of events, organizations, and principles which made the city of Detroit the incubator of emancipation.

Detroit, founded in 1701, received the definition of her historical social and moral significance in American history eighty-six years later in the Northwest Ordinance of 1787, which established the Northwest Territory. In this ordinance, the territory received the first known sanction by act of the federal government that here would be a land

73

in which no man should be slave to another. Article VI of the ordinance read:

> There shall be neither slavery nor involuntary servitude in said territory otherwise than in the punishment of crimes whereof the Party shall have been duly convicted: Provided always that any person escaping into the same, from whom labor or service is lawfully claimed in any one of the original States, such fugitive may be lawfully reclaimed and conveyed to the person claiming his or her labor or service as aforesaid.[1]

Article III read in part as follows:

> Religion, Morality and knowledge being necessary to good government and the happiness of mankind, schools and the means of education shall forever be encouraged.[2]

These two articles destined Detroit, Michigan, and the Canadian province of Ontario for the unique influence which they were to exercise upon events in the United States from 1833 until the full constitutional recognition of citizenship for all Americans in the Fifteenth Amendment to the Constitution of the United States. This was ratified in 1870. The Thirteenth Amendment, the abolition of slavery amendment, had received almost its exact wording from the Northwest Ordinance.

Prohibition of slavery being the *a priori* condition for the development of a climate of universal respect for man in the United States, and the encouragement of religion, morality, and knowledge being the necessary *a posteriori* condition for the production of free men and a free society, the two articles projected Detroit and Michigan into a particular opportunity. The conflicts, tensions, near disasters, and eventual successes of Detroiters as they ad-

[1] Clarence Edwin Carter (ed.), *The Territorial Papers of The United States* (Washington: U. S. Government Printing Office, 1934), II, 49.

[2] *Ibid.*, II, 47.

74

dressed themselves to these articles, provided a living testimony of a democracy's search for fulfillment.

The first complication about Article VI of the Northwest Ordinance was that it provided for the apprehension and return of fugitive slaves. This made it, at the same time, one of the first explicit fugitive-slave acts in the United States, antedating the federal Fugitive Slave Act of 1793. The second complication was that slavery had existed in the territory, and specifically in Detroit, since shortly after the arrival of Antoine de la Mothe Cadillac, the founder. It would continue until about 1836. It is significant that even though there were large numbers of slaves (about 175 in 1783 diminishing to 30 in 1830) and though slavery was not a matter of economic concern as it was in the South, the question of slavery in the form of address to the *status of a class of mankind* was ever present and persistent in all of the critical decisions in and about the territory and the state of Michigan.

Two years after the enunciation of the Northwest Ordinance, every effort to incorporate a prohibition of slavery article into the United States Constitution failed. Moreover, no attempt had been made to enforce the ordinance because of unresolved questions about the Illinois and Indiana territory. In 1792 the Canadian government passed an act abolishing slavery while Detroit was still under the dual jurisdiction of Canada and the United States. But in 1796 when, under the Jay Treaty, Detroit came exclusively under American jurisdiction, pro-slavery forces wrote a clause into the treaty which permitted slaveholding in Detroit by British residents who had slaves on or prior to July 11, 1796.

The treaty clause directly contravened Article VI of the Northwest Ordinance and raised the interesting question of whether the Northwest Ordinance was still valid, since it had been apparently superseded by the adoption of the United States Constitution. In 1802, a specific effort was made by pro-slavery forces in the territory to repeal Article VI. The effort failed, but slavery continued.

In 1805, under conditions of complete confusion and disaster, Detroit assumed her new role as capital of the newly created Michigan Territory. On July 4, Augustus B. Woodward arrived to assume the post of Chief Justice of the Michigan Territory and began a stormy and confused nine-year period of joint government with General William Hull as Governor. Father Gabriel Richard was already an established institution in the city, and his immediate and pressing concern was to rebuild the city devastated by fire and to protect the people from famine. Governor Hull, on the other hand, was concerned about military protection.

The first dispute between Woodward and Hull occurred over plans for the rebuilding of the city. Immediately upon the heels of this dispute there followed a concern about labor for the physical task of building a city and about militia for protection. In this atmosphere of confusion, in 1807, Justice Woodward heard his first fugitive slave case before the Michigan supreme court. He rendered an elaborate opinion, which he based upon the Northwest Ordinance, Article VI; but the effect of the decision was to reverse the construction of the ordinance article and incorporate the clause of the Jay Treaty into a decision which denied the claimant's right and set the fugitive free. This decision which had the effect of denying the fugitive slave apprehension portion of Article VI, while making exception to the prohibition of slavery section, set the stage for tension and struggle over the next half-century. The decision presaged a climate that made Detroit and Michigan "God's Country" and "The Promised Land" for fugitive slaves, but made residence in Detroit and Michigan tenuous and uncertain for Negroes who were not slaves. For example, in 1808, a small group of Negroes who had come from Canada volunteered and were accepted by Governor Hull for service in the militia. But, as a consequence, Justice Woodward sought to have Governor Hull impeached for incompetency. This ambiguity had the effect of pushing the moral dimension of the question of slavery to a new ground.

Slavery was not an economic issue here: it was a matter of social classification. This circumstance of reference crystallized in an act of April 13, 1827, titled: "An Act to regulate Blacks and Mulattoes and to punish the kidnapping of such persons." The impact of the act was to make explicit the legal proposition that, although Negroes could not be legally held slaves, this fact did not recognize their status either as residents or as persons with civil rights to be respected. Residency in Michigan was given a specific definition in the 1827 act as follows:

Section 1. Be it enacted by the Legislative Council of the Territory of Michigan, That from and after the first day of May, next, no black or mulatto person shall be permitted to settle or reside in this Territory, unless he or she shall produce a fair certificate, from some court within the United States, of his or her actual freedom, which certificate shall be attested by the clerk of said court, and the seal thereof annexed thereto by the said court.

Section 2. That every black or mulatto person, now residing in this Territory, shall, on or before the first day of January next, enter his or her name, together with the name or names of his or her children, in the office of the clerk of the county court, in the county in which he, she, or they reside, which shall be entered of record by said clerk, and thereafter the clerk's certificate of said record shall be sufficient evidence of his or her freedom: Provided . . . nevertheless, That nothing in this act contained, shall bar the lawful claim to any black or mulatto person.

Section 3. That if any person or persons shall harbor or secrete any black or mulatto person, the property of any

person whatever, or shall in anywise hinder or prevent the lawful owner or owners, from retaking and possessing his or her black or mulatto servant or servants, such person shall, upon conviction thereof before any justice of the peace in the county, be fined in a sum not less than ten, nor more than fifty dollars, at the discretion of the Court, one half thereof for use of the informer, and the other half for the use of the township where the offence shall have been committed, excepting Wayne, when the same shall be appropriated as is provided for in the fifth [eighth] section of this act. ". . . paid into the county treasury, and be appropriated for the purchase of lands, and the erection of poor-houses on the same."
Section 6.   That no black or mulatto person shall be permitted to emigrate into and settle within this Territory unless such black or mulatto person shall, within twenty days thereafter, enter into bond, with one or more freehold sureties in the penal sum of five hundred dollars, before the clerk of the county court of the proper county, in which such black or mulatto person may wish to reside, to be approved of by the clerk, conditioned for the good behavior of such black or mulatto persons, . . . and if any black or mulatto person shall migrate to this Territory, and not comply with the provisions of this act, it shall be the duty of the overseers of the poor of the township where such black or mulatto person may be found, to remove immediately such black or mulatto person, in the same manner as required in the case of paupers . . . .[3]

It held, in fact, that all Negroes must register with the county clerk. No immigrant Negro could be considered a resident unless he, first, produced a legal certificate of his being free, and, second, posted bond of five hundred dollars for good behavior. The stringency of the act was such that it was unenforceable, but it reflected a climate of such

[3] *Territorial Laws, Michigan* (Lansing: W. S. George and Co., 1874), II, 634-36.

growing denigration and hostility that it contributed directly to the city's first race riot.

Around 1831, slave insurrections had begun to increase in the South under the direction of Denmark Vesey and Nat Turner. Of significance to Detroit was the fact that large numbers of dedicated anti-slavery Quakers had moved into Detroit from Niagara, New York, in 1832 and 1833. Both pro-slavery and anti-slavery sentiments were so sharply focused as to eventuate in a riot which has been called the Blackburn Riot of 1833, even though the number of slaves in Detroit had diminished to a negligible few. Mr. and Mrs. Thornton Blackburn were arrested on fugitive slave charges on June 14, 1833. Negroes resisted the execution of the law and effected the escape of the Blackburns to Canada. Disorder ensued. General Cass, then Secretary of War, called out the militia to restore order.

The Blackburn Riot so stung the conscience of the city that anti-slavery sentiment became institutionalized. Detroit now had reached the juncture of opportunity to assume its role as the anti-slavery and abolitionist capital of the United States. She now would re-define slavery in terms of moral law. In 1834, Erotius Parmalee Hastings got together the first organized anti-slavery group in Detroit (not the first in the nation: a convention in Philadelphia in 1831 organized the Anti-Slavery Society). By 1837, the Michigan Anti-Slavery Society became a formal organization with Judge Shubael Conant as president. The organization had really been founded and developed by two dedicated women: Mrs. Mary Margaret Chandler and Mrs. Laura Haviland. It was Mrs. Laura Haviland of Adrian who provided the "higher law" moral dimension of the anti-slavery operation when she made the following appeal the foundation of its work:

I presume, if the slave claimant should come with a score of witnesses and half-bushel of papers to prove his legal right, it will avail him nothing, as we claim a higher law than wicked enactments of men who claim the misnomer of law by which bodies and souls of men, women, and children are claimed as chattels.[4]

The name of Sojourner Truth of Battle Creek, the Negro abolitionist and Underground Railroad conductor, also bears special significance in this amplification of the meaning of the anti-slavery movement. Her most dramatic moments were associated with women's suffrage, an achievement which was not to be consummated until the Nineteenth Amendment to the United States Constitution in 1920. She was a most incisive defender of women's equal rights organizations against the "superiority" arguments of men. This reach beyond the physical emancipation of slaves was to be more clearly enunciated to a larger world audience by Frederick Douglass in his eloquent speeches and editorials, and by Harriet Beecher Stowe in her immortal novel and drama, *Uncle Tom's Cabin.* Douglass, who himself escaped slavery in 1834 to become later the greatest abolition orator, chief recruiter of Negro soldiers for the Union Army, and eventually Marshal of the District of Columbia and Minister to Haiti, framed the question of slavery in the following way:

> I have held all of my life and shall hold to the day of my death, that the fundamental and everlasting objection to slavery, is not that it sinks a Negro to the condition of a brute, but that it sinks a *man* to that condition. I base no man's right upon his color and plead no man's right because of his color. My interest in any man is objectively in his manhood and subjectively in my manhood.[5]

Again:

My sympathies are not limited by my relation to any

[4] Laura Smith Haviland, *A Woman's Life Work* (Cincinnati: Walden and Stowe c. 1881), p. 93.

[5] Philip Foner, *Life and Writings of Frederick Douglass* (New York: International Publishers, 1955), IV, 117.

race. I can take no part in oppressing and persecuting any variety of the human family. Whether in Russia, Germany, or California, my sympathy is with the oppressed, be he Chinaman or Hebrew.[6]

Miss Stowe writes:
What is peculiar to slavery, and distinguishes it from free servitude, is evil, and only evil, and that continually.[7]

And again:
At different times, doubt has been expressed whether the representations of "Uncle Tom's Cabin" are a fair representation of slavery as it presently exists. This work, more, perhaps, than any other work of fiction that ever was written, has been a collection and arrangement of real incidents,—of actions really performed, of words and expressions really uttered,—grouped together with reference to a general result, in the same manner that the mosaic artist groups his fragments of various stones into one general picture. His is a mosaic of gems,—this is a mosaic of facts. . . .

The writer acknowledges that the book is a very inadequate representation of slavery; and it is so, necessarily, for this reason,—that slavery, in some of its workings, is too dreadful for the purposes of art. A work which should represent it strictly as it is would be a work which could not be read. And all works which ever mean to give pleasure must draw a veil somewhere, or they cannot succeed.[8]

From 1833 to 1870, a succession of events in and emanating from Detroit had a definite progression and a paradoxical quality which helped produce the fact of emancipation as a national achievement. Immediately following the Blackburn Riot, the Anti-Slavery Society and the

[6] *Loc. cit.*
[7] Harriet Beecher Stowe, *Uncle Tom's Cabin* (Boston and New York: Houghton Mifflin Co., 1896), II, 253-54.
[8] *Ibid.*, II, 255.

Underground Railroad emerged as genuine social forces. The 1835 Constitutional Convention was persuaded to retain the Anti-Slavery Article and the Encouragement to Education Article of the Northwest Ordinance, but it could not be persuaded to include citizenship for Negroes or Indians.

By 1837, there were no more slaves in Detroit, but 1836 saw the beginning of racial segregation as a social fact when a separate Colored Baptist Church, now Second Baptist Church, was established. By 1839 there was a separate Lafayette Street African Methodist Episcopal Church, now Bethel A.M.E. Church, and later, in 1847, a Colored Episcopal Church, St. Matthews. Meanwhile, Negro children were excluded from the common schools. In 1842, the Detroit public school system was organized to pull the education system out of a steadily worsening condition of lack of financial support. The following plea was issued:

> . . . There is not a hard-handed and toil worn laborer within the precincts of all Detroit destitute of the heart and spirit, and the will, and who will not earn and freely contribute his dollar for the emancipation of the rising generation from the thraldom of vice and the slavery of ignorance.[9]

The part of the school ordinance approved on February 17, 1842, which was used to justify separate colored schools was contained in Section 9 of the ordinance as follows:

> The board of education shall have full power and authority, and it shall be their duty, to purchase such school houses, and apply for and receive from the county treasurer or other officer, all moneys appropriated for the primary schools and district library of said city, and designate a place where the library may be kept therein.

[9] Sister Mary Rosalita, *Education In Detroit Prior to 1850* (Lansing: Michigan Historical Commission, 1928), p. 326.

The said board shall also have full power and authority to make by-laws and ordinances relative to taking the census of all children in said city between the ages of five and seventeen years; relative to making the necessary reports and transmitting the same to the proper officers as designated by law, so that said city may be entitled to its proportion of the primary school fund; relative to visitation of schools; relative to the length of time schools shall be kept, which shall be less than three months in each year; relative to the employment and examination of teachers, their powers and duties; relative to regulation of schools and the books to be used therein; relative to the appointment of necessary officers; and prescribe their powers and duties; relative to anything whatever that may advance the interest of education, the good government and prosperity of common schools in said city, and the welfare of the public concerning the same.[10]

This authority was used one month later by the Board of Education in its "Introductory Report Together With Rules and Regulations" to make the following provision for colored schools:

1. In addition to the two classes of schools hereinbefore enumerated there shall be established a school for the education of the colored children of this city, under the direction and subject to the control of this board.

2. Said colored school shall be open to all the colored children of every age in the city and shall receive from the public moneys under the control of the board a sufficient sum of money to support the same for — months in each year.

3. The teacher of said school shall be chosen by the board; and it shall be under the particular charge and direction of a committee for the purpose to be annually

[10] *The Revised Rules and Regulations of the Board of Education of The City of Detroit,* February 20, 1846 (Detroit: Charles Willcox, 1846), p. 21.

appointed by the President, which committee shall consist of three members.

4. The regulations of this school shall be the same as those of the other schools of the city. Its teacher shall be subject to the same rules, shall perform the same duties and be under like responsibility to the board as are the teachers of the other schools established by the board; except that the teachers shall be authorized to admit scholars to such schools, subject to the decision of its committee.

5. The committee of said school shall perform the same duties, in relation to this school as the respective committees of the other classes of schools are required to perform toward the schools under their control. Its teacher shall be examined and certified as competent by the committee on qualifications of teachers, as in the other schools; and, it shall be the duty of the committee on school houses to see that a suitable room is furnished, and to perform the same duties in relation to this school as to other schools of the board.[11]

Section 4, Article 5 of the "Rules" reads in part as follows:

... Scholars must, as a general rule attend the school located in the district or part of the city where they reside: for good cause this rule may be departed from by a decision of a majority of the committee on admissions.[12]

By this language, Detroit became organized and defined as one school district, but that definition did not include Negroes. In fact, one of the first *de facto* separate education systems in the United States was incorporated into the interpretation of the Detroit School Ordinance of 1842. A separate district called Number 8 had been established for colored children in 1839, and the Rev. William

[11] *Detroit Board of Education, Introductory Report Together With Rules and Regulations,* March, 1842 (Detroit: Bagg and Harmon Co., 1842), pp. 25-26.
[12] *Ibid.,* p. 21.

C. Monroe was charged to be the teacher. No funds were available for District 8. It was not until 1865 that two colored teachers, Miss Fannie Richards and Miss Delia Pelham, were hired and paid as regular teachers. Quite coincidentally, the later United States Supreme Court "separate but equal" decision in the *Plessy vs. Ferguson* Case of 1896 was written by a Detroiter, Justice Henry B. Brown.

The Negro population of Detroit trebled between 1837 and 1840, and its drive for citizenship began to take concrete form. The domestic question now rested not upon slavery, except in relationship to the fugitive slaves, but squarely upon the questions of citizenship and the recognition of the dignity of person. Therefore, by 1843, Negroes organized to this end. On October 26-27, 1843, a state convention of Negroes was held in the Bethel A.M.E. Church to petition the legislature for full citizenship. The petition was denied, but this beginning was not to diminish until the final achievement of the goal in 1870.

There was even organized a political organization called the Liberty Association whose sole purpose was to get anti-slavery and liberal candidates elected to the legislature. This party enjoyed considerable success with Henry Bibb of Detroit and Windsor, publishing his newspaper *The Voice of the Fugitive* in Windsor.

The year 1850 was a particularly paradoxical year because of one domestic and one national event which, though negative, gave the strongest positive thrust to the emancipation process. The second Michigan Constitutional Convention was held in 1850, and a coalition of Negro and white petitioners sought to secure an article enfranchising Negroes. Indians and immigrants were accorded citizenship, but Negroes were again denied. In addition, the United States Congress passed the infamous Fugitive Slave Act of 1850.

The enactment of the Fugitive Slave Act was almost a

direct consequence of two earlier events in Detroit and Marshall, Michigan. In 1846, David Dunn, a man from St. Louis, Missouri, an affluent businessman, influential in Missouri politics, came to Detroit to apprehend his reputedly brilliant ex-slave, Robert Cromwell. By a ruse, he tricked Cromwell into the courthouse and had the court clerk lock the door. Cromwell eluded Dunn and ran to the window yelling "Murder!" Thereupon William Lambert and George DeBaptiste, active Negro abolitionists, began to break open the locked door. The clerk threw them the key. Cromwell was transported to Canada. Dunn was chased down Jefferson Avenue and subsequently arrested for attempted kidnapping. Dunn was incarcerated for six months before he was narrowly acquitted of the charges. He returned to Missouri a very angry man and told his story to Senator Thomas H. Benton, who introduced the bill into the United States Senate which was to become the Fugitive Slave Law.[13] The bill did not pass immediately, but Detroit now had the firm reputation in the South as a hotbed of radical abolitionists.

In the same year, 1846, a case similar to that of Cromwell-Dunn occurred in Marshall. Frank Troutman, a southerner, led a group of slave agents on a rampage in Marshall, where they shot some Negroes and severely beat others. They captured Adam Crosswhite and his family, who had earlier fled Kentucky and taken residence in Marshall. Citizens of Marshall were outraged and attacked the agents. The Crosswhites were sent on the Underground to Canada. Violence was averted only by the influence of the Quakers. In a conciliation meeting, Troutman took the names of everyone present and later entered a case against them in federal court, after he had been arrested for failure to leave Marshall peaceably.

The case carried over to 1848 when, as fortune would

[13] "Negroes In Detroit, Compiled from Burton Historical Collection," pp. 23-25.

have it, General Lewis Cass, former Governor and now United States Senator from Michigan, ran for President. To secure the nomination it became politically necessary for him to establish the image of Michigan as a friend of the South. This political circumstance weighed directly upon the Marshall case, and the citizens whom Troutman had charged were convicted. The Marshall citizens won a moral victory because Cass was defeated, and the case strengthened the abolitionist cause.[14] Nevertheless, by 1850, Henry Clay and other southerners used the Cromwell-Dunn and the Crosswhite-Troutman cases to secure passage of the Fugitive Slave Act, in a form more oppressive than previous forms which had not passed the Congress.

The act of 1850 was so extreme that it prescribed that all a person needed to claim another as property was an affidavit. Naturally, many persons were claimed in this way who had never been slaves. In addition, prison and heavy fines were prescribed for anyone sheltering or hiding a fugitive, and commissioners were appointed by the federal government to apprehend fugitives. These commissioners were empowered to deputize citizens to assist them, and such citizens were subject to arrest and fine if they did not cooperate. Commissioners were also given quasi-judicial powers, and they were paid ten dollars for every slave captured, but only five dollars if a claim was refused and the accused fugitive released—a nice inducement to assist in the perversion of justice.

This type of act and denial of justice provided the backdrop for the emergence of the eloquent and profound Frederick Douglass and William Lloyd Garrison, bitter foes of the Fugitive Slave Act. These two men, along with Gerrit Smith and United States Senator Charles Sumner, became the giants of the emancipation drive.

[14] *Ibid.*, pp. 25-27.

By 1855, enough liberals had been elected to the Michigan legislature to secure an act called the Personal Liberty Law, which prohibited the use of county jails to house fugitive slaves and prescribed that prosecutors must defend them in courts. In the previous year, the Refugee Home Society was organized by the dedicated group of Detroit abolitionists. The society purchased land near Windsor and built homes for some fifty fugitive and indigent families to start farms. The work of the society continued to 1872. In the same year, 1854, the Republican party, which was later to send Abraham Lincoln to the Presidency, was organized in Jackson, Michigan, on July 6.

The crowning events in this process occurred in 1858 and 1859. William Lambert, Negro organizer of "The African American Mysteries," an anti-slavery organization predominantly of Negroes, which reached a membership of one million in the United States and Canada, had become the key contact between the city of Detroit and John Brown, who brought fugitive slaves over the railroad. The Rev. William C. Monroe, minister and teacher, had become the key contact between Detroit and Frederick Douglass. These four men and other citizens of Detroit and Chatham were to exercise vital roles in the precipitation of the Civil War and in the pressure for the Emancipation Proclamation.

In 1858, William Lambert called together a national convention of followers of John Brown in Chatham, Ontario. Monroe presided. The products of that convention were the drawing-up and adoption of a constitution for a democratic state to be set up for ex-slaves, and a commitment of men, money, and arms to John Brown. Lambert was elected treasurer.

In the following year, on March 12, 1859, by a kind of coincidence which appears to be design, Frederick Douglass was scheduled to lecture at the Colored Baptist Church (Second Baptist) under the auspices of Monroe.

John Brown arrived in Detroit with five followers and nineteen fugitives whom he delivered to Elijah Willis in Windsor. Harriet Tubman, planning to meet John Brown here and go with him to Harper's Ferry, was detained by illness in New York and Philadelphia. (She later served the Union Army as an intelligence agent and actually fought with the Fifty-Fourth Massachusetts Regiment which captured Fort Wagner in 1863.)

After Douglass' lecture, held at Old City Hall instead of the church, John Brown, Douglass, Rev. William Monroe, Elijah Willis, George DeBaptiste, John O. Richards, William Lambert, and Dr. Joseph Ferguson, met at the home of William Webb at 185 E. Congress (where the commemorative historical marker now stands) in a secret meeting to discuss for the last time together John Brown's proposal to raid the Harpers Ferry federal arsenal, although Brown and Douglass met twice again for earnest discussion in Rochester, New York, and Chambersburg, Pennsylvania.[15] Brown detailed his plans and requested money and volunteers. Douglass dissented and proposed an intensification of the nonviolent method of political and moral persuasion. Douglass' argument did not carry, and Brown could not be dissuaded. Brown received volunteers. History records that on the following October 16, the unsuccessful raid was undertaken. John Brown was captured and subsequently executed on December 2, 1859. This event, which inspired the classic hymn, "John Brown's Body Lies a-Mouldering in the Grave," set in motion the chain of circumstances which became the Civil War.

Frederick Douglass, on the other hand, made his overtures directly to the President. In the course of events, he became the chief recruiter of Negro soldiers for the Union

---

[15] Benjamin Quarles, *Frederick Douglass* (Washington: Associated Publishers Inc., 1948), pp. 176-80.

Army and the chief pressure agent upon Lincoln for the Emancipation Proclamation.

Fourteen Negro soldiers were decorated with the Congressional Medal of Honor during the Civil War, even though their enlistment was not really accepted until 1863, after the Proclamation had been issued.[16] Among the participating Michigan regiments was the 102nd United States Colored Regiment, organized in Detroit. The regiment participated in ten engagements in Florida and South Carolina.

Several facts about the Emancipation Proclamation itself must be placed in perspective in relationship to Detroit's role. The relevant part of it read:

> That on the 1st day of January A.D. 1863, all persons held as slaves within any State or designated part of a State the people whereof shall be in rebellion against the United States, shall be then, thenceforward, and forever free; and the Executive Government of the United States, including the military and naval authority thereof, will recognize and maintain the freedom of such persons and will do no act or acts to repress such persons, or any of them, in any efforts that may make for their actual freedom.[17]

The reference to "all persons" did not specify Negroes because there were white slaves and indentured servants, and there were and had been Indian slaves. There were also instances of Negro and Indian owners of slaves fighting on the side of the Confederate Army. Moreover, the Proclamation was thought by some to be a universal declaration, when in fact it was addressed specifically and by name to states and counties of states which were in rebellion on the date, January 1, 1863.

[16] Benjamin Quarles, *The Negro In The Civil War* (Boston: Little, Brown and Co., 1953), p. 210.
[17] John G. Nicolay and John Hay (ed.), *Abraham Lincoln, Complete Works* (New York: Century Co., 1894), p. 287.

The President was cautious and concerned to win the war and preserve the territorial and political unity of the United States government. The Proclamation was as much a tactical instrument as it was a moral edict. It prescribed emancipation, but it did not recognize citizenship. Douglass was aware of this, but so also were those who were intolerant of the possibility that all Americans should be recognized as full citizens.

Douglass turned to the Negro people and tried to instruct them as to the difference between the Proclamation's address to the state and the necessity for Negroes to recognize and secure their *own* freedom. He proposed, in effect, that the latter recognition is the necessary *a posteriori* condition for the *state* to recognize their freedom. In Douglass' words:

> If there is no struggle there is no progress. Those who profess to favor freedom, and yet depreciate agitation are men who want crops without plowing up the ground. . . . This struggle may be a moral one; or it may be a physical one; but it must be a struggle. . . . Power concedes nothing without a demand. It never did and it never will.[18]

The reality of this as a fact of life was demonstrated in Detroit almost immediately after the issuance of the Proclamation. Two of the first and largest demonstrations of it were held in Detroit at the Lafayette Street A.M.E. Church, January 1, 1963, and at Second Baptist Colored Church, January 6, 1863. The celebration momentarily galvanized the entire city into a unity of reverential joy. The pressure for enlistment in the Union Army and the adulation of the President reached a zenith. But this moment was not to last.

In the midst of the joy about the Emancipation Proclamation and the urgency on the part of Detroit Negroes to

[18] Foner, *op. cit.*, p. 153.

share in the mammoth military effort to secure the Union, there came a stark reminder that there was a marked difference between emancipation and full recognition of citizenship, even in a state where there were no slaves. Michigan was still a state where Negroes were not yet accorded citizenship rights. Sentiments for continued denial of these rights had been supported by the United States Supreme Court in the Dred Scott case (*Scott vs. Sandford*) of 1857.

In the famous Dred Scott case, Chief Justice Taney had ruled that United States citizenship was enjoyed by two classes of individuals: (1) white persons born in the United States as descendants of "persons, who were at the time of the adoption of the Constitution recognized as citizens in the several States and (who) became also citizens of this new political body," the United States of America, and (2) those who, having been "born outside the dominions of the United States," had migrated thereto and been naturalized therein. The States were competent, he conceded, to confer State citizenship upon anyone in their midst, but could not make the recipient of such status a citizen of the United States. The Negro, however, according to the Chief Justice, was ineligible to attain United States citizenship either from a State or by virtue of birth in the United States, even as a free man descended from a Negro residing as a free man in one of the States at the date of ratification of the Constitution. That basic document did not contemplate the possibility of Negro citizenship. By the Fourteenth Amendment this deficiency of the original Constitution was cured.[19]

Detroit had also become the home of one of the first expressly anti-Negro, as distinguished from pro-slavery, organizations, called the Knights of the Golden Circle. Its

[19] *Constitution of The United States* (Washington: U. S. Government Printing Office, 1952), pp. 963-64.

avowed purpose was to resist conscription into the Union Army and to spread anti-Negro sentiment. This sentiment unfortunately received support from a prominent local newspaper which was accused of being one of the precipitants of the Faulkner Riot, which occurred on March 5, 1863.

This riot is still recorded as the most savage and violent racial episode in Detroit history. It was a tragic reminder to the city and to the nation that emancipation and freedom were of different dimensions. They could not be equated. A second sharp reminder came in 1865 when, in the year of cessation of the hostilities of the Civil War, Negroes again petitioned the Michigan legislature for citizenship and the petition was again denied.

The final recognition came only after the Fifteenth Amendment to the United States Constitution clarified the language of Article VI of the Northwest Ordinance, which the Constitution had recovered in the Thirteenth Amendment; reinforced the relationship of law to citizenship prescribed in the Fourteenth Amendment; and made final recognition that the right of citizens of the United States to full participation in American political life shall not be abridged by a state. This was the essence of the Fifteenth Amendment. Herein lies the distinction between the absence of slavery and the presence of freedom. In full citizenship and full exercise of franchise alone is there the possibility of the achievement of the equal dignity of person which is essential to the recognition of freedom either by the person or by the state.

Michigan sealed its pledge to this end when she ratified the Fifteenth Amendment to the United States Constitution in 1870. Negroes voted for the first time in Michigan on November 8, 1870, after Detroit and Michigan had made themselves for eighty-three years a precursor and thirty-seven years a participant, a taskmaster, and a testing ground for the complete spectrum of complex struggles and counter-struggles represented in the historical fact of the Emancipation Proclamation. Even so, it took fifty more years to accomplish the enfranchisement of women. The imperative moral meanings of the difference between slavery and liberty, freedman and resident, resident and citizen, citizenship and the right of franchise, were all in some wise written in the city of Detroit.

Detroit again has all of the moral nuances and all of the actors. She stands at the portal of opportunity again to be a stage and model to the nation for the full amplification of the Encouragement to Education Article to achieve the further meaning of the difference between citizenship and the equal dignity of man in the reciprocity of freedom. There is a present opportunity and a present imperative.

II

THE NEGRO
IN A CHANGING
SOCIETY

As was pointed out in the first part of this book, the United States has always been a changing society, but the position of the Negro did not change very much until about the time of the Second World War. Since then, change has been occurring more and more rapidly.

It is the purpose of this portion of the book to present a description and analysis of facets of this recent change through the eyes of competent social scientists. Gunnar Myrdal points out that what is happening in the United States has its parallels in large parts of Africa and Asia in the elimination of colonialism and the demand for equal opportunity to strive for the good things of life. G. Franklin Edwards specifies the recent occupational changes of the American Negro. The physical segregation of the Negro in the slums of the large cities is the problem tackled by Robert C. Weaver. This problem has political as well as economic roots: James Q. Wilson delves into the political position of the Negro in the American social structure. The dramatically changing basis of court decisions is both a cause and a result of changes in other spheres of social life; the pertinent court decisions are analyzed here by Charles W. Quick and Donald B. King. To complete the survey of recent changes is the essay by Rayford W. Logan, who considers education in a broad context.

These surveys of recent social change are not intended to be comprehensive, but merely to sample the nature and extent of the changes. Social scientists tend to study change much as they study a static social structure: They see the objective facts and report them adequately, but usually fail to examine the underlying dynamics of the change. The result is a fairly static picture which does not allow for prediction of the future course of change. Of course, predictions often fail, even when based on careful analysis; so social scientists usually do not wish to take the risk.

THE WORLDWIDE
EMANCIPATION OF
UNDERDEVELOPED NATIONS

Gunnar Myrdal

There are striking similarities between the emancipation of the Negro slaves in America and the freeing of the peoples in the colonies from metropolitan rule. For one thing, these new nations suddenly emerging as independent political entities are all colored. In the new era of independence, this fact is usually soft-pedalled in the scientific as well as in the political and popular discussion of their problems, both by the articulate people in these nations themselves and by the white people in the rich countries who come in contact with them or who otherwise express views on their problems. This fact has important social, ideological, and political implications. It gives its tone and temper to almost every ideological issue. In the protest against colonialism we will almost always find the word "racialism" joined together with "imperialism."

In addition to this fact that the people of the new

nations are colored, as are American Negroes, and feel themselves to be separate from the whites, there are other significant similarities in the historical processes of their liberation. In both instances, freedom came to colored peoples as the result of a big war, the biggest and most devastating war that had been fought up until that time, but a war in which they themselves had not taken much of a part.

The Civil War in America had not been waged by the victorious northern states in order to free the slaves, even though the peculiar institution of Negro slavery in the South was one of the many conditions creating tension and disunity between the North and the South. Abraham Lincoln had at the outbreak of the war been very emphatic in stating that the intention on the northern side was not to disrupt the institution of slavery in the rebellious South but to preserve the Union. Nevertheless, he was brought, by the logic of events, to take one step after the other to end slavery. The first major step was the Proclamation of September 22, 1862, that the Negro slaves in the rebellious states should be free.

In the same way, the liberation of the colonial peoples was definitely not a war aim of any country when the Second World War broke out in 1939, or even later in the course of that war. Nevertheless, the end of that war left the colonial powers unable to prevent a political avalanche that in a rapid sequence of events led to the emancipation of many hundred millions of colored people from colonial rule. The process of emancipation is not entirely consummated yet, but there is no doubt that in a few years' time all colonial peoples will be politically independent.

The colonial power system, that had developed over many centuries and that had had its widest expansion and strongest manifestation in the period of the "new imperialism" in the decades around the turn of the century up until the First World War, will disappear from the earth and belong entirely to history, as does Negro slavery in the United States. Indeed, the collapse of that political power system will one day be seen as by far the most important result of the Second World War. The reverberations of it will change conditions for life and work in every corner of the world and will in a decisive way determine world development till the end of this century and even beyond. Its importance cannot be overestimated. We have as yet only seen the beginning of its world-shaking effects; and, as I shall indicate, we have by means of biased scientific approaches protected our minds from grasping the seriousness of what has happened and what will happen.

In the wake of the abolition of slavery in the United States there were high hopes expressed, far-reaching declarations made, and political decisions undertaken, some of these latter in the form of changes in the constitutional law of this country, all aimed at rapidly establishing real social, political, and economic liberty and equality of opportunity for the Negroes now no longer held in the bondage of formal slavery. After a few confused years of Reconstruction, however, these attempts were given up almost entirely. In the national compromise towards the end of the seventies, the great majority of the Negroes who lived in the South were delivered as unprotected pawns into the hands of the defeated, embittered, unreconstructed southern whites. Even in the North the Negroes were not given many new openings even though their lot was much better than that of their brethren in the South.

For sixty years thereafter, until about the time when I happened to be finishing my study of the Negro problem in America, the status of the Negroes remained almost unchanged. Only during the last twenty years has there been again a consistent trend upwards that gradually has begun to give more reality to the hopes, declarations, and decisions following the Civil War.

In hindsight, the frustration of the urges during and after Reconstruction to give reality to the American creed in respect to the Negroes is not difficult to explain. Those efforts not only met the sullen determination of the southern whites, who even after defeat in the Civil War held the positions of social and economic power in the region. In the victorious northern states we can see an increasing lack of devotion to the ideals that had served as banners during and immediately after the Civil War.

Behind the extemporized political and legal action in the Reconstruction period there was not much serious, searching analysis or planning. There was no real preparedness to undertake large-scale social and economic reform, which would have had to imply, among other things, redistributional intervention and, in particular, what we are now trying to preach to, and press upon, the underdeveloped countries: land reform. In the absence of a will to large-scale induced social and economic change, the initial political revolution, implied in the abolition of slavery, petered out, leaving things very much as they were, except in form. "Fifty acres and a mule" never became anything more than an empty slogan.

What then happened to a few million Negroes in one country may now be happening on a vastly bigger scale to many hundred million colored peoples in the liberated colonies. The American Negroes lived enclosed together with their former white masters within one country, that was left to pursue an undisturbed national life in a political vacuum behind the protection of the two oceans. What is now happening and will be happening in the former colonies occurs not only on a vastly larger scale but also in a heavily charged political world situation, of which the Cold War is an element, and which more generally is the very opposite of the political vacuum in which America lived during the nineteenth century. On the world scene there are other aggravating circumstances not present in

America a hundred years ago, for instance the population explosion in all the poor countries.

As I said before, neither the freeing of the Negro slaves in the United States, nor the liquidation of the colonial power system in the world at large was a war aim, though these far-reaching changes occurred as a result of the two wars. In both cases, however, the resultant changes had behind them a long development that had gradually made the situation ripe for such changes.

In both cases, the developments leading to the collapse of a previous power system were of a complex nature with many cross currents. Curiously enough, in both cases it had for a time seemed as if the system had been strengthened. We know that in the United States the slavery institution, already on its way to decay, had early in the nineteenth century got an underpinning of stronger economic interests to uphold it through technological changes in cotton agriculture. I have already mentioned, too, how the "new imperialism" of the last decades of the nineteenth century had implied the widest extension of the colonial rule and the most intensive use of it for economic exploitation.

The First World War set a limit to further growth of the colonial power system, even if its liquidation was still far off. Mr. K. M. Panikkar, the Indian statesman-historian-philosopher, is probably right when he expresses the opinion that it was only the outbreak of the First World War that prevented the French and the British from consummating—after a long series of mutually agreed infringements—the final division of Siam between themselves. It is his opinion that the war alone stopped the great powers from splitting China into colonies without leaving it even the appearance of being an independent nation. It is always a difficult and, indeed, impossible task to ascertain in a binding way what would have happened if a major development had not occurred, but there is much that makes this view credible.

In any case it is clear that, historically speaking, the First World War marks the end of expansion and intensification of colonial rule and the beginning of a new trend in world history. The "new imperialism" from the seventies had been developing continually up till that point. Now the further advance of colonialism was brought to a stop. If we look a little closer, we can also see that the First World War demarcates the time when developments both in the metropolitan countries themselves and in some of the colonies began, or, when the beginning was earlier, gained a momentum that in the end released the avalanche of world-wide emancipation for the colonial peoples. So far as developments within the colonies themselves are concerned, there are wide discrepancies, which I shall touch upon later.

At this stage of the argument I want first to comment upon the character of the emancipation of the colonial peoples as a movement with the force of an avalanche. Once started, it rapidly spread out in such a way that the winning of freedom in one part of the world acted as a trigger to unstabilize the colonial power system in one region after another, until the masses of colored peoples everywhere in the world joined in the movement, even in colonies where there had been little or no internal development foretelling what was going to happen. Everywhere the barriers, built to preserve the *status quo* in the interest of the white people in the metropolitan countries, mainly in Western Europe, crashed as if they were constructed of straw.

In some parts of the world, as in most parts of Africa, the avalanche came as a surprise to everybody concerned. In the Belgian Congo, to take an extreme example, the Belgians, only a few years before the collapse of their regime, sincerely believed that they had found the formula of colonial exploitation through beneficent husbandry, effectively insulating the colony and making it safe against the outbreak of rebellious movements. They believed that they had perfected a political and economic dependency that contained no germs of conscious dissent and that also stopped the influx of dangerous ideas from abroad. Most outside observers at that time shared their view.

But suddenly the rebellion swept into the country, which almost instantaneously was in full flame. The colonial rulers were helpless. If they thought that an equally rapid political retreat would prove the necessity of their presence in command, the indigenous people having been more systematically prevented there than anywhere else from acquiring the skills to care for themselves, they were, as we know, grossly mistaken.

The world-wide avalanche was unleashed by the liberation of the South Asian countries. In South Asia the quasi-voluntary withdrawal by the British from their domination of British India, Ceylon, and Burma foredoomed to complete failure the attempts of the Dutch in the Netherlands East Indies and the French in Indochina to resist rebellion. British policies in their colonies had, more than the Dutch and French policies, made the indigenous people "prepared for independence." In a rather close correlation with this, organized liberation movements in the British colonies were generally more frequent. As the avalanche spread out to other regions, it increasingly set in motion dependent peoples who were even less "prepared" and among whom, until almost the moment of liberation, there had been no organized liberation movement.

The general conception I have wanted to convey is that the emancipation of the colonial peoples is a development of the Second World War, but that developments in the outside world and particularly in the metropolitan countries as also in some of the colonies themselves, going far back and becoming accentuated by the First World

War, must be looked into in order to understand why the Second World War had this result and why it had the character of an avalanche.

One main factor was undoubtedly the relative weakening, economically and politically after the First World War, of the Western European countries that of old were the colonial powers. The rising economic and political power of the United States, with its inherited anticolonial ideology, was another force weakening the colonial power system. This ideology was in various ways qualified; the United States was itself a colonial power, mainly through its political dominance of the Philippines. But its intention of giving up that colony was declared and, a little later, decided and agreed upon. In regard to West European colonialism the dislike and distrust of it by the Americans was more unqualified. In regard to the economic exploitation by American business concerns in some Latin American countries, which often took a character similar to colonialism, there were continual criticism and pangs of conscience in the United States. On the whole, there was also, in the period between the two wars, a gradually increasing reluctance to back up these economic interests by governmental power.

Another main factor was, of course, the appearance on the world scene of the Soviet Union, with an ideology strongly opposed to colonialism and a political interest directed toward destroying the colonial power structure. The Leninist theory, borrowed from Hobson more than from Marx, of colonialist imperialism as a late stage of capitalism provided an easily popularized ideology for liberation movements in the colonies. In one or another form and degree it has influenced every one of these movements and, indeed, every articulate individual active in them. Even if the Soviet Union for a long time was not strong enough to act as a political force in the world arena, its very existence in defiance of the Western world's intensive dislike, along with its aggressive propaganda against the capitalist and imperialist countries, was a disturbing thing that weakened the inner morale in the metropolitan countries and at the same time provided a spur to liberation movements in those colonies where such movements rose to importance.

Since the Second World War, the rising power of the Soviet Union and the Soviet bloc has undoubtedly been a main cause of the avalanche I have talked about. More important than direct political influence in the various colonies through its propaganda and through other means has probably been the firm reliance that every rebellious movement could have upon Soviet backing in the international organizations, and, on the part of the Western countries—not least the United States—the competitive interest in the pursuance of the Cold War, where they had to be careful not to be maneuvered into a position in which they would seem to be standing against freedom. The very existence of the Soviet Union and the Soviet bloc has thus been a mighty force in speeding up the emancipation of the colonial peoples.

But let me return to the developments before the Second World War which, in hindsight, stand out as main causal factors for what later happened. The West European countries had for a long time been on the way to becoming full-fledged democracies with universal suffrage. That development was consummated at the end of the First World War, when restrictions on the right to vote, confining it to the upper strata, were generally abolished. Parallel to that development, the welfare state came into being, implying a growing concern and responsibility on the part of organized society for the underprivileged strata at home. It became an ever more weighty moral burden to stand for a system of government and for colonial policies in contradiction to the ideals and aspirations becoming ever more commonly accepted in the home countries and actually more and more applied in practical policy.

One effect of this ideological and political trend in the metropolitan countries was an intensified export to the intellectual elite in the colonies of radical ideas and ideals which must have made revolt against the colonial system even more enticing. Almost everywhere, though to varying extents, the colonial powers had been brought to create an educated class for service in their administration and as professionals. In some of the colonies, particularly in South Asia, where the avalanche later was to be released, the colonial governments began to share power by permitting members of the educated class to become administrators even of higher rank and by setting up consultative assemblies with appointed and/or elected members from the indigenous educated elite. When in varying degrees the colonial governments began to adopt welfare measures in the colonies, this action implied engaging that elite more fully in responsibilities for their own people. As the elite grew, they came to press for more posts for themselves and for more responsibility at higher levels. About this whole development, which in some countries like the British colonies in South Asia had gone far but in others had hardly begun, the most important observation in the present context is that it introduced a trend which is in contradiction to colonial rule.

Whether more generally there was a decrease in the economic interest of having colonies is a moot question. There probably was in some colonies but not in others. To the Dutch, who had made, relatively speaking, great investments in the Netherlands East Indies, the economic interest in holding on to colonial domination was considerable until the very end; and this interest partly explains their stubborn resistance to independence for Indonesia.

The French economic interests in Indochina and, particularly, in North Africa were probably, objectively assessed, much smaller, if not negative.

On this point we have to remember, however, that one effect of a rising liberation movement in a colony is an increase in the cost of retaining it under colonial rule. Equally important is the observation that while the cost had to be carried by the whole nation—insofar as the colony was not brought to carry it completely—the profits from colonial exploitation went to restricted groups of nationals who had settled there, or to shareholders and business people in the metropolitan country. When these groups who held the vested interests in retaining a colony were able to influence the press and the legislators—sometimes, as in France, by illegitimate means—they could determine policy.

The general political trend, however, since the beginning of this century and more definitely since the end of the First World War was, as I pointed out, that the broad masses, who had little economic stake in the exploitation of the colonies, become politically more powerful. And as the general costs—military costs and also some welfare costs—were rising rapidly and more and more becoming costs on the budget of the metropolitan country, this trend towards political democracy at home must in general have weakened the determination to hold on to the domination of the colonies.

Looking back on recent history in this period when colonialism was approaching liquidation, it must strike us as remarkable how little comprehensive and intensive analysis there was of the economic consequences to the metropolitan countries of having colonies: in terms of profits and costs and their distribution among different groups and classes, and, indeed, how little public discussion there was of these matters. There has been very little of it even later. These problems still remain open ones calling for research, which will now have to be of an historical nature.

Instead, in all the metropolitan countries the issue was debated in terms of national honor, civilizing mission, political principles, and, in the end, practical possibilities and necessities, not in terms of economic interests, except by means of very sweeping and unsupported slogans. Generally speaking, none of the colonies were given up voluntarily in a true sense, i.e., by a decision to do it in response to democratic ideals and in a situation where the choice of not doing it was felt to be open. They were either hopelessly lost, often after resistance to the last; or it was seen that they could not be held without prohibitive cost.

This was true even of the early British surrender of colonial dominance over British India, Ceylon, and Burma, which played such a tremendously important role in releasing the avalanche. The British government was aware of the fact that holding on to British India and to Burma would have required deploying there an increasingly big army and police force and keeping an increasing number of Indian and Burmese patriots in prison. Ceylon was calmer, but it could be foreseen that even there a liberation movement would rise, particularly if there were a rising tide of unrest in India. Sooner or later the financial and moral burden would have been overwhelming; and the British calculated—correctly as we have seen—that they would have greater possibility of protecting their enterprises and capital assets and greater opportunity to repatriate capital, if they settled the independence issue amicably and without struggle unto the bitter end. The British were cool and rational when giving up these colonies, more than generous and idealistic, and they have in the main followed the same policy in regard to their other colonies in other parts of the world. The French and Dutch acted differently, to their own great disadvantage.

When pointing to the rational motives for giving up the colonies, the importance of which rapidly increased in an accelerating pace, we should not forget that in Britain the development towards greater democracy and towards the welfare state at home had softened the ideological ground for having colonies. It probably meant something also, at least for the timing of the surrender, that Britain after the war had a Labour government.

There were, as I pointed out, parallel changes in the colonies: the growth of an indigenous educated class, the sharing to an increasing extent of political and administrative responsibilities with that class, and a continuous and gradual redirection of policies toward giving greater consideration to the interests of the indigenous people. On the one hand, these changes implied a preparation for independence. On the other hand, they made the continuation of colonial rule more difficult. Directly and indirectly they fostered the liberation movement.

When one after another of the South Asian colonies had won independence, overcoming more or less resistance from the metropolitan country, it became impossible to prevent a similar development in West Asia. The Communist takeover in China and the consolidation of a strong and independent central government there had some traits in common with the decolonization in South Asia. In any case, it was often so conceived in the underdeveloped regions and understandably spurred events elsewhere. The most remarkable and until then most unexpected development was, of course, the spread of the emancipation movement in Africa and then even to parts of that continent where there would seem to have been least preparation not only for an independent regime but for the rise of a rebellion. In Latin America almost all countries, even the poorest and most backward, have been politically independent for a long time. The reverberations of events in the rest of the underdeveloped world are manifested there in movements with various blends of radicalism and nationalism but where protest against foreign economic domination is always an ingredient.

In remarking on the economic, social, and political situation in the former colonies, I may be excused for wanting to point out something which I should perhaps have said right at the start. To speak briefly about such a large part of humanity embroiled in such a dramatic development requires me to make broad generalizations without any possibility of accounting for differences or making proper qualifications.

Having made this *reservatio mentis*, I venture to state first that the masses of these people live in great poverty with levels of living, in all respects, so low that they can hardly be grasped by people in the rich countries. Ordinarily, their living levels are not rising, at least not very rapidly. The income gap between the rich and the poor countries in the world that has been growing for a century is now growing faster than ever. On President Kennedy's proposal, the Assembly of the United Nations declared the sixties to be the Development Decade. What has actually happened during the last few years has been a slowing down of the already slow development in most of those countries which had had any development at all, and stagnation or regression in the others. Meanwhile production and consumption in the Western countries—with a few exceptions, among them the United States—is rising fast.

An aggravating factor is population development. Medical science has made available exceedingly cheap means of preserving life, fairly independently of the living level. This implies that the level of living where the Malthusian checks start to operate has been radically lowered. While mortality has been decreasing, and will continue to decrease, natality is preserved and occasionally even raised. In none of the underdeveloped countries, even in those few where the government has come out for a policy of spreading birth control, are there rational reasons to expect that fertility will decrease substantially, reestablishing a new balance between births and deaths. As the age composition of the populations is heavily biased towards a preponderance of young people, population increase has a tremendous momentum and will imply a doubling of the populations in thirty, twenty-five, or even twenty years.

In most of these countries—though with considerable variations—there is great social and economic inequality. There have been on the whole few effective reforms aimed at establishing greater equality. Economically, at least, the trend has rather been toward greater inequality. There is this great difference, though, in the situation of the masses of poor people in the former colonies from that of the Negroes in the United States after Emancipation and Reconstruction, that their masters are not usually white any longer but indigenous. This state of affairs becomes increasingly common as the general tendency towards economic nationalism asserts itself.

In all the emancipated new nation-states, the articulate classes are craving for economic development towards greater equality with the rich nations, and planning for development is a program everywhere. Only in a few underdeveloped countries has there been much planning, and even there planning has not succeeded in spurring rapid economic growth.

Politically, there is much tension and uncertainty in almost all of these countries. Initially, they generally accepted as the basis for their nationhood the boundary lines established by the colonial powers. Drawn to meet political and administrative needs of rival powers, these boundary lines are often arbitrary and artificial. Since there are also other causes for friction between neighboring countries, numerous conflicts are to be foreseen.

There are also conflicts between different ethnic groups within each country which tend to break out or worsen, with the end of colonial domination. Even apart from ethnic tensions, the internal political situation is mostly not very stable. In general, all the former colonies tended to opt initially for full democracy, for civil rights, and for radical redistributional reforms in the direction of reaching towards the modern western welfare state. But with the masses living in great poverty and illiteracy, with a weak administrative machinery and the social and political power held by a privileged few, there is usually a wide and often widening gap between ideals and pretensions, on the one hand, and accomplishments, on the other.

There is visibly a trend toward a more authoritarian regime, often founded upon the army. Such a regime can, however, represent a very different direction of actual policies. It may be a reactionary government bent upon preserving the *status quo* in the interest of the top military officers, administrators, landlords, and industrialists; or it may have a more revolutionary inclination. In any case, it is mostly not founded upon a firm basis; factions may develop even within the army.

In most or, indeed, in all underdeveloped countries, it is impossible to know what sort of regime there will be ten or even five years from now.

To these short remarks I should like to add some reflections about the way in which social, economic and political facts in the underdeveloped countries are recorded and analyzed by research. We should first note the tremendous increase during recent years in research activity focused upon these countries. The study of underdeveloped countries is almost entirely a new branch of the social sciences developing after the Second World War. Now, as we know, it engages a large part of our total research personnel and other research facilities. This is particularly true of economic research.

By itself this should surprise no one who has had his

attention focused upon how closely our research interests are steered by the political inclinations in the surrounding society. These countries were about as poor in colonial times as they are now and as much in need of economic development. But the colonial power system was not of the type to call for and encourage our research interests. Obviously, this new redirection of our scholarly activity is not simply a spontaneous development in our sciences but is itself caused by the avalanche of emancipation from colonial rule. The rich countries feel anxiety about the effects for their own security and other vital interests of what has happened, and this anxiety is enhanced by the Cold War and the competition for the souls of men. The internal developments in the underdeveloped countries become therefore of importance in the rich countries.

The fact that a political development has had such a tremendous influence upon the direction of our scientific interests should make us alert to the possibility that even our approach and our way of observing facts and drawing inferences may have been influenced in the same way. This would, however, imply systematic biases in our research activity. I cannot enter upon a discussion of this important problem in this context, and have to restrict myself to stating the conclusion I have reached, that there are such systematic biases.

They usually go in an optimistic direction. Part of this is a sort of diplomatic tendency in research, which we see reflected in the use, even in scientific literature, of terms like the "developing countries" or the "free world." The absence even at our great universities of critical study in the fields of the sociology and the philosophy of knowledge and science has made it more possible than it ought to be for social scientists to be helplessly naïve in regard to the need for protection against the tendencies to bias emanating from the surrounding society.

In this particular case, the tendency to optimistic

biases has had the support of the rapidity by which this new branch of economics has had to be developed. When in the last fifteen or twenty years we economists swarmed into the study of underdeveloped countries, it was natural that we applied the approaches, concepts, and theories we had developed for the study of our developed economies. In our countries, attitudes and institutions have accommodated themselves to a degree of rationalism that makes it possible to carry out economic analysis without much regard to them. While we have criticized on theoretical grounds the concept of the "economic man," he has gradually become a reality.

When applying our modern, western approaches, concepts, and theories to this study of underdeveloped regions —and even collecting statistics defined in these terms— we come, however, to abstract from some of the most awkward facts in the underdeveloped countries facts which stand as inhibitions for development. They are almost always in the sphere of attitudes and institutions, modes and levels of living. The optimistic opportunism of our modern research is demonstrated in the fact that we succeed in having a large literature on the underdeveloped countries while hardly mentioning even the climate factor, which played such a large role in earlier writings on the colonial economy.

In regard to the scientific development, I am hopeful. There is a self-purging force in scientific work. In ten years' time, we are going to have quite other approaches to the study of underdeveloped countries, more adequate to the reality there. We will then be more aware than we are now of how tremendously difficult the situation is for the emancipated colonies.

All the emancipated underdeveloped nations are "unprepared" to rule themselves in a way that corresponds to their development goals and other ideals which they have set up. Many of them are, indeed, very unprepared to do it. One can dream about how different the situation would now be, if one generation ago the colonial powers and the whole western world had had more foresight about what would happen, and if they had, as a consequence, pursued a rationally planned policy of doing whatever could be done to prepare the colonies for independence. Only in a few colonies and only to a limited extent was anything accomplished in this direction.

Another dream would be that there existed a substitute for colonialism, some sort of collective international responsibility for the colonies carried out in the interest of their smooth and rapid development. To a limited extent the trusteeship rule over the colonies of defeated Germany after the First World War and those of Italy after the Second World War would perhaps seem to correspond to this dream. But before the Second World War the territories under trusteeship rule were managed very much as ordinary colonies with a limited supervision on the part of the League of Nations. When once the avalanche of emancipation had been put in motion, after the Second World War, trusteeship rule became nothing more than a transitory arrangement which had rapidly to be changed to full independence. The United Nations' recent activity in the Belgian Congo resembles the assumption of collective international responsibility for a colony that is palpably unable to rule itself. It has been very expensive and not very successful—except perhaps in preventing something much worse—and we have not seen the end of that experiment yet.

There are several reasons why the thought of a collective international responsibility for a former colony, carried out in an unselfish way in the interest of the emancipated people, preparing it for independence and putting it on the road to development, must remain a dream. For one thing, if such a responsibility were undertaken on a large scale it would necessarily be an expensive affair, and the rich countries which would have to defray the costs would hardly be willing to do so. Unselfishness cannot be taken for granted and will, anyhow, not be trusted among the former colonies who have had to fight their way to independence. There is, indeed, an unquestioned principle in all the former colonies of feeling solidarity with every rebellion against remaining colonial authority in any corner of the world. Full independence is the self-evident goal accepted in regard to every dependent people, however badly prepared to rule itself. Added to this is the existence of the Soviet bloc and the Cold War. Cooperation between the Western countries and the Soviet countries in any type of collective international responsibility for the emancipated former colonies seems not a likely thing.

What international responsibility we have for these countries is technical assistance and financial aid, to a small extent channeled through the organizations within the United Nations family but to a larger extent given unilaterally. It would take me too long to discuss this activity in detail. There is a mixed assemblage of motives behind it: commercial, financial, political, and humanitarian. It is probable that the Cold War is responsible for the size this aid has reached; but the Cold War has also given a peculiar direction to it.

About this aid I want to stress only two things. First, the very idea of international redistribution—aside from subsidies in war, help in emergencies as after an earthquake, and the work done by the missionary institutions—is an entirely new thing in the world. Until the very end, colonies were in principle supposed to be profitable or, at least, to pay for themselves. There are hopes that in the rich countries this new principle can be fortified in people's minds.

From that point of view it is deeply regrettable that so many political leaders in America show such eagerness to stress and reiterate that foreign aid is of the nature of subsidies in the Cold War, saving military expense to the United States. I have always been convinced that to a large extent this is a self-deception of the type I have called perverted Puritanism. The Americans want to pretend selfish motives even when they act on humanitarian impulses. The matter is important; for if, in the long run, we want to increase our aid to underdeveloped countries and to plan our aid in a rational way, we must build it upon a foundation of human solidarity as we do when we plan social policy within our own countries.

My second point is that all this aid activity, apart from its obvious and large-scale maldirection, is much too small to meet the needs. And we have not come far in what matters much more than technical assistance and aid: a reform of our way of doing business with the underdeveloped countries. If we were prepared to reconsider our commercial policies and open our markets by giving them a preferential treatment, that would mean much more than all aid. The additional income would be channeled right into the economies of these countries without passing through the government offices.

We are probably approaching a most critical period in the life of the underdeveloped countries. They will feel increasingly frustrated in their development efforts. Several of them will experience a lowering of their living levels, particularly those of their broad masses. There might be radical changes in their political systems and many conflicts between neighboring countries. At least in some parts of the underdeveloped world political developments will not go in the direction we wish. Meanwhile, I feel sure that our research will become more realistic and convey a truer picture of what the situation really is. I believe we are on the point of an awakening to dangers implied in present trends but not yet realized by most people, even among those specializing in development problems.

What we should then hope is that the rich countries in the world will rise to the challenge and be prepared to accept real sacrifices in order to make possible a change in the discouraging trends.

CHANGES IN OCCUPATIONS
AS THEY AFFECT THE NEGRO

G. Franklin Edwards

In considering the relationship of the Negro in America to the structure of American society, attention should be directed to the work life of the Negro as knowledge of it is gained from an analysis of his occupational status. Occupations correlate highly with all status-conferring variables, and from this single item one is able to gain some measure of an individual's and group's position in the society.

In elaboration of this, it is only necessary to point out that occupations are ranked hierarchically, so that some are accorded more prestige than others; social honor and esteem are conferred upon persons, in part at least, according to the occupations they follow. Occupations are related to money income and material possessions, and, in a society which places a high valuation upon these, the work in which one is engaged is of extreme importance. In line with this, occupational status determines one's life chances and those of his descendants, affecting the circumstances under which he is born, his life expectancy, educational attainment, and style of life. It should be pointed out, finally, that the occupation one follows helps to shape his self-conception and thus is importantly related to his conduct.

There is, to be sure, an important relationship between ethnicity and the occupational structure. Minorities in this country have occupied special niches which are associated with the historical circumstances related to their entry into the work force. Mexican Americans, for example, are identified with agriculture in the Southwest and migratory labor elsewhere. Their movement to cities entailed some upward mobility, generally to blue-collar occupations. The Orientals came first in large numbers to perform much of the heavy work associated with railroads. They later settled mainly in the Far West as agriculturalists and small businessmen. The same general point may be made for other minorities which have had a longer history in this country, including most of the white Protestant groups from northern and western Europe, which over time have become well assimilated. The Jewish population from eastern Europe is associated with the needle trades, and Hungarian-Americans and many of the southern and eastern European immigrant groups have been identified with heavy unskilled and semiskilled work in steel, rubber and other manufacturing industries and mining, as their arrival in large numbers coincided with the upsurge of the American industrial revolution.

All of these groups, some more than others, were later affected by changes in the economic structure of the country. What is important, however, is that most of them entered the world of work at the lowest reaches of the occupational structure and developed middle classes at first around professional and business occupations, oriented primarily to serve their own ethnic communities.

They later achieved a break-through in the wider world of work. The rate of assimilation for these groups varied, of course, and some of them are only now in the process of a "take-off" from their lowly occupational origins.

The Negro's relationship to the work world shows all of the characteristics common to other minorities, but in some respects his is a special case. Our concern in this paper will be to review the historical forces which have determined the present occupational and economic status of this minority, an emphasis which is in keeping with the spirit of these commemorative exercises; and to assay some evaluation of the forces which are destined to influence its occupational position in the decades ahead.

Brought to this country mainly as a slave to do the heavy work of plantation agriculture, the Negro was predominantly an agricultural worker until relatively recent times. While his occupational status was in general related to the dominance of agriculture in the economy, he was at the bottom of the agricultural ladder. The hope of many Negroes to become independent farm-owners after the Emancipation was not realized in the terms in which it was envisaged. On the contrary, at the turn of the century three-quarters of the Negroes in agriculture were tenant farmers, the majority of them sharecroppers. As this development occurred mostly in the South, it meant also that the Negro was subjected to the most severe system of economic exploitation and, owing to the succession of events which followed the withdrawal of federal troops from the region, his hopes for climbing the agricultural ladder were almost completely eliminated.

The system of segregation which developed in the South meant poor schools, limited educational achievement, and a loss of hope for entering occupations other than those permitted by the color-caste system. Most of the jobs outside agriculture were as artisans and in service capacities. The great tragedy of the years immediately following the Reconstruction, as Myrdal observed, is that efforts at political reform in behalf of the Negro were not matched by comparable efforts at social and economic reform.[1]

In time the great mass of black peasants lost any hope of gaining a substantial hold in agriculture as owners. Several million left southern farms for cities in the North during the First World War and another million and a half went to southern cities and towns during the 1910-20 decade. The status of those who remained was affected by the Depression and by government agricultural policy in the 1930's, and subsequently by changes in agricultural technology.

The Depression seriously restricted agricultural markets and reduced the need for tenants. Many indebted owners could not meet their mortgage payments and lost their farms. New Deal policies for agriculture led to the reduction of crop acreages. A large proportion of the acreage retired from production was farmed by tenants. A most important fact was that American cotton, the chief crop which claimed the labor of Negro farmers, was losing its competitive position in the world markets with the opening of new cotton lands in Brazil, Egypt, and India. Better fibers were being produced in those countries, with cheaper labor. Many of the older cotton lands, particularly in the Southeast, were turned over to cattle production, and Negroes found no place in the transition.

One vital factor serving to reduce the number of Negroes in agriculture by more than one-half in the last fifty years has been the application of new labor-saving devices. One of the earliest of these was the tractor, but others followed. The size of the average farm increased steadily with the introduction of new machinery, but fewer workers were required. By 1950, California ranked

[1] Gunnar Myrdal, "The Changing Status of the Negro," *Howard University Magazine*, IV, No. 4 (July 1962), 5.

fourth among the states in the production of cotton, a fact which was due mainly to newer land and the application of machinery to larger-scale operations.

The Negro today is not a vital force in American agriculture. His decline as an agricultural worker is related in part to the decline of agriculture in general as it claims a smaller proportion of the labor force. But his traditionally marginal position in these operations has meant that he was more seriously affected by the complex of forces already described—changing markets, economic fluctuations, government agricultural policies, and new technologies. These forces, either singly or in combination, have affected the Negro's relationship to the occupational structure in other work areas as well.

At the time of Emancipation, Negroes did most of the skilled labor in the South. In 1860, there were five times as many Negro artisans as white. The economic liberation of poor whites, however, provided an opportunity for them to enter the skilled trades in large numbers, and with this development the number of Negro artisans declined sharply in the twenty-five years after Emancipation. The rise of craft unions in the 1880's resulted in the segregation of Negro workers into auxiliary unions and prevented them from having access to much of the large-scale construction involving new materials and new technologies. They remained in the trowel trades and worked on small-construction jobs.[2] In the North, vigorous opposition was expressed by immigrant workers to Negroes in the skilled trades; and union policy, in this region as in the South, seriously handicapped Negroes who wished to become artisans. In many of the newer skilled operations so vital to the functioning of urban civilization—plumbing, electrical and metal work, transportation—Negroes were, for all practical purposes, excluded.

[2] Robert C. Weaver, *Negro Labor: A National Problem* (New York: Harcourt, Brace & Co., 1946), p. 12.

The toehold which Negroes gained in northern industry during the First World War was due mainly to industrial expansion related to the war. Many immigrant workers had either gone home to fight or had shifted from the unskilled and semiskilled jobs to more skilled operations either in the same industries or in the munitions industries. The vacuum at the lower work levels was filled by Negroes. Post-war recessions and, finally, the Great Depression seriously restricted their rise in these industries. The industrial unions of the 1930's offered greater hope for their upgrading, but the seniority principle espoused by these organizations meant that the Negro worker was the first to be laid off in periods of recession and technological displacement.

By and large, the Negro worker until the beginning of the Second World War was concentrated in agriculture, service industries, and in manufacturing operations. His status was affected by changes in the American economy, union policies with their discriminatory tendencies, and technological innovations. He was cut off almost completely from the expanding area of clerical and sales work and the larger world of finance and business. His adventures in business and the professions developed mainly as monopolies to serve the segregated Negro community, and the number and size of business enterprises and the number of independent professional persons were determined mainly by the capacity of the Negro community to support their services. There were fewer than four thousand Negro physicians and less than half this number of lawyers prior to 1950. There were only a handful of engineers and architects, for these skills were oriented to the larger world of work. By and large, the Negro had a small middle class of professional workers, mainly teachers, clergymen, and small businessmen. The great mass of Negroes, in effect, were unskilled and semiskilled workers. The occupational distribution of the group was reflected in money income, with Negroes having only approximately one-half the median income of whites.

Under these circumstances, the traditional conception of the Negro worker was that of an unskilled or, at best, semiskilled worker. He did the dirty work of the society. Moreover, he was unable either to afford or secure the necessary education or training for entering many new positions; and, as often as not, these were closed to him if he possessed the educational requirements or skills. The vicious circle in which the Negro found himself had an important bearing on his occupational position; but, even more importantly, it conditioned his motivation and his perceptions of the opportunity structure. The Second World War set in motion a chain of events which produced changes in the American economy and the Negro's relation to it. It is to these developments that we now turn our attention.

A first observation is that the preparation for war and the later full mobilization of American industry favored the upgrading of Negro workers. Full employment demands and government policy of nondiscrimination in war industries permitted Negroes to enter many occupations for the first time and to be upgraded in others. This was true of aircraft and metal work, for example. The index of dissimilarity in the occupational distributions of white and nonwhite workers, which had been increasing slightly since 1920, began to show a decline.[3] These gains were accompanied by a rapid shift of Negro workers to urban centers where most of the defense plants were concentrated, so that by 1950 more than three-fifths of the Negro population was living in urban places, and 72 per cent were urban dwellers by 1960. There was, moreover, a

[3] Much of the discussion in this section is based upon Nathaniel Hare, "The Changing Occupational Status of the Negro in the United States: An Intracohort Analysis," unpublished Ph.D. dissertation, Department of Sociology, University of Chicago, 1962.

notable shift of the Negro population from the South to the North and West. Negro communities of considerable size began to develop for the first time in the West during the forties and fifties.

It is significant to note that the gains experienced by Negroes were in those socioeconomic categories in which the economy is generally expanding: in professional occupations, clerical services, and skilled work. The movement was from occupations in which Negro workers were over-represented to those in which they were underrepresented, a fact which suggests the opening of many job areas formerly closed to them.

The tendency toward convergence in white and nonwhite occupational distributions was most evident for the younger workers—those between the ages of 25 to 34, and 35 to 44. What is suggested by these statistics is that younger workers are entering the labor force with more formal education and better general preparation. But even when educational attainment is standardized for white and nonwhite workers, Negroes continue to occupy a disproportionate share of the lower-status jobs. Negro workers with some college training and those who have graduated from high school, for example, are overly represented among semiskilled workers.

In the fifties Negroes maintained many of the gains experienced during the war years. Continued high-level employment associated with increased domestic consumption in housing, appliances, automobiles and other items, the expansion of defense industries connected with the "Cold War" and the Korean War, and our foreign-aid programs contributed to this result. In addition, it should be observed that there was during the period a more vigorous effort on the part of government, both federal on the one hand and state and local on the other, to push for equality of opportunity in employment.

This complex of factors—the state of the economy, the

role of government, and the preparation of the Negro worker—is so intimately connected with the status of the Negro in the work force that each is deserving of further comment.

The first Fair Employment Practice measure was advanced as a war measure in response to Negro pressures to be included in the war effort on a more significant scale than was true during the First World War and to insure needed production increases at a rapid pace. Later executive orders during the Truman and Eisenhower administrations followed. The most recent and strongest of these orders is Executive Order 10925, issued by the present administration in 1961. This promises to be the most effective of all such orders in the fight against discrimination in employment as a result not only of its sanction permitting termination of contracts with those who fail to comply with the merit hiring and promotion provision and the barring of such contractors from further work, but also because of the apparent will of the federal government, through its Committee on Fair Employment Opportunity, to enforce it. With more than one-half of the federal budget earmarked for defense spending, considerable leverage is available to the government to implement its policy of fair employment. The executive order, moreover, applies to federal agencies which now employ nearly two-and-a-half million workers. The scope of the order is interesting, as contrasted with previous orders, because of its conception of what is required for an implementation of government policy in this area. Compliance is required not only of contractors, but of their major subcontractors and the labor unions with which they work as well. To a considerable degree, the coverage of subcontractors and labor unions closes some of the escape valves to the training, merit hiring, and promotion of minority-group workers. The early reports of the committee suggest that under its influence, upgrading of Negro workers is already taking place.

The more vigorous role of the federal government in its efforts to guarantee equal employment opportunities is a response to several factors. One is our international posture, which has been affected by charges of discrimination against Negroes in employment and other areas. A second underlying reason is that more vigorous governmental action becomes necessary in face of the mounting pressures from organized Negro groups for first-class citizenship. Economic improvement always has been regarded as one of the avenues by which this might be achieved. Today the concern with economic advancement is part of a larger movement which encompasses the fight for integration of educational facilities, effective use of the suffrage, and other goals as well. With 72 per cent of the Negro population residing in cities, a disproportionate number of whom are concentrated in large metropolitan centers, and with the group's being better educated and politically more sophisticated today, the pressures upon the federal government are more forceful than in previous periods. Similar political pressures are being applied by Negroes to state and local governments, with employment in many areas now considered as a right rather than a privilege. Moreover, the sit-ins, boycotts, and selective buying campaigns are directed against private establishments as expressions of disapproval of established employment practices by an extremely self-conscious group. In all of these actions one observes the growing interplay of political power and economics.

Turning now to education and training, it is clear that equality of employment cannot be attained unless there is an increase in the formal education and training experiences of Negro workers. Since 1940, there has been a tendency for the educational attainments of Negroes and whites to show some convergence, but there remains a considerable gap between the two groups. For persons twenty-five years of age and over in 1960, whites approximate eleven years of schooling, while the median for Negroes is approximately eight years, or roughly a grammar-school education.

What is important in the context of the present discussion is that jobs in the skilled trades, clerical services, and other areas in which the occupational structure is expanding require somewhat more formal education and training than was true for qualifying for unskilled and semiskilled work. The fact that many adult Negroes do not now meet the fundamental requirements for white-collar work positions is an important barrier to their absorption in the work force. The percentage of both whites and Negroes with less than a fifth-grade education has declined steadily since 1940, but for each of the past three decades the percentage of Negroes with this level of educational attainment has been four times the comparable white percentage. In 1960, approximately one-fourth of all Negroes over twenty-five years of age had not completed the fifth grade. The proportion of the Negro and white populations having one to three years of high-school training is approximately the same, but twice as many whites as Negroes are high-school graduates; and twice as many whites as Negroes, proportionately, have some college training.

This general condition has led one student to the following conclusion:

> Whatever the future may hold with regard to the oncoming cohorts of young Negroes, the performance to date, together with the postulate that educational attainment is a "background" characteristic [for employment], enables us to make a most important prediction: the disparity between white and nonwhite levels of educational attainment in the general population can hardly disappear in less than three-quarters of a century. Even if Negroes now in their early teens were to begin immediately to match the educational attainment of

white children, with this equalization persisting indefinitely, we should have to wait fifty years for the last of the cohorts manifesting race differentials to reach retirement age.[4]

The movement to cities is helping to eliminate some of the observed educational lag, as indicated by the larger number of younger Negroes who remain in school. At the upper educational levels, increased scholarship and fellowship funds are of assistance in helping many Negroes secure undergraduate and professional degrees. What is more, the opening of professional schools in the South to Negroes, as in medicine, law, and engineering, provides access to professional education in nearby communities. Many of these opportunities were not available to Negro students until the past decade.

The expanding opportunities for training experiences, as well as for formal education, may be illustrated by what has been occurring to Negroes in the medical profession. In 1947 there were only ninety-two Negro physicians who were members of medical specialty boards. In 1959, there were 377 medical specialists among the group, 357 of whom represented recent graduates. This fourfold increase during the dozen years resulted from the ability of larger numbers of young medical graduates to remain in training after their internship period. Equally, it resulted from the expansion of opportunities for residency training which became available to young Negroes during the period. Before 1940 most Negro medical graduates were forced to take their internships and do their residency training in Negro hospitals. In 1959, the 74 graduates of

[4] Otis Dudley Duncan, "Population Trends, Mobility and Social Change," a paper prepared for the Seminar on Dimensions of American Society, Committee on Social Studies, American Association of Colleges for Teacher Education, p. 52. Quoted with the permission of the author.

the Howard University School of Medicine took their internships in 33 different hospitals, with only thirteen of them serving in Negro hospitals. The 67 graduates of the Meharry Medical College in the same year were doing their internships in 29 different hospitals, with only eighteen of these graduates serving in Negro hospitals.[5]

We may summarize these remarks on education and training as they relate to employment by stating that existing differentials between Negroes and whites have an important bearing on the Negro's chances for jobs. There must be an upgrading of both educational and training experiences if Negroes are to qualify for jobs in many of the areas which are expanding. This is true in both a quantitative and qualitative sense. The movement to cities, with stricter attendance requirements for public education and better school systems, is helping with this process. More important, however, is that the desegregation of public education has provided a better quality of education for the Negro child and new occupational models for both the child and his parents. The incentive to remain in school as a prerequisite for qualifying for high-level jobs is nurtured by the prospect that such jobs will, in fact, be available as the society develops the more egalitarian ethic that the use of Negro manpower is not only morally right but economically sound. One of the remaining bottlenecks is admission to apprenticeship training programs formerly closed to Negroes through union policies. There is evidence that some gains are being made in this area.

The third factor upon which we wish to comment is the state of the economy. Negroes and other minorities, including women, have made their greatest occupational gains during periods of economic expansion. The years since 1940, with periodic exceptions, have been marked by

[5] Data supplied by Dr. W. Montague Cobb, ed., *Journal of the National Medical Association.*

generally high-level economic activity. The gross national product rose steadily until 1957, but its rate has been slower since that time. It is estimated that our economy requires an annual growth rate of 5 per cent, instead of the present 3½ per cent, to absorb the large number of new workers entering the labor force. The 67 million now in the labor force will expand to 86 million by 1970. Twenty-six million young people will enter the labor force during the 1960's. This expansion of the work force, in face of a slowdown of economic growth, poses serious and challenging problems for the nation. For minority-group workers it represents a serious threat to their retention and upgrading. The government's concern with the problem is evidenced by the Manpower Act of 1962 and the work of the Area Redevelopment Administration as it seeks to retrain workers for jobs which offer the prospect of employment. How successful the retraining programs will be remains to be seen.

Automation has been one component contributing to the high unemployment rates of Negro workers, for they have been unduly concentrated in those jobs which have felt the impact of changing machine processes most heavily. Unless the displaced workers can be retrained quickly and successfully for other jobs, the prospect of a hard core of unemployed persons is real. What is especially significant is that the present unemployment rate of 11 per cent among Negroes is twice the comparable rate among whites, and the full impact of automation has not yet been felt. These rates are particularly high among the youngest workers with limited education and training experiences, being twice as high as the average among workers 14 to 19 years of age and a third larger than the average for workers 20 to 24 years of age. It should be observed that it is not only the application of machinery to certain classes of work which is of concern, but also the prospect of restricted markets overseas with the recovery of the European economy, the development of the common market, and possible cuts in foreign-aid programs. The notion of an affluent society will have to be rethought. There is no question of the fact that government will have to play a more important role in the economy of the future. It is only necessary to remark in conclusion that with the marked increase of the urban population the services which cities must supply in education, sanitation, health care, and protective services will be enlarged, thus producing additional jobs. In line with previous comments regarding the Negroes' growing political power in cities and their view that government employment is a "right," it follows that Negroes will have greater access to jobs in this category than heretofore.

The over-all gains being made by Negroes in the work force may be expected to continue in the future. This is true despite the fact that the American economy is undergoing marked changes at the present time and these pose serious problems for Negro workers. For a variety of reasons, not the least of which is the insistence of Negroes on equal treatment, they may be expected to find a larger place in those areas of expanding opportunity. Negroes will be taken on in increasing numbers as clerks and salesmen as the stereotypes of their employment in these areas are altered. They will be found in increasing numbers in medicine, dentistry, law, social work, and engineering, as training opportunities and job prospects increase. And a beginning will be made on a significant scale in many positions in business enterprise formerly closed to them—in banking, insurance, and utilities.

The over-all effect of these developments, in line with general trends, is that larger numbers of Negroes will be found in white-collar employment, and the base of the Negro middle class will be broadened. Most significant of all, the Negro will be taken from his isolation and will work alongside the white, so that the traditional conception of Negro jobs will disappear in time. He will lose the quasi-monopolistic hold he now has on certain of the professional services, for example, but the result will be a higher level of performance born of broader training and more acute competition. It remains to be pointed out that these developments will have a salutary effect on Negro family life and every other institution of the Negro community. There will be a closing of the gap between Negro and white income and higher morale as Negroes perceive an opportunity structure which becomes measurably broadened.

These conclusions can be reached only if one accepts the fact that they will not all be realized in the next decade or two. It is enough to point out that progress in the last two decades has been made at a much faster pace than in the preceding eight, and that the general direction in which the society is moving lends support to this prediction.

THE CHANGING STRUCTURE
OF THE AMERICAN CITY
AND THE NEGRO

Robert C. Weaver

Until fifty years ago, the Negro remained, for the most part, outside the process of urbanization. He was primarily an American peasant—perhaps the only basically peasant component in the nation. In the last fifty years, however, he has joined the march to the cities and has caught up with and surpassed even the white rate of urbanization.

Negroes have become mobile, but their mobility is still very different from that of other Americans: it, too, is a search for a better life, but it is still a search more confined and bounded, more subject to disaster and tragedy and uncertainty than other Americans find. Urbanization has set the stage for a new and better life for Negroes, and over a third have realized this in economic terms. But the development of a really viable life pattern in the cities remains largely unfinished business for the majority of Negro Americans.

It is estimated that 69.5 per cent of the United States population was urban by 1960; among Negroes, 72.4 per cent were urban. But even these figures underestimate the urbanization of Negroes; for while almost all urban Negroes live in central cities, about a quarter of urban whites live in suburban areas. The movement out of the South, to the northern and western cities, has been steady from 1910, when four-fifths of the nonwhites lived in the South, to today, when just over half live in the South. Even in the latter region the majority of Negroes now live in cities.

The basic cause of the northward migration was undoubtedly economic. Great waves of Negro migration have been stimulated by periods of economic growth, particularly by the expansion of assembly line production during each of the two world wars and the decades immediately thereafter. Northern industries actually solicited the migration of Negroes during the First World War. But even without solicitation, it has been the search for full-time employment and higher wages that brought the Negro migrant to the city from the southern farm. Within the South, too, it is the search for jobs that has urbanized the Negro population.

These great waves of migration may now be tapering off. The period from 1955 to 1960 appears to have been one of lessening movement from the South to the North. From 1950 to 1955, three and four times as many nonwhite males between the ages of 25 and 34 migrated to Chicago and Detroit respectively as entered in the next five years. Unemployment in these and other mass-production cities of the North was clearly evident in the latter half of the fifties as automation grew more widespread and other technological changes occurred.

On the other hand, there were increasing employment opportunities in many parts of the South where new industrial and commercial activities were located. During the last decade, in the South, the rural Negro population declined by 11 per cent, but the urban Negro population increased by 36 per cent. Thus, while the tide of migration to the North subsides with decreasing job opportunities in that region, there is a strong rural-to-urban migration movement within the South in response to job opportunities.

Viewed against the background of general population mobility in this country, the nonwhite rate of migration is not high. In the year beginning March 1960, while 3.4 per cent of the white population moved from one state to another, only 2.3 per cent of the nonwhite population made such a move. Nonwhite migration is more apparent to us and more striking because until recently it has been directed to only a few destinations, while white migration has been composed of many more currents and cross-currents.

There is another difference in the movements of whites and nonwhites. Once the nonwhite arrives in the northern and western city, he moves around *in the city* more than the white does. In 1960, in central cities of metropolitan areas, 15 per cent of the white population moved from one house to another within the same county; but among the nonwhites, 20.6 per cent moved to a different house in the same county. In Chicago and Los Angeles, more than one-quarter of the nonwhites move, in a single year, from one house to another; less than one-sixth of the whites do so. This shuffling of one-quarter of the nonwhite population within some central cities represents, I fear, a desperate scramble for shelter among those who must play a game of musical chairs with a restricted supply of housing continuously affected by demolition, conversion, and losses for other reasons. For some, however, it also reflects a movement into areas of improved housing, particularly during recent years as more normal rates of vacancies have developed.

To date, nonwhite migration has been primarily a

search for new and better jobs. Once the destination is reached, the nonwhite is apparently less likely to move again to another city or state than the white. The migration of the white population, on the other hand, is more often represented by a move to a new place where a job has already been secured and residence is easily exchanged. The white residential mobility in all the regions of the country reflects the availability of jobs and housing in the whole wide reach of the American scene. The mobility of the Negro is still a steady move to urbanization, relatively unmitigated by cross-currents between urban areas. The white mobility contains many moves between areas by persons already urbanized, and one may conjecture that many white families move from one suburb to another without ever touching the central cities.

What is the effect of these great movements of people between country, city, and suburb? For the white middle class, these migratory moves are probably beneficial. In addition to the economic gains, they probably contribute more to family stability than they take away. This, at any rate, was the point of view of the participants in a conference on American middle-class migration conducted by the Brookings Institution a while ago.

Another point made at the conference is of particular interest to this analysis. Two groups of long-distance movers, it seems, have difficulty in a Chicago suburb— New Yorkers, who were not accustomed to small-town "mass participation in community problems," and southerners, who missed the "easy sense of community they left behind at home."

But if migrant white middle-class families in Park Forest, Illinois, have these difficulties, how much more serious must be the difficulties of a lower-class Negro rural family? For after the urbanization that is recorded in statistics—the simple move from country to city—must come the social and cultural urbanization, the change in life patterns, the development of skills, and the evolution of values inherent in an urban way of life. And when this has to take place under conditions of hostility, overcrowding, and poverty, the adverse effects of the migration often balance out, at least for a time, the beneficial.

Urbanization for American Negroes has meant, among other things, the bringing of willing but unskilled hands into American cities. We have less need for unskilled workers today than ever before in our history, and our new technology eats up unskilled and semiskilled jobs at a frightening rate. The first Manpower Report recently presented to Congress by the President sums up the resulting situation authoritatively:

> In 1962 non-whites made up 11 per cent of the civilian labor force but 22 per cent of the unemployed. On the average there were 900,000 non-white workers without jobs during 1962, with an unemployment rate of 11 per cent, more than twice that for white workers. [Among adult men] the non-white workers' unemployment rate was two and one half times higher than that of the white . . .
> In part, this is due to the heavy concentration of Negroes in occupations particularly susceptible to unemployment . . .
> Nevertheless, within each broad occupational group, unemployment is disproportionately high among non-white workers, partly because these workers tend to be near the bottom of the skill ladder for their occupational group.

Persistent discrimination in employment, in training, and in upgrading harass Negro Americans. We often hear that the situation is improving, and it is for the well-prepared colored American. The reverse is true for the untrained. Each ten years the Census records the fact that the gap in median earnings between whites and nonwhites is wide and sometimes wider than before. The economic situation of the Negro in the United States, taken on the average, is not improving as rapidly as the situation of the white.

Averages, however, are misleading. They can be meaningless if there is high frequency at either extreme or at both. The latter is the case in this instance. Thus the median income figures actually represent remarkable economic progress of Negroes at higher income levels at the same time that there has been retrogression among low-income groups. In 1959, for example, there were some 1,160,000 nonwhite families earning $5,000 or more in the United States; 154,000 had incomes from $10,000 to $15,000; there were 28,000 with incomes from $15,000 to $25,000, and 6,000 earned $25,000 or more. It has been said that Negroes in the United States have a total annual income from 15 to 20 billion dollars.

At the other extreme, in 1959, some 1,200,000 nonwhite families earned under $2,000 a year, and another 1,400,000 earned between $2,000 and $4,000. The majority of these faced poverty and almost all had too little resources to sustain a decent standard of living. This latter status was almost universal among those families earning less than $4,000 and residing in urban areas, unless they were single-person families.

What is the future for these people? What are the lessons of the past?

It is revealing experience to dip back into the literature of the early industrial revolution, when rural migrants were crowding the cities. They lived under conditions and with results very similar to those we find today. William Blake was not referring to our Harlems and our ghettos, when he wrote:

> I wander thro'each charter'd street
> Near where the charter'd Thames does flow,

And mark in every face I meet
Marks of weakness, marks of woe.[1]

Hogarth and Dickens painted a picture of urban misery and poverty, of social disorganization and disease, which was greater than anything we have to face today. In this country, from the 1840's on, European immigrants were crowded into our cities; and the same frightful toll was taken in the disruption of families, in illegitimacy, in the desertion by husbands, in disease and alcoholism and madness. We need only read the descriptions of the urban ghettos by Jacob Riis and his contemporaries to discover that some of our problems are not new. They are more shocking and dangerous, however, because they occur and continue at a time when ours is an affluent society.

When finally Negroes began to move out of the social backwash of the South and into the northern cities, they became the latest in the sequence of people to undergo urban misery. One indicator of the social disorganization incident to the Negro's move into the city is the incidence of family disorganization. But this is not a recent or a racial phenomenon; it is one of the most predictable consequences of rapid urbanization under crowded and impoverished circumstances.

Everything we see today in crowded Negro urban settlements was noted by social workers in the crowded immigrant quarters of our cities at the turn of the century—whether these were Jewish, Italian, Polish, or what have you. There was overcrowding; unrelated people living in the same households; poverty and discouragement; and the observable consequences. And we can go further back, to seventeenth-century England. The rate of illegitimacy then was so disturbing that Sir William Petty, one of the fathers of political economy, proposed a system of govern-

[1] "London," *The Poetical Works of William Blake* (London: Oxford University Press, 1913) p. 102.

ment maternity hospitals for pregnant unmarried women, and urged that the illegitimate children born in them become wards of the state.

Today, the strains upon the nonwhite family continue to be aggravated by overcrowding. In 1960, in the metropolitan areas, 28.5 per cent of the nonwhite households in rental units lived under crowded circumstances, compared to only 11.1 per cent of the whites. It is particularly significant that even at the income level of $6,000 to $7,000 the crowding remains just as high, and the disadvantage, compared to white households, as great.

If family stability is judged by the presence of both husband and wife, it declines with migration and increases with rising income. Among southern rural nonwhites, for example, there is considerably more stability than in northern cities at every income level. And in both South and North, the stable nonwhite families become more numerous as income rises.

In the northeastern and midwestern cities, very high percentages of households with female heads occur among the poor nonwhites. Thus, if households with incomes under $3,000 and whose heads are in the 35- to 44-year age bracket are considered, 1960 census data reveal that over 50 per cent have female heads; for families with incomes between $3,000 and $4,000, the percentage drops, but is still over 20 per cent; for families with incomes between $4,000 and $5,000, the percentage drops further, to between 10 and 15 per cent.

Among southern rural nonwhites, in the poorest families with incomes under $3,000, the percentage of families with female heads is only 20 per cent; and it falls in higher brackets to about 5 per cent. Thus, it may be said that in northern cities there is, by one measure, approximately two-and-a-half times as much instability among nonwhite families as in southern rural areas; and among the poorest families there is about four or five times as much instability as there is among those better off.

The 1960 census figures for Detroit offer convincing proof that as the Negro acquires education and becomes integrated into the economic life of our cities, family life becomes more stabilized. Indeed, after Negro families achieved a relatively moderate income, $3,000 to $5,000 a year, the degree of family stability among Negroes in Detroit was as high as among whites, using our measure of proportion of husband-wife families.

The urbanization of the American population is an accomplished fact; yet, our society still has a nostalgic longing for the rural life. The family farm and its supposedly happy, well-adjusted family are still an ideal, presented weekly to the American public in the form of "Lassie" and "The Real McCoys" and the like. Reacting to our urban ghettos, it is easy to assume that nothing in a rural background could have been as bad; that the urbanization of the Negro in America has separated him from a source of strength, stability, and serenity. But it is important to view the relative merits of the urbanization of the Negro population, not because we can turn back the tide or change the fact, but because we can modify society's attitude toward this development.

The rural population of the South is undereducated, underemployed, and underpaid as compared with its urban counterpart. It is served with less adequate medical facilities, and even in terms of minimal comfort it is poorly housed. If we look at education, for example, the northern urban nonwhite has on the average three-and-a-half more years of education than the southern rural Negro. And in terms of income, the relative position of the urban Negro, either in comparison with his white prototype or southern Negroes, is undeniably much superior.

Nor is this the only economic gain resulting from urbanization. The movement of Negroes to the North during the First World War resulted in their entering American industry. True, they were concentrated in the heavy and dirty areas of production and in unskilled occupations, but even this type of employment represented a great advance over the status of peasant. The Great Depression, of course, wiped out many of the gains achieved during the war and post-war periods, but these were recouped and extended during the economic expansion for defense and the Second World War. By the end of the war, Negroes had achieved a place in many light and clean industries, had become, in a significant measure, semi- and single-skilled workers, and were slowly moving into skilled jobs.

At the same time, the Negro became a functioning part of organized labor; and as of today, it is estimated that well over 1,500,000 Negroes belong to unions. Concurrently, Negroes are entering engineering, technical, and white-collar jobs at a continually increasing rate. Since they started from a low base in these higher occupations, their proportions in the totals are still small. But it must be noted that in many of the highly-trained occupations, there are more opportunities than qualified nonwhites.

Under these circumstances, the transfer of disadvantaged Negroes to the areas where people have more advantages represents a gain. It brings the problems they face to light, forcing the attention of society to the contrasts they represent and causing acute discomfort. It is quite natural that society should choose to think that it is the transfer which creates the problems. It is important to recognize, however, that the transfer merely exposes the problems to view. In a word, the urbanization of the rural southern Negroes has created a situation which has more potential for growth and improvement than their continued isolation from the mainstream of society.

144

But even for the Negro families themselves there are positive aspects of urbanization, despite the apparent misery of many in their initial situation. It is in the cities that many Negroes have learned the skills of the twentieth century and an increasing number have achieved middle-class economic status, if not social acceptance. The substantially higher educational attainment of the northern urban Negro over the southern rural Negro can be partially explained in terms of the increased educational opportunities available to the children of migrants and the longer period of schooling of the second and third generation of Negroes. This, too, is a result of their living in an area where the quality of education is of a higher level. It is in the cities that the broadened employment and educational opportunities exist. And finally it is in the cities that the Negro population has been large enough to exercise a political influence.

The last may well be the most important of the benefits of urbanization. James Q. Wilson's penetrating analysis of the methods employed in various cities in coping with their new Negro voters makes it plain that "Negro politics" is just a subdivision of the political apparatus in each city. But the significant growth of Negro political power in the cities has been a comparatively recent thing. Today it is a fairly nationwide phenomenon, evidencing itself in southern as well as northern cities. For in large southern cities almost one-third of the voting age population was non-white in 1960. In some northern cities the proportion is one-fourth. Of course, the Negro has faced fewer impediments in enjoying the ballot in the North; and, as a consequence, his lesser proportion among potential voters has been translated into greater political influence.

It has been said that most recent urbanization of Negroes has come too late to help them in terms of the need for labor, and the unemployment figures indicate that without drastic improvement in our economy and the upgrading of skills among nonwhites this is true. But in the political arena the urbanization of the Negro is coming at a time when the redistribution of legislative power and the end of the county-unit system enhances the power of the cities to determine their own fate.

Urbanization is neither the salvation nor the damnation of Negro Americans. It occasions many problems of adjustment and generates serious and baffling social difficulties for newcomers who are still permanent exceptions to the melting-pot theory. But it is also the *sine qua non* of the Negro's participation in the mainstream of national life. If the color line is eradicated, that participation, like most progress in race relations, will occur in urban areas.

Meanwhile, class differences and conflicts among urban Negroes will continue to develop. There will be continuing social disorganization. Poverty will stalk a large segment of the colored community. Relationships between whites and nonwhites will probably become increasingly strained. But all of this will occur in the complex where decisions are made, where power resides, and where nonwhites are becoming a part of the decision-makers. Urbanization, with all its growing pains, offers Negroes a chance to change and improve their status in this nation.

LEGAL CONCEPTS IN THE QUEST EOR EQUALITY

Charles W. Quick and *Donald B. King*

Many phases of the legal position of the Negro might be re-examined in this centennial year. One might contrast the legal status of the Negro just prior to emancipation with his contemporary position. Here Chief Justice Taney's acid comment in the Dred Scott case that the Negro had "no rights which a white man was bound to respect," could be contrasted with recent Court equalitarian pronouncements. The false jurisprudential basis of the "separate but equal" doctrine and the historical setting of its enunciation by the United States Supreme Court in *Plessy v. Ferguson*[1] might also be re-examined. In considering that decision, we might question the strange reluctance of the Court to extend the doctrine to the "true equality" which logic seems to have required, and the subtle racial bias reflected in that opinion. One could also

[1] 163 U.S. 537 (1896).

trace the gradual revival over the intervening years of the federal concept of individual rights. Or one might take as a topic the great counterattack against segregation which came about in the thirties and forties, or emphasize the development of civil rights in cases in the 1950's and early 1960's.

Nevertheless, as valuable and as intellectually stimulating or appropriate as such topics might be in this centennial year, it may be even more interesting to consider contemporary equalitarian legal concepts. For the use of such concepts will assure continued progress toward the ideal of liberty.

The growth during the past half-century of legal theory to buttress the ideal of equality has taken place in three major areas. One is the developing of new content for the concept of equality and liberty. The second is the determination of what constitutes unconstitutional "state action" within the purview of the Fourteenth Amendment, which provides for "equal protection of the law" and freedom from state discrimination. The third is the adoption of a continually developing concept of "due process" more closely attuned to the enlightened social conscience of the modern community. It includes the issuance of new safeguards against what has been characterized as the tyrannous pressures of officialdom.

The Supreme Court's earlier view of the constitutional requirement of equal protection was very superficial. So long as the physical facilities afforded the Negro were equal or substantially equal in a purely physical sense the Fourteenth Amendment mandate was considered satisfied. The Court, with but few exceptions, followed this naïve and myopic view for nearly half a century.

The Court was patently wrong; for in determining equality in settings involving human beings, with the myriad of social factors involved, it is obvious that a much more refined analysis is necessary. Indeed, the only absolute equality that may be found is that expressed in terms of mathematical equivalence or chemical formulae. Even here it is of an abstract and purely symbolic nature. To come even close to equality in comparative sociological settings, an infinite number of factors must be taken into account. Not least among these is the psychological effect of conditions upon individuals. And wherever possible, the existence of two separate settings or the separation must be eliminated. Yet for nearly half a century, the Court clung to its crude standard of "observable physical facilities."

In the late forties and early fifties, however, the Court began to take cognizance of some of the intangible factors entering into equality. In *Sweatt v. Painter*,[2] a case involving a Negro applicant to the University of Texas Law School, the Court observed that there were many factors "incapable of objective measurement" that must be considered. In *McLaurin v. Oklahoma State Regents*,[3] it noted that the separation of a graduate student from others could affect his learning and studies. In the words of the Court, such restrictions "impair and inhibit his ability to engage in discussion and exchange views with other students, and, in general, to learn his profession." Likewise, in the *Henderson*[4] case, involving the partition of a railroad dining car, the Court called attention to the emotional impact of segregation upon the individual.

The Court thus has emphasized that equality must be considered in terms of the intangibles. It further recognized that discrimination or segregation could have an emotional effect. In this manner, it recognized that equal protection must be viewed in light of the individual's total reaction. The sense of inferiority which accompanies segregation is one major factor making any separate facilities

[2] 339 U.S. 629 (1950).
[3] 339 U.S. 637 (1950).
[4] *Henderson v. United States*, 339 U.S. 816 (1950).

"inherently unequal." Although not further amplifying this point, the Court was in fact recognizing that in separate sociological settings true equality is difficult if not impossible.

The adoption of this concept of equality removed the legal underpinning of segregation legislation. Statutes requiring segregation of public transportation, public libraries, public parks and other public recreational facilities were thereafter speedily invalidated. The concept still promises to be invaluable for the future. In addition to clarifying the goal of equality conceptually it may be applied in all areas where segregation remains. One example for immediate application is that of sex and miscegenation laws based on shabby logic and used for ignoble purposes.

The use of this concept of equality may be extremely important in resolving situations not normally viewed as within the ambit of the Fourteenth Amendment, such as *de facto* segregation in the schools. As a practical matter, segregation continues with its badge of inferiority and the emotional reaction of both teachers and children placed therein. Neighborhood boundaries may and often do reflect all the evil effects of historical segregation; moreover, in most such areas schools are inferior in all aspects.

In addition to developing and applying this concept of equality, the Court emphasized the applicability of the concept of liberty. This conceptual consideration has received scant notice. For the most part, the case *Bolling v. Sharpe*,[5] is viewed only as making the results of the school segregation cases effective in the District of Columbia. It is true that the Court's decision was undoubtedly based in large part upon the realization that any decision concerning desegregation must be nationwide in scope and that such a result could not be impaired by reason of the federal status of the District of Columbia. Yet the reasoning of the

[5] 347 U.S. 497 (1954).

Court has prophetic significance in holding that the individual should be able to exercise his liberty with only reasonable and nonarbitrary governmental restrictions. Segregation, in the eyes of the Court, was clearly an arbitrary restraint upon the liberty of the individual.

Practically, the doctrine may serve to aid the Court in making difficult determinations as to constitutional doctrine to be followed in the hazy area between public and private action.

The second area is that of clearly and fully determining what is "state deprivation." Indeed, it would seem that much of the attack for equality must center around the continuing development of this concept. Those opposing integration, having lost the major battle relating to problems of equality, rely on "non-governmental action." Even here, however, the initial skirmishes have been lost by the segregationists as a result of a steadily enlarging concept of state deprivation. Because of the significance of state deprivation, it is desirable to view the various theories which have been or may be used in making this over-all concept more meaningful.

State action has classically been contrasted with individual action and only the former held constitutionally proscribed. It was in the *Civil Rights Cases* of 1883 that the Court invalidated a large portion of the Civil Rights Acts (1875) by holding that the denial of rights by individuals acting in a "private" capacity was permitted by the Fourteenth Amendment. Historically, there is ample evidence that the draftsmen intended it to apply to private action; moreover, as Justice Bradley indicated, some types of individual action backed by custom or by executive or judicial sanction of the state constitute state action. While it is true that the doctrine has been greatly expanded over the years, the requirement of governmental action and the distinction of "state v. individual" deprivation continues.

At a very early date, the doctrine of state action extended to the actions of particular state officers. In 1880, it was held that a Negro defendant was deprived of due process by the state judge who excluded Negroes from the jury. Not until over half a century later, however, was it established that acts of state officers under color of law constituted state action even though in excess of their authority or prohibited by state law. The question remained as to whether a state officer was acting officially, though perhaps wrongfully, and when he was acting purely in his private capacity. In one case, involving religious rather than racial persecution, a chief of police removed his badge to administer brutal treatment. The trial and appellate courts, however, considered him still acting in his official capacity.

The concept of governmental action has been greatly expanded in recent cases. In one of the latest sit-in cases, the majority of the Court held that the statements of the superintendent of police and of the mayor relating to segregation at lunch counters and in restaurants were, because of their official status, "coercive," and thus constituted the proscribed state action. This reasoning is significant because the act of excluding Negroes from lunch counters was taken by private businessmen otherwise unconnected with the state. The decision means that if southern political leaders or local governmental officials make pronouncements asking businessmen or others to segregate, the resulting segregation may be considered as an indirect result of state action. This new rationale, although not yet developed, may have potential use in the near future.

Another major component of state deprivation rests upon the receipt of state benefits which may further the discriminatory purposes of private individuals. Perhaps the most recognizable application of this over-all theory is found where the state has given private individuals possession of property and the private individuals have discriminated in their use of it. In the recent *Wilmington* case,[6] discrimination by the lessee of space for a restaurant in a public building was held to violate the Fourteenth Amendment. Even though the state may have given the lease in an arm's-length transaction and may have had no express purpose of furthering discriminatory practices, it remains undeniable that the lessee is receiving some benefit from his use of state property. The fact that he might have leased property from a private individual and discriminated is not particularly relevant. (If he wishes even to attempt such practices then he may follow this course rather than utilizing property which belongs to the state and all of its people.) Arguably the state action may have consisted of the failure of the city to have insisted upon a nondiscriminatory clause in the lease.

A less apparent, but equally applicable, form of state action is where the private individual who discriminates is the beneficiary of state powers or has received some form of governmental assistance. A forceful argument can be made that state deprivation exists wherever the power is used by an individual or organization which discriminates. While action has been taken by agencies of the federal government to prevent discrimination on the basis of this rationale, the potential of such a theory has yet to be utilized by the courts. The use of state powers of eminent domain or other powers necessary for the creation or existence of the instrumentality or organization which discriminates should be recognized as state deprivation. Where the purchase of a home is made possible or made easier through federal assistance or insurance, the purchaser should not be able to utilize this advantage or benefit and still sell his home in a discriminatory fashion. In effect, the government has subsidized his house and should not have to subsidize his ability to own or resell it if he is

[6] *Burton v. Wilmington Parking Authority*, 365 U.S. 715 (1961).

acting in a discriminatory manner. The fact that he could have secured private financing is not the answer—for he has indeed utilized governmental benefits.

The state deprivation theory, it may be urged, should be applied in the future to tax-exempt organizations which discriminate. An effective argument can be made that a tax exemption is in fact a form of governmental subsidy. If an organization has as one of its purposes, or a part of its rules, the furtherance of segregation, it should not be subsidized by the government. If it wishes to give up the tax exemption or subsidy in order to avoid the presence of any element of governmental action, that is, of course, its choice.

Another major aspect of state deprivation is found in the use of state judicial processes by private individuals to further their own discriminatory practices. It was in the landmark case of *Shelley v. Kramer*,[7] decided in 1948, that the Court emphasized this theory. Interestingly enough, it had been noted years earlier by Justice Harlan in his dissent in the *Civil Rights Cases*. In *Shelley* a private third party sought court enforcement of a restrictive covenant. In the words of the Court, the Constitution "confers upon no individual the right to demand action by the state which results in the denial of equal protection of the laws to other individuals." The Court pointed out that the state was not merely abstaining from action. Rather, in the use of the state's judiciary there was to be found "the clear and unmistakable imprimatur of the state." In its language the Court also pointed up the full theoretical expanse of the state action concept. "State action," it said, "as that phrase is understood for purposes of the Fourteenth Amendment, refers to exertions of state power in all forms."

The full potential range offered by the finding of state action in judicial enforcement of private discrimination is

[7] 1334 U.S. 1 (1948).

yet to be achieved. Most forms of segregation and discrimination depend ultimately upon the ability of the private individual to obtain legal enforcement thereof. Where the individual utilizes any of the law-enforcement machinery or the judiciary in order to enforce his private philosophy of segregation, clearly state action is involved.

Instead of avoiding a decision in the sit-in cases on a constitutional basis, the Court could have utilized this reasoning and held that the use of law enforcement officials and the use of judicial sanctions constitutes state action. Since judicial action encompasses the whole range of human activity no discriminatory action, save the purely voluntary, may be exempt from its effects. For this reason, the *Shelley v. Kramer* rationale may prove to be of the greatest significance in attacking the heart of discrimination.

Another theory of state deprivation rests upon use of the power given through state licensing. This theory, now gradually developing, may find use in a number of varying instances. Where a particular union is licensed or given statutory sanction as the bargaining agent, the Court has indicated that it cannot discriminate against Negroes who are not members. While the decision itself rests upon the Court's interpretation of congressional intent relating to particular labor legislation, the Court has indicated that were it not to place its holding on this narrow ground the issue of constitutionality would have to be considered. Even though the union may be the exclusive bargaining agent, it would seem that the state action is found in the statutory creation and regulation of it, in any event.

Just as the union may be considered as a creature of the state or as being licensed by it, so might be corporations or businesses. Both the corporation and individual businessman must obtain the sanction and permission of the state for doing business. Although this privilege is extended on a widespread basis and without discrimination, it represents nevertheless the granting of state permission for conducting business. Justice Douglas, in particular, has been an advocate of this type of reasoning. In one of the most recent sit-in cases, he pointed out the broad powers of the state in relation to business and concluded that there is no constitutional way by which the state "can license and supervise a business serving the public and endow it with the authority to manage that business on the basis of apartheid which is foreign to our Constitution." Where the license is purely regulatory, however, and not one which gives the individual the power to do business with the public of the state, deprivation by the state may not be considered to exist to a sufficient degree in the application of this general theory.

Still another rationale which has not been fully utilized in defining the state deprivation concept relates to the undertaking of public functions by private individuals. In the famous case involving the Jay Bird party, the Court seemed to adopt such reasoning as one of the bases for its decision. Within Texas, Negroes were denied their right to vote over a period of many years—first directly, then by private parties conducting the primaries, under state law, and finally by private parties holding "pre-primary elections" which controlled the ultimate outcome. The Court held that the state, by permitting private individuals to undertake such a public function, was permitting them to exercise a form of state action; hence, the arbitrary exclusion of Negroes from participating in this party activity was a violation of the Fourteenth Amendment. In another case, involving religious rather than racial discrimination, the Court held that a corporation engaged in the public functions of managing and owning a company town was within the ambit of the Fourteenth Amendment.

Related to this theory is the reasoning that all businesses engaged in public services are performing a type of state function and are included in the state deprivation concept. Public carriers and innkeepers may be held to violate the Fourteenth Amendment through discriminatory practices since the state is letting them perform business considered vital to the public. Justice Douglas has noted recently, in a concurring opinion in one of the sit-in cases, the historical genius of the legal doctrine which viewed the services of innkeepers and carriers as a public trust and impressed upon them the duty to serve all. In light of the changing society and the increasing dependence of people upon one another for services, he indicated that extension of such a doctrine might be possible. In any event, he pointed out that "the day has passed when an innkeeper, carrier, housing developer, or retailer can draw a racial line, refuse service to some on account of color, and obtain aid of a State in enforcing his personal bias by sending outlawed customers to prison or exacting fines from them."

While this theory relating to the public nature of businesses has yet to be decisively and clearly set forth and supported, its potential is apparent. In contemporary society there are a number of businesses performing functions of an equally vital and public nature. It is quite possible that in the future this rationale may be used to strike down discriminatory practices on a large scale.

A theory which may see possible use in the future and give added meaning to the state deprivation concept is the "negative state action" or the "inaction" theory. The state, through inaction, may be giving sanction and force to discriminatory practices just as much as if it had affirmatively participated or aided in them. Legislative history and early court language gives some support to such a theory. Even Justice Bradley in his majority opinion in the civil-rights cases spoke of a deprivation by a private individual as a private wrong if it was not done under state authority and "if not sanctioned in some way by the state." It is clear that he did not expect the state to stand idly by but to offer protection. As he stated, such wrongs "may presumably be vindicated by resort to the laws of the state or redress . . . ."

In more recent times, the inaction of the state of Texas in sanctioning the discrimination by the private Jay Bird party may be looked upon as a form of state inaction. It seems relatively clear that at least part of the Court's reasoning in that case was based upon the inaction of the state in permitting the private discrimination. It would seem both logical and reasonable that certain state inaction would be considered as a state deprivation of rights under the Fourteenth Amendment. For example, if police officials were to stand idly by and watch private citizens injure or kill another individual in an expression of racial hatred, it would seem that this inaction should be considered as state deprivation of due process and equal protection. If the state fails to furnish protection to one exercising constitutional rights—whether they be rights of free expression, freedom to travel, or any other—there is state deprivation. The tremendous potentialities of this particular theory have yet to be recognized or used to advantage. It necessarily posits the assumption of affirmative duties by the state to protect its inhabitants in their constitutional rights. It is quite possible then that if the state stands idly by while private citizens inflict harm upon others or if it fails to take affirmative steps of prevention or provide relief, there is a state deprivation of equal protection and liberty.

The third area is the expansion of "due process." A component of the Fourteenth Amendment, due process is an elusive concept. Its content is determined by contemporary notions of fair play. From generation to generation it is an ever expanding concept gaining new meaning from the social conscience of the community. As early as 1880 the Court utilized the due process clause to strike at inequality in *Strauder v. West Virginia*.[8] Here the Court found that the exclusion of Negroes from the jury selection processes vitiated the conviction of the Negro defendant by violating the due process concept of the Fourteenth Amendment. But for almost fifty years the concept lay dormant and unused.

In the last several decades, however, there has been a tremendous breakthrough on this front. These safeguards are especially significant for the assurance of fair play to all minority groups, including the economically under-privileged as well as the racial or religious minority. Since those of a majority group are generally protected by eco-nomic circumstances as well as the ballot, these rights have relatively little significance to them. While not specifically dealing with racial equality, concepts providing for fed-erally protected rights to a nondiscriminatory jury, for an expansion to the right of counsel, and for the right of con-frontation have an especial significance to a member of a minority group.

So, also, has the expansion of protections designed to safeguard the individual from the tyrannous pressures of officialdom. While the doctrine of the *Mapp* case[9] that state officials may not use evidence illegally obtained ap-plies across the board, the cold hard truth of the matter is that in an urban community and in the South especially the Negro is the butt of illegal searches and seizures. It was not fortuitous that the vicious acts of the police in *Mapp v. Ohio* were directed against a Negro woman nor that the police practice in Detroit of illegal investigative arrests was directed against the Negro community nor that the juveniles from whom confessions were obtained by physical and mental coercion were Negroes and Mexicans. Throughout the nation, the cases embodying the most far-

[8] 100 U.S. 303 (1880).
[9] *Mapp v. Ohio*, 367 U.S. 643 (1961).

reaching judicial reforms, such as the *McNabb* and *Mallory* cases,[10] which required the police to follow legal procedures in arraignment, bear the names of members of racial minority groups. In Michigan, for example, it is no coincidence that the *Hamilton* case[11] setting forth a similar requirement for state police officials in Michigan involved an Iranian student.

The concept of due process has gradually evolved and become more refined over the years. Right of indigent defendants to counsel in state courts was first established in 1932 in a case arising out of gross violations of the rights of Negro defendants. Since that time, the principle of counsel for indigent prisoners has been centered upon noncapital cases. Opinions of some of the justices indicate that in the near future provision for counsel must be provided by the state for the indigent at first contact with officialdom. In the area of coerced confessions, there has steadily been a refinement of the concept of due process so that even very subtly coercive techniques may be held to violate the Constitution. In the jury-exclusion area the concept has been extended to cover grand jury proceedings as well. In the area of illegally obtained evidence, it has been extended so as to fix the exclusionary rule on the states. There is even reason to believe that due process, as a concept, may continue to become more refined and thus to protect the primary victims of oppression—the Negro and other minority group members. Indeed it might even provide a new rationale for striking at segregation practices by groups or individuals acting as quasi-public officials. With the extension of the state deprivation concept and the recognition that segregation interferes with the liberty of the individual, the unfairness and bigotry

[10] *McNabb v. United States,* 318 U.S. 332 (1943); *Mallory v. United States,* 354 U.S. 449 (1957).

[11] *People v. Hamilton,* 359 Mich. 410, 102 N.W. 2d 738 (1960).

inherent in such practices may be legally condemned under the due process concept.

The development of new standards of due process has been accompanied by a modifying of old principles and a refusal to stand on legal technicalities. In cases such as those where non-Negro southern attorneys have failed to assert the constitutional rights of their Negro defendants, the Court has been able to afford protection to the accused by ignoring the legal problems of waiver.

There are ample resources of legal concepts and reasoning for use in the future quest for full equality and the realization of rights. As occasions arise in the near future, it can be expected that the Court will draw upon this body of legal theory and give fuller meaning to the concepts of equality, liberty, and state deprivation. This is not to say that there will not be a need for hard thinking and a recognition of the problems involved in extending this rationale. Yet it may not be remiss to note that contemporary problems may appear more difficult than they actually are and may become clouded through present emotional feelings.

In the light of history the problems in this area may not appear difficult of solution. It might be briefly pointed out, however, that the Court has already in a number of cases been confronted with the conflicting values of achieving equality on one hand and the use of one's private property as he so desires, on the other. As the Court has noted, constitutional rights of owners of property must be balanced against the constitutional rights of others. Where freedom of press and religion conflict with property rights, the Court has recognized that the former must prevail. In the light of the extreme harm and impairment of liberty caused by discrimination, it is only proper that these personal freedoms should outweigh certain property rights. Further, the Court has noted that the power of the state to enforce property interest must be exercised within the boundaries defined by the Fourteenth Amendment. In other areas extensive curtailment of the individual's private property rights, whether they be in business or real property, has taken place; yet, there is a point where personal and property rights become so entwined that careful balancing and decision-making will be necessary.

The significance of legal rationale and theory to the status of the Negro is that it makes change possible. Legal theories of the past when effectively marshalled and used have brought the Negro much closer to equality and human dignity. Already existing legal concepts afford ample opportunity for significant progress in this quest. If properly developed and given effect, they will make it possible for all to partake of the many fruits of liberty.

THE CHANGING POLITICAL POSITION OF THE NEGRO

James Q. Wilson

It requires no special insight to know that the political position of the Negro is changing rapidly, and that, for the most part, the change is in the direction of a greater assertiveness, a heightened sense of expectancy, a more general awareness of rights and the barriers to the enjoyment of those rights, and a broader and deeper commitment to social change.[1] Negroes everywhere, but particularly in the South, expect and demand better treatment, and this expectation has imparted a more militant tone to their political and civic life. Boycotts, sit-ins, protest marches, law suits, voter registration drives, and agitation for new legislation can be found on every hand.

Although the fact of this growing militancy is both

[1] See, for example, the lengthy account in the *New York Times*, April 23, 1963, p. 20.

obvious and indisputable, the reasons for it may not be. I propose to examine some of those reasons, not simply as an academic exercise in *post factum* explanation, but because a clearer appreciation of some of these reasons may permit us to understand better the direction in which events are moving and more particularly the implications of these events for the social and economic position of the Negro. As a result of dwelling on these matters, I hope to leave you with a question rather than a conclusion: to what extent is militant Negro political and civic action likely to lead to a significant improvement in the lot of the mass of Negroes? I will suggest that there are some reasons for answering that question pessimistically. However morally desirable and personally satisfying Negro militancy may be, it may confer relatively few tangible benefits on most Negroes.

The first reason for a heightened sense of militancy is, of course, that change itself begets pressures for more change. As many others have observed, revolutions are not made by persons who are utterly dispossessed and despairing, but by those who have already gained something, who hope for more, and who have reason to believe (because they have seen it before) that change is possible. The gains of one generation of Negroes stimulate the expectations of the next; the pioneering success of one leader becomes the hardly tolerable *status quo* to his successor; what was daring militancy to parents becomes servile accommodation to their children.

These considerations indicate the kind of impact that recent events in the South have had on Negroes everywhere. The sit-ins, boycotts, and protest marches have been dramatic actions directed towards simple goals—usually, access to public accommodations. Indeed, much of the drama of these efforts has been the result of the simplicity of the objectives and the consequent clarity of the moral issue.[2] There are few scenes more compelling than a photograph of Negroes seated at a segregated luncheon counter, enduring the hostile stares and loud jeers of a tense white mob. Such events create pressure among northern Negroes for equally dramatic action even though Negro goals in the North—where access to most public accommodations is no longer at issue—are far more complicated, involving entry into certain occupations, industries, and neighborhoods where convenient and visible targets for, say, a sit-in campaign are often lacking.

A second reason for the heightened militancy of Negroes is that the education of Negroes has been advancing more rapidly than their economic growth. In education, Negroes have been catching up with whites far faster than they have been catching up in income. In 1940, young white men averaged four years more of schooling than nonwhites of the same age; by 1960, that difference had been reduced to one-and-a-half years, and it continues to decrease. In the same period, the average income of a nonwhite man increased from 41 per cent of a white's in 1940 to 61 per cent in 1950, in great part as a result of the wartime demand for manpower. Since 1950, however, nonwhite income has not increased at all relative to white income (although of course it has increased in absolute terms); in fact, it may have decreased slightly.[3] Negroes have *kept* up but not *caught* up. Furthermore, the differences between white and nonwhite income are greatest in professional and managerial occupations—precisely in

[2] See Daniel C. Thompson, *The Negro Leadership Class* (Englewood Cliffs, N. J.: Prentice-Hall, 1963), especially chaps. vii and x; and M. Elaine Burgess, *Negro Leadership in a Southern City* (Chapel Hill, N. C.: University of North Carolina Press, 1962), chap. vii.

[3] Herman P. Miller, "Is the Income Gap Closed? 'No!' " *New York Times Magazine*, November 11, 1962, pp. 50, 52.

those occupations where the rewards of education are supposed to be the greatest.[4]

This disparity is resulting, I think, in the creation of a kind of "intellectual proletariat" among Negroes, consisting of young men and women who are educated beyond their current earning capacity (when compared to equivalent whites) and beyond their present opportunity to participate in all aspects of American society. These are young Negroes who have been given in college a glimpse of the Great Society and its economic and social advantages but who feel that they are denied equal access to that society. In my experience, these people usually form the activist cadre of the more militant race-relations organizations, seeking by protest tactics to compel society to redistribute opportunities for income, power, and access to life's amenities and to affirm, by such redistribution, the self-esteem of the Negroes who seek it.

This growing intellectual proletariat is further disposed toward militant civic action by the fact that, to much greater extent than among other minority groups, Negro economic progress is more professional than entrepreneurial. The rate of capital formation among Negroes is low and very few Negroes own businesses that are anything more than small (and often marginal) retail and service establishments. The conservative attitudes and constraints which are associated with entrepreneurial activity will be found to a lesser extent among Negroes than among whites; young Negroes, for a variety of reasons, are recruited into professions (such as law, teaching, government service, and the like), the members of which have always tended to have a higher commitment to social change than is characteristic of businessmen.

A third reason, and one related to the foregoing, for

[4] Irving B. Kravis, *The Structure of Income* (Philadelphia: University of Pennsylvania Press, 1962), pp. 48-49.

increased Negro militancy is that Negro civic associations (such as the NAACP branches) are generally so small, so poorly financed, and so lacking in paid staff that much of the civic effort must be done, if it is to be done at all, by volunteers. Such volunteers are typically the most highly motivated members; and these, in turn, are often the members with the highest commitment to the goals of the organizations. In short, the structure of Negro civic associations makes them highly vulnerable to a growth in the number of potential militants in the community. Because of the shortage of paid workers and the difficulty in mobilizing more than a tiny fraction of members, enthusiasts and militants can dominate the activities of the branch even though they may not control its offices. At election time, more conservative members who can control blocs of votes through their affiliation with churches, business firms, and even political parties can often reassert control over at least the offices, if not the activities, of the organization.[5]

Even among race-relations organizations which do rely heavily on a paid staff (as, for example, the Urban League does), there is likely to be an increase in militancy as younger staff members are recruited. The restraints imposed by the necessity of raising a large budget and protecting one's own job are in part offset by the increasingly cosmopolitan background of staff members. They are college-trained, but to an increasing extent, I suspect, in general universities rather than all-Negro schools, and in the North rather than in the South. These professionals are also likely to be trained in one city, begin their career in a second, and continue it in a third. There is an increasing movement from city to city and from agency to agency and a growing tendency to regard themselves as profes-

[5] James Q. Wilson, *Negro Politics: The Search for Leadership* (Glencoe, Ill.: The Free Press, 1960), pp. 63-65, 281-94.

sionals who are to a significant extent eager for and even dependent on the approval of fellow professionals elsewhere.

Fourth, the Negro masses in many areas are, to an increasing extent, willing to participate in direct civic action —perhaps because they now are more keenly aware of the disparity between their own lot and the attainments of society as a whole, perhaps because social change has been rapid enough to dispel to some extent the fears and pessimism which hitherto restrained them from testing the *status quo*. Particularly in the South, Negro intellectuals have been able to assume leadership over several mass movements, the participants in which, once brought together, have generated pressures on their leaders for vigorous, quasi-revolutionary action. In the North, such mass efforts have been rare, in part because there are fewer appropriate targets for such demonstrations, in part because there are in the North many existing political and civic organizations which resist being displaced by Negro intellectuals and ministers, and in part because the goals of middle-class and lower-class Negroes are less likely to coincide in the North than in the South.

In the North, the chief effort to organize the Negro lower classes has been made by the Black Muslims, a movement which uses frankly racist and anti-white sentiments to instill a sense of self-respect in the Negro. By persuading him that he is superior to whites, the Muslim leaders give him a sense of his own dignity sufficient to make him expressively, if not economically, middle class. Many whites, who are impressed by the ideology but fail to understand its function, are alarmed by the Muslim movement and see it as a threat to peace and order. In fact, the Muslims disavow political or civic action (because it must take place in a system created by whites and can therefore only serve white ends). Further, the ideology which is their strength is also their weakness: it is probably too esoteric and restrictive ever to permit the recruitment of large numbers of members.[6]

Finally, Negro militancy will continue to increase as the urban political party continues to lose control of those resources with which to buy off (or, more politely, co-opt) politically ambitious Negroes. Big-city machines have all but vanished. Party control over patronage, nominations for elective office, and access to government has everywhere been weakened and will be weakened even further. Less and less are party leaders able on their own terms to appoint or nominate Negroes to office; more and more, they must be appointed or nominated on the Negroes' terms.

Almost every large city government needs to make its decisions appear legitimate in the eyes of its constituents; almost every large city government resorts, in some measure, to group representation as a way of achieving this legitimacy. Where the city government lacks other sources of power—as it does to an increasing extent today with the breakup of the power which in the past was informally centralized by the party machine—it must attach a high value to the legitimacy conferred by group representation. If such a city has a large Negro population, the political leaders must seek out and appoint those Negroes who have the greatest prestige as a result of their participation in *nonparty* activities—voluntary associations, churches, education, and so forth. Such Negroes discover that political rewards come to those who conform to the expectations, not of party leaders, but of voluntary association leaders. These expectations, for reasons I have already discussed, are likely to require a certain degree of militancy.[7]

[6] This paragraph and the one that follows are adapted from Edward C. Banfield and James Q. Wilson, *City Politics* (Cambridge: Harvard University Press, 1963).

[7] James Q. Wilson, "The Strategy of Protest: Limits of Negro Civic Action," *Journal of Conflict Resolution*, V (September 1961), 291-303.

These tendencies toward militancy, particularly insofar as they involve political action, are not unrestrained.
The political facts of life do not change as rapidly as the
aspirations of would-be leaders. In both the North and the
South, the Negro, if he is to play politics at all, must still
do so under the rules and within the systems which were
created by whites and which change slowly if at all.

The current emphasis on ending barriers to Negro
registration and voting in the South tends to obscure the
long-run limitations on the effectiveness of political participation. In the North, where the Negro has had the vote
for generations, his political effectiveness is constrained by
the political system of which he is a part and by the fact
that politicians and political organizations develop interests not always consistent with the interests of the most
militant Negro activists. In the South, where the battle for
the vote is far from won, Negro leaders must contend with
a vast potential Negro electorate consisting, in the main,
of very poor, ill-educated persons, who have no tradition
of political activity and who are hard to organize and hard
to lead.

In the North, the Negro vote seems firmly wedded to
the national Democratic party. Although the degree of
enthusiasm may vary from election to election(it was low
in 1956 and high in 1960), the variation is relatively small.
Because Negroes are concentrated in key urban areas
(eight states with 210 electoral votes are now 6 per cent or
more Negro), they have been referred to as holding the
"balance of power." While it is true that in several important states—California, Illinois, Michigan, and New
Jersey, among others—the Kennedy margin among Negro
voters was greater than the margin by which he carried
the state as a whole, his margin among various other
groups of voters (for example, Catholics, workers, and
Jews) was also of this character. Any one of these groups
could be called the "balance of power"; and if any could,

then none is.[8] Although Negroes are clearly an important part of the national electorate, it is easy to exaggerate that importance by using such phrases as "the balance of power" and ignoring the extent to which their importance is diminished by the unswerving commitments of the bulk of Negro voters to one party. Votes need not be bargained for when they can be taken for granted.[9]

Within the large cities, further constraints operate. Although Negroes have elected Negro councilmen in many cities and influenced the behavior of white councilmen in many others, there are limits to this influence even in cities which have a large Negro minority. For example, in more than half of the cities of 250,000 population or more, candidates for city council must run at large and on a nonpartisan ballot. This means that in most cases the effort to elect a Negro to the city council, or the effort by Negroes to affect the policies of a white candidate for the council, is inhibited by the fact that the candidate must run with the whole city as his constituency (in which whites are the majority) and without the benefit of a party label.

In those cities where Negroes have been most successful in electing Negroes to local offices, that very success has usually been purchased at the price of a certain degree

[8] Richard M. Scammon, "How the Negroes Voted," *New Republic*, November 21, 1960, pp. 8-9. See also Roberta S. Sigel, "Race and Religion as Factors in the Kennedy Victory in Detroit, 1960," *Journal of Negro Education*, XXII (1953), 436-47.

[9] This problem is illustrated by the two senatorial campaigns of Jacob Javits of New York. An outspoken defender of civil rights for Negroes, Javits did as well in Negro areas of New York City when he ran in 1956 against another outspoken liberal, Robert F. Wagner, Jr., as he did when he ran in 1962 against a conservative Democrat, James Donovan, who had an unclear position on civil rights. In seven predominantly Negro assembly districts, Javits' percentage of the two-party vote increased less than two percentage points—from 32.8 per cent in 1956 to 34.5 per cent in 1962. (Data courtesy of Professor Robert Peabody of Johns Hopkins University.)

of political indifference to militant demands for social change. Cities with the largest number of Negro city councilmen—such as Chicago, Cleveland, and St. Louis— are also cities in which Negro politics is the special province of professional politicians, who in most (though not all) cases must temper the demands of militant civic leaders to suit the realities of party discipline and organizational maintenance.

Negroes in American cities are thus confronted by two different kinds of constraints. In cities with nonpartisan, at-large elections and weak or nonexistent party organizations they find it exceptionally difficult to elect Negroes to public office. In cities with partisan elections, small council districts, and strong party organizations, Negroes win elective office fairly easily but often under conditions which place a high value on caution and party loyalty and a low value on political protest.[10]

In the South recent events have suggested that, for the time being at least, urban Negroes may escape to some degree from this dilemma. Perhaps because Negroes in many southern cities have only recently won (or chose to exercise) the vote, the use of that vote has been strongly influenced by the conditions under which it was obtained. When the vote is not (as it is in the North) taken for granted but is viewed as a prize in an intense political conflict over civil rights generally, then it is likely that the vote will be cast less out of casual party attachment or traditional loyalties and more out of a preoccupation with furthering the civil-rights struggle.

Fragmentary evidence bears out this interpretation. Southern Negroes show much less attachment to the national Democratic party than northern Negroes. In the 1956 presidential election, for example, a survey by the National Association for the Advancement of Colored

[10] Wilson, *Negro Politics*, chap. ii.

People showed that the vote for the Republican candidate for President increased by 36.8 per cent among Negro voters in twenty-three southern cities but only by 9.9 per cent among Negro voters in forty northern and western cities. For example, in Chicago the Negro vote for Eisenhower increased from 29.5 per cent in 1952 to 37.2 per cent in 1956; in Atlanta, by contrast, it increased from 30.9 per cent to 85.3 per cent.[11] In 1960 the Negro vote in both the North and the South was heavily Democratic.

The degree of selectivity among Negro voters in southern cities is often remarkable. In the 1961 mayoralty election in Atlanta, for example, the white candidate endorsed by the Atlanta Negro Voters League received, in the Negro precincts, 31,224 votes while his opponent (who got about half the white vote) received only 179. In these precincts, *over 99 per cent* of the Negro voters voted for the same candidate—an almost incredible plurality. Many other examples can be found in the South of a comparable high level of race consciousness among Negro voters.[12]

Although Negro leaders are increasing in number, saying, as the Rev. Martin Luther King recently remarked, that the most significant step Negroes can take is in the "direction of the voting booths," it would be easy to exaggerate the long-term gains to be expected by Negro voting

[11] Henry Lee Moon, "The Negro Vote in the Presidential Election of 1956," *Journal of Negro Education*, XVI (1947), 219-30.

[12] The Atlanta case is from Donald R. Matthews and James W. Prothro, "Negro Voter Registration in the South," a paper presented at the Duke University Conference on the Impact of Political and Legal Changes in the Postwar South, Durham, North Carolina, July 1962 (mimeo). See also Douglas S. Gatlin, "A Case Study of a Negro Voters' League," *Political Studies Program: Research Reports*, No. 2, March 1960 (University of North Carolina Department of Political Science); H. Douglas Price, *The Negro and Southern Politics: A Chapter of Florida History* (New York: New York University Press, 1957); and Henry Holloway, "The Negro and the Vote: The Case of Texas," *Journal of Politics*, XXIII (August 1961), 526-56.

participation in the South. The extensive studies of Professors Donald R. Matthews and James W. Prothro of the University of North Carolina have shown that a great deal (over one-fourth) of the variation in Negro voter registration levels in southern counties can be explained by social and economic factors.[13] High levels of voter registration (much less participation) cannot be expected among a group which, like urban southern Negroes, had, in 1959, a median income less than *half* that of southern whites and less than two-thirds that of Negroes living in northern and western cities.[14] As Professors Matthews and Prothro conclude in their own study,

> . . . reformers should not expect miracles in their efforts, through political and legal means, to increase the size and effectiveness of the Negro vote in the South. The Negro registration rate is low, in rather large part, because of the social and economic characteristics of southerners—both Negro and white. These facts are not easily and quickly changed by law or political actions.[15]

Furthermore, success in electing Negroes to office in the South will create a new set of constraints. There is no reason to believe that Negro politicians in the South will be exempt from the general tendency of politicians everywhere to place the necessities of re-election above the interests of the most passionate exponents of militant civil-

[13] Donald R. Matthews and James W. Prothro, "Social and Economic Factors and Negro Voter Registration in the South," *American Political Science Review*, LVII (March 1963), 42.

[14] *United States Census of Population, 1960: General Social and Economic Characteristics*, United States Summary: Final Report PC(1)-1C, Table 139.

[15] Matthews and Prothro, "Social and Economic Factors and Negro Voter Registration in the South," *op. cit.*, p. 43. See also Leonard Reisman, K. H. Silvert, and Cliff W. Wing, Jr., "The New Orleans Voter: A Handbook of Political Description," *Tulane Studies in Political Science*, Vol. II, pp. 68-72 (1955); Thompson, *op. cit.*, pp. 86-96; and Holloway, *op. cit.*, p. 544.

rights action. Nor is there any reason to believe that, once the battle for the vote is won, it will be any easier in the South to arouse, organize, and lead the mass of lower-income Negroes than it has been in the North. Finally, electoral success will probably be purchased at the price of unity. Whereas the Negro vote can be powerfully united when the choice is between two white candidates, or between a white and Negro candidate, it must be expected that this unity will be considerably less when it is between two Negro candidates.[16]

These constraints on effective Negro political action—traditional party loyalties, the self-interest of politicians, and the difficulties inherent in organizing voters who have little income, education, or political experience—are powerful indeed. Nonetheless, they are only constraints and not barriers. Although the militant spirit will not be shared as widely or expressed as loudly as the most impassioned Negro leaders might prefer, it will exist to an ever greater extent as success breeds the expectation of further action, as the size of the Negro intellectual proletariat increases, and as political parties continue to lose those resources which make it possible to carry on politics without recourse to issues or ideology. For example, even all-Negro constituencies with partisan elections are electing Negro politicians who, like Adam Clayton Powell, Jr., in New York and Charles Diggs in Detroit, engage in extreme protest activities because in their areas the older style of party organization has been weakened or destroyed to the extent that militancy is no longer inhibited by organizational constraints—indeed, it is actually encouraged.

From a practical standpoint, the consequences of this increasing militancy are more important than the reasons for it. It is, of course, too early to tell what all these consequences will be. Thus, my remarks here must be largely

[16] Gatlin, *op. cit.*, p. 28.

conjectural. I believe, however, that there is some evidence to bear out my most general point—that the social consequences of Negro militancy will in part be determined by the particular reasons for that militancy.

First, Negroes will increasingly seek means to make their demands for change more visible, more dramatic, and more immediate. Although law suits, court proceedings, and legislative campaigns will continue and even increase, there will be a growing emphasis on direct action. This shift in emphasis will result in part from a desire of Negroes to give expression to their own increased sense of urgency, in part from their restlessness with the slow pace and prosaic quality of legalistic action, and in part from their disappointment with the results of laws, rules, and court orders. "Passive resistance" campaigns, sit-ins, picketing, and boycotts, which in the South have been dramatic efforts to attain simple goals, will be increasingly adapted in the North to more complex (and perhaps less appropriate) goals.

Second, white and Negro politicians will have an increasing incentive to offer certain general programs to Negroes in order to win and hold their political support. The old style politics of the big-city machine, now fast dying, provided no such incentive. So long as jobs, favors, and other personal benefits were given to individual voters (Negroes and white), politicians could count on getting the votes they needed. Today, except in a few places, the politician cannot rely on such personal benefits—he has been deprived of his control over these resources. He must rely either on rational argument to sway the voters or (what is much more likely) he must offer collective inducements to general classes of voters.[17] The politician will be under pressure to offer to middle-class Negroes, who need

---

[17] Banfield and Wilson, *op. cit.*, chap. xxii.

not worry about sheer economic survival, general civil-rights legislation which in the South will remove legal barriers to integration and which in the North will outlaw barriers which arise from the preferences of white citizens. These laws will have the general effect of conferring, at least symbolically, access to jobs, housing, and public facilities on Negroes who demand an affirmation of such rights, even though many (perhaps most) of them may not plan to avail themselves of these rights.

Lower-class Negroes, who probably regard legally-protected "opportunities" to buy twenty-thousand-dollar homes, work in large law firms, and stay at fancy hotels as irrelevant to their daily preoccupations, will expect the politician to offer, in addition, programs that redistribute income in their favor. The politician will be under pressure to support and expand various welfare policies (such as general relief, aid to dependent children, and unemployment benefits) and to restrain or improve police activities in lower-class Negro areas.

Indeed, the allegation of "police brutality" or "police neglect" is becoming, rightly or wrongly, one of the few major political issues which can both unite middle- and lower-class Negroes (middle-class Negroes find that, because of their color, they are often treated by the police like lower-class Negroes; thus, they have both a self-interest and a community interest in altering police practices) and arouse many normally apathetic or uninterested Negro voters. The mayoralty contests of 1961 in both Detroit and Los Angeles were fought out in great part over the issue of police treatment of minority groups; the winning candidates received heavy Negro support and, in at least one case, initiated important changes in police operations as a result.

A third consequence of the growing militancy of Negroes will be, I think, a widening gulf between Negroes and some of their traditional white liberal allies.[18] Although Negroes will continue to have the general support of white liberals, I foresee an increasing restlessness and discontent among both partners to what was once a fairly close alliance. To an increasing extent, white liberals will express openly (as they have long expressed privately) a concern for the tendency of Negro leadership to emphasize militant civic action directed towards integrationist goals at the expense of civic action directed towards the improvement of conditions within the Negro community itself. White liberals will also, I suspect, begin to distrust what they take to be the growing nationalism and extremism of some Negro leaders. On their part, Negro leaders will increasingly regard with suspicion what they take to be the unwillingness of white liberals to go the whole way with them—an unwillingness which Negroes will interpret as the result of white moderation, white caution, and white paternalism.

In the past it was typically the white liberal who complained at the moderation, caution, and even lack of interest of his Negro ally.[19] Today, I believe the roles are being reversed as the number of young militant Negroes increases and the intensity of their feeling deepens. The restlessness is compounded, one suspects, by the quite human view of many Negroes that they ought not to take advice or be placed in a subordinate position in a cause which is peculiarly their own and that no one who is not a Negro can really understand their feelings on these issues.

Recent efforts to bring about an organized political alliance between white liberals and Negroes within the

[18] See, for example, Loren Miller, "Farewell to Liberals," *Nation*, October 20, 1962, pp. 235-38, and Murray Friedman, "White Liberals' Retreat," *Atlantic*, January 1963, pp. 42-46.

[19] Wilson, *Negro Politics*, pp. 149-65.

Democratic party of certain cities and states have frequently foundered, in part on the differences in interests between lower-class Negro voters and middle-class white liberal politicians and in part on the differences in attitudes and strategies between middle-class Negro and white leaders. Such, for example, appears to have been the case in both New York City and Los Angeles.[20]

If these are the directions in which Negro political life is moving, it is important to ask what difference these changes are likely to make in the life of the Negro community and, for that matter, in the life of the white community. It is hard to give simple answers to this question if for no other reason than that while there are under way profound changes in both the Negro's socioeconomic position and his political role, it is by no means clear which is cause and which is effect. It is entirely possible that economic improvements among Negroes have caused a shift in political strategy, not that enhanced political power has caused governmental action which has led to economic improvement.

I incline to the former rather than the latter interpretation. One can, of course, find examples in which governmental action—taken in great part, although not entirely, out of a regard for Negro political power—has made an important difference in the life prospects of large numbers of Negroes. The 1954 Supreme Court school desegregation decision precipitated events which contributed to the admission, in seven years, of more than two hundred thousand Negro school children into formerly segregated schools. Almost all of these children, however, were in the so-called border states; practically none, except in Texas, was in the eleven states of the Old Confederacy where to-

[20] James Q. Wilson, *The Amateur Democrat: Club Politics in Three Cities* (Chicago: University of Chicago Press, 1962), pp. 277-88.

day far less than one per cent of Negro school children are in integrated schools.[21]

The removal of federal restrictions on the insuring of mortgages has probably contributed significantly to the great increase in the number of Negroes who are now buying rather than renting their homes. In one Ohio city where a survey has recently been completed, nearly three-fourths of all Negro families in the oldest portion of the city were buying their homes; better than half of these were making use of various government-insured mortgages.[22] The ending, in 1948, of the judicial enforceability of racially restrictive covenants in real estate deeds has undoubtedly greatly accelerated the movement of Negroes into better-quality homes (although *not* into neighborhoods which have remained integrated).

Although examples such as these are well known, I would argue that their total effect on the position of the average Negro in America has been relatively slight. Of much greater importance, it seems to me, has been the economic improvement of Negroes which has resulted not from governmental responses to Negro political power but from the continued growth of our economy. The median income of male Negroes living in cities increased about 58 per cent between 1950 and 1960; the proportion of male Negroes with incomes of $10,000 a year or more, living in cities, more than tripled in the same period. This is roughly the same gain as registered by whites during this period.

The effect of governmental policies designed to stimulate the growth of the economy may have profound effects

---

[21] United States Commission on Civil Rights, *Education: 1961 Report*, p. 238.

[22] James B. McKee, "Changing Patterns of Race and Housing: A Toledo Study," *Social Forces*, XLI (March 1963), 256. The U. S. Census Bureau reports that between 1930 and 1960, the percentage of nonwhite dwelling units which were owner-occupied rose from 25.2 to 38.3 in the nation as a whole.

on improving the Negro's economic position; whether policies which aim at improving that position simply by eliminating racial discrimination have much effect is at least debatable. The great increase in the Negro's economic position, both absolutely and relative to whites, occurred in the decade 1940 to 1950, *before* most state fair employment practices acts were placed on the statute books. The great gains in Negro employment were made during this time in occupational groups which were rapidly expanding in size—where, in short, a demand for certain skills was great enough to create a demand for Negro workers in areas previously closed to them.[23] Negroes as a whole have substantially improved their economic position when the society as a whole has improved its position and not, insofar as we know, when Negroes were made the beneficiaries of legislation aimed at ending discrimination.

Every northern industrial state now has a fair employment practices law of some consequence; yet, the effect of these laws on most Negroes seems hardly discernible. Over half of all Negro families living in cities had, in 1960, an income of less than $3,000 per year. The unemployment rate among Negroes has regularly been two to two-and-a-half times that of whites throughout the last decade. Negroes are heavily concentrated in the unskilled and semiskilled occupations; yet, it is precisely in these occupations that the fewest new jobs are being created as automation to an ever-increasing extent provides machines to do jobs formerly done by men. For most Negroes, laws intended to eliminate discrimination in employment may succeed only in integrating the bread line.

Essentially the same situation prevails in housing. New

[23] Norval D. Glenn, "Changes in the American Occupational Structure and Occupational Gains of Negroes During the 1940's," *Social Forces*, XLI (December 1962), 188-95. But compare Morroe Berger, *Equality by Statute* (New York: Columbia University Press, 1952).

York City was the first community to enact a "fair housing" or "open occupancy" ordinance banning discrimination in the sale or rental of all housing except owner-occupied duplexes and rooms in private homes. Since 1957, more than two dozen states have followed suit with roughly similar legislation. Yet, the effect of all this seems thus far to be negligible. In the first three years of its operation, the New York City law adjusted slightly more than two hundred complaints to the satisfaction of the Negro complainant. This to be sure is a gain, but it is a trivial one when viewed in the perspective of the nearly one million Negroes in that city. Most of the Negro complainants were middle-class Negroes in white-collar or professional occupations; lower-class Negroes, for whom the housing problem is perhaps most severe, hardly participated in the benefits of the open-occupancy law at all. And finally, nearly half the complaints were from Negroes who were already living in areas that were overwhelmingly white—from Negroes, that is, who had already broken out of the ghetto before they had recourse to the law.[24]

Ending discrimination in all its forms—particularly discrimination that has the sanction of law or governmental custom—is a moral necessity. Insofar as the rising militancy of Negro leaders is directed to that end, it is all to the good. But militancy is not enough. The problems which confront the mass of American Negroes will, I strongly suspect, remain for many years even if every major political goal of Negroes is attained tomorrow. If every city and state adopts and enforces to the best of its ability laws preventing discrimination in employment, housing, public accommodations, and medical facilities; if every school district in the North and the South were desegregated in fact as well as in name; if every level of

[24] Harold Goldblatt and Florence Cromien, "The Effective Reach of the Fair Housing Practices Law of the City of New York, *Social Problems*, IX (Spring 1962), 365-70.

government spent generously on welfare payments to indigent Negro families—if all these things occurred tomorrow, we would still be confronted with a social problem of considerable proportions.

For some time to come, we would still be confronted with the fact that unskilled Negro laborers cannot compete effectively in the labor market; that in many sectors of the economy job opportunities go begging because there are no qualified Negroes available to fill them; that the majority of Negro families are at the very lowest income levels and live in the poorest housing; that Negroes, while only one-tenth of our urban population, commit over one-third of all serious crimes in our cities;[25] that Negroes comprise the vast majority of welfare recipients in most large cities; and that Negroes constitute a disproportionate share of those young people who drop out of school before completing at least their secondary education.

About twenty years ago, when Gunnar Myrdal was writing his classic book, *An American Dilemma*, he entitled one section "What the Negro Gets Out of Politics." His conclusion was this:

> Unquestionably the most important thing that Negroes get out of politics where they vote is legal justice— justice in the courts; police protection and protection against the persecution of the police; ability to get administrative jobs through civil service; and a fair share in such public facilities as schools, hospitals, public housing, playgrounds, libraries, sewers and street lights.[26]

[25] Calculated from Federal Bureau of Investigation, *Uniform Crime Reports*, 1960, p. 95, for the seven "Part I" crimes. In 1960 Negroes were 11.0 per cent of the population of all urban places of 2,500 population or more.

[26] Gunnar Myrdal (with Richard Sterner and Arnold Rose), *An American Dilemma* (New York: Harper & Bros., 1944), p. 497. A more optimistic view of the power of the vote to solve major social problems can be found in Henry Lee Moon, *Balance of Power: The Negro Vote* (Garden City, N. Y.: Doubleday, 1949), p. 9.

The experience of twenty years does not require us to change this judgment. Myrdal believed then, as I believe now, that giving Negroes legal justice is a moral and practical necessity. But his conclusion also suggested, as I have tried to suggest, that political and civic action, no matter how militant, cannot by itself deal significantly with other important social problems. Neither civil rights legislation nor a steady increase in welfare payments will solve the most fundamental problems facing Negroes today.

Legal justice means the elimination of prejudicial barriers to the full enjoyment of citizenship. Political action over the last twenty years has contributed substantially to great progress in this area. But today, Negro militancy is increasing dramatically at the very time when militant political and civic action is approaching the limits of what is possible. Dramatic struggles will still be waged, and dramatic victories won, so long as the South lags behind the North in the granting of legal justice. But when it has caught up—as catch up it will, although perhaps not in our lifetime—problems will remain which cannot be dealt with by dramatic victories. Unless we address ourselves more urgently to the undramatic, prosaic, but crucial problem of continued and broader economic progress and cultural development, the day when there are no more political and legal victories to be won will be a day, not of exultation, but of bitter disappointment.

EDUCATIONAL CHANGES AFFECTING AMERICAN NEGROES

Rayford W. Logan

The title of this essay requires a definition of terms. The Fourteenth Amendment defined American Negroes in terms of citizenship but wisely refrained from entering the biological thicket. State laws, however, have foolishly attempted to fill the void left by the federal Constitution and Congress. In some states Negroes are persons who may have less than one-sixteenth of Negro blood; in other states, more than one-eighth; in Virginia, an "ascertainable" degree of Negro blood. These laws, as stupid and as inhuman as those of Nazi Germany and, today, of South Africa, evoke derision from scientists, lawyers, and men of good will. In this essay American Negroes are those persons who accept discrimination and segregation imposed upon Negroes.

Education means the acquisition of knowledge. Formal education consists of knowledge gained in schools. Informal education includes knowledge acquired in homes and in churches; on the job; by self-study; by visits to legislatures and courts, to museums, zoological gardens, to theaters and musical concerts; by participation in politics. Informal education includes also knowledge gained through mass media and travel, through changes in American society and in international affairs. During the past several years, freedom-rides, sit-ins, wade-ins, lie-ins, kneel-ins, boycotts, and street demonstrations have added a new dimension to the meaning of education. In brief, as John Dewey put it: "Education is life."

Among the more important changes in the character of education are the increased percentages of students seeking formal education; token desegregation, massive resegregation and token deresegregation, if I may coin a word; and the rapidly growing impact of informal education.

Before undertaking a detailed analysis of formal education, I shall examine some changes in education outside of the classroom. Parents, in too many instances, have abdicated their responsibilities for the preparation of students for serious study. Many sociologists attribute Negro juvenile delinquency and the large number of Negro high school drop-outs and failures in college to the urban pathologies of Negro slums. A revealing article, "Where's the Party—Let's Crash It!" by Robert Wallace in *Life*, July 5, 1963, makes clear that the affluent society also produces these social ills. Mr. Wallace wrote: "The violence of the suburban teen-ager often exceeds that of his delinquent cousin in the slums." The author cited two particularly relevant recent incidents:

> In Grosse Pointe, a wealthy suburb of Detroit, party-crashers invaded a handsome house, were asked to leave and did—but not before smashing the kitchen furniture, overturning the stove and breaking all the kitchen windows.

In Detroit's Northwest Side a teen-ager arranged a small party while his parents were absent. Presently more than 100 boys and girls, almost all of them un-invited, were in the house. They destroyed the wall-paper and wall decorations by splattering them with beer, then slashed the furniture and carpeting with knives: damage, $3,000.[1]

Evidence of the lack of interest in serious study by some teen-agers in the gilded ghettos does not solve the problems of Negro teen-agers in the slums. But this evidence does suggest that the problems of Negro slum dwellers are not inherently racial. Remove the causes for antisocial behavior, and parents in both the suburbs and the slums can better use the home as a positive educational force.

But what about middle-, upper middle-class, and the few wealthy Negro parents? Are they as guilty of parental neglect as were the parents of the teen-agers of Grosse Pointe and Northwest Detroit? Do they inculcate a love of learning or do they foster a false set of status symbols such as cotillion balls, for example? Do they live in modern homes which have a recreation room and a bar but no library? If they have a library, what reading material does it provide for themselves and their children? Since Detroit has had for many years an active branch of the Association for the Study of Negro Life and History, I can be easily convinced that many Negro homes there receive the *Journal of Negro History*, the *Negro History Bulletin*, and have a shelf of books on Negro history. I can be easily convinced also that at eventide Mom and Dad, instead of going out for a game of bridge, or bingo, or poker, inspire their children with the thrilling saga of the Negroes' quest for equal rights. Since many earnest educators have not

[1] Robert Wallace, "Where's the Party—Let's Crash It!" *Life*, July 5, 1963, p. 64. Quoted with the permission of *Life*.

decided whether Negro history should be taught as a separate subject, as an integral part of diluted social studies of traditional courses in history and, hence, frequently it is not taught, parents have an inescapable responsibility to provide their children with stimulating, well-written, non-propagandistic reading materials.

Parental ignorance and indifference, added to inadequate courses in history, explain an experience that I had a few years ago. I asked a class in Negro history at Howard University who was Dr. William Edward Burghardt Du Bois? Not one student in a class of some twenty juniors and seniors could give a specific answer. They had never heard of *The Souls of Black Folk*, of the Niagara Movement, of the *Crisis* or of the Pan-African Congresses. How many parents have made their children commit to memory the clarion call of Du Bois at Harpers Ferry in 1906 when he asserted in more eloquent terms than any present-day leader the rejoinder to Booker T. Washington's "Compromise" address at Atlanta on September 18, 1895? Du Bois, in 1906 an authentic American radical, long before he espoused the cause of the Soviet Union, warned: "We will not be satisfied to take one jot or tittle less than our full manhood rights. We claim for ourselves every single right that belongs to a freeborn American, political, civil and social; and until we get these rights we will never cease to protest and assail the ears of America." I would hope that this clarion call might be placed on the walls of homes as a reminder that the so-called "New Negro" has not formulated more incisively or more eloquently the demand for first-class citizenship than did Du Bois more than fifty years ago.

Most white churches are still one of the principal bulwarks of segregation. You know better than I do the extent to which predominantly white churches in Detroit—except perhaps the Unitarians, the Quaker Meeting Houses and the Ethical Societies—have extended a warm hand of fellowship to Negro members. Washington's record is probably as bad as that of Detroit.

Two recent major developments offer encouragement. Even when a few prominent white church leaders began to preach the social gospel in the latter part of the nineteenth century, they rarely included the Negro in their concept of the Brotherhood of Man on earth. In recent months some leading white churchmen have gone to jail for their participation in freedom rides, sit-ins, and street demonstrations. Belatedly, a few white church leaders have publicly declared that segregation is a moral wrong.

In recent years also, some Negro pastors have been in the vanguard of the quest for civil rights. Their activities have shocked advocates of the *status quo*; for during slavery and, indeed, well down into the twentieth century the Negro pastor and the Negro school principal were looked upon by the white power structure as instruments of control to "keep Negroes in their place." Today an increasing number of Negro pastors have revived the tradition of Bishop B. W. Arnett of the African Methodist Episcopal Church, who was elected to the Ohio legislature in 1885 and led the fight for the repeal of that state's "Black Laws." I doubt that any present day Negro church leader has preached as powerful a sermon as did Nathaniel Paul, pastor of the African Baptist Society of Albany, New York, on July 5, 1827. Paul admonished:

Did I believe that it [slavery] would always continue, and that man to the end of time would be permitted with impunity to usurp the same undue authority over his fellow, I would disallow any allegiance or obligation I was under to my fellow creatures, or any submission that I owed to the laws of my country; I would deny the superintending power of divine Providence in the affairs of this life; I would ridicule the religion of the Savior of the world, and treat as the worst of men the ministers of the everlasting gospel; I would consider my Bible as

189

a book of false and delusive fables, and commit it to the flames; nay, I would go still farther; I would at once confess myself an atheist, and deny the existence of a holy God.[2]

This sermon is in *Negro Orators and Their Orations*, edited by Dr. Carter G. Woodson in 1925. The book is hard to find, a fact which suggests that in these days of paperbacks and of Xerox-produced books, there is little reason that Negroes should fail to underwrite publication of this and other books.

Mass media—newspapers, magazines, movies, the radio, and television—have become even in this era of paperbacks the most powerful instrumentalities of informal education. Indeed, I would not violently challenge those who say that the total impact of mass media is greater than that of the schools. On balance, American Negroes have profited from the impact of mass media, which have both molded and reflected attitudes and opinions about the Negro. The changing character of this educational force is most evident in newspapers, for the image of the Negro there portrayed has a longer history in the development of American thought than that of other mass media.

During the last quarter of the nineteenth century most northern newspapers lampooned and stereotyped Negroes almost as viciously as do rabid southern segregationist newspapers today. Most of these northern newspapers opposed Negro migration to the North and supported President Hayes in his policy of leaving the "Negro question" to the "great mass of intelligent white men in the South." The Detroit *Post and Tribune*, later the *Tribune*, was one of the few newspapers that supported Justice John Marshall Harlan's famous dissenting opinion in the Civil

[2] Carter G. Woodson (ed.), *Negro Orators and Their Orations* (Washington, 1925), pp. 72-73.

Rights decision of 1883. The *Tribune* was also one of the few newspapers that rejected Henry W. Grady's distorted picture in 1886 of the "New South" which, he said, treated the Negro with equality and justice. Most papers approved the rulings of the Interstate Commerce Commission, 1887, 1888, and 1889, in favor of separate but equal accommodations for Negroes. In the last decade of the nineteenth century, northern newspapers again opposed migration of Negroes from the South to the "Northern land of ice, snow and blizzards," the admonition of the Chicago *Tribune*. They opposed the Blair Bill for federal support of public education and the Lodge Bill for federal supervision of federal elections; condoned the enactment of southern constitutional amendments which disfranchised large numbers of Negroes while permitting large numbers of equally unqualified whites to vote; praised Booker T. Washington's "Atlanta Compromise Speech" and generally ignored the Supreme Court decision, *Plessy v. Ferguson* (1896), in which the Court for the first time sanctioned the principle of separate but equal accommodations. These papers stereotyped Negroes as clowns and criminals. While the papers did not often use pejorative terms in news articles, they did use such words as "coon," "darkey," "pickaninny," "uncle," "aunt," "nigger," "niggah," in anecdotes, jokes, cartoons, and narratives.

My investigations have revealed a slightly less derogatory treatment of the Negro by the end of the First World War. Increasingly since that time, northern newspapers and some southern newspapers presented a more favorable image of the Negro until 1954 when the Supreme Court decision declaring segregation in public schools unconstitutional, and subsequent decisions in behalf of civil rights for Negroes renewed vicious attacks by southern newspapers hardly exceeded by earlier condemnation of Abolitionists. By contrast, many northern newspapers have supported the quest for civil rights more forcefully than they did the campaign for the abolition of slavery.

The metamorphosis of magazines with national circulation has been perhaps even more dramatic than the change in the policies of newspapers.

In the last quarter of the nineteenth century, *Harper's*, *Atlantic*, *Scribner's*, and *Century* vilified Negroes—and to a much less degree foreign-born whites and their descendants—in a manner that can be believed only if one has read their editorials, short stories, articles, anecdotes, and cartoons. Like northern newspapers, they generally opposed the Negro and supported the "New South" and the "Road to Reunion." The following compilation of names and titles taken from these leading literary magazines during the last quarter of the nineteenth century affords an idea of the way in which they lampooned Negroes:

> Negroes were made ludicrous by the bestowal of titles, names of famous men or of folk expressions. Among the choice ones were Colonel, Senator, Sheriff, Apollo Belvedere, George Washington, Webster, Abraham Lincum, Napoleon Boneyfidey Waterloo, Venus Milo Clevins, Columbus, Pomp, Caesar, Lady Adeliza Chimpanzee, Prince Orang Outan, Hieronymous, Ananias, Solomon Crow, Piddlekins, Sosrus Dismal, Asmodeus, Bella Donna Mississippi Idaho, Violetta Marie Evalina Rose Christian, Nuttin 'Tal, Had-a-Plenty and Wan-na-Mo. The ultimate was achieved in Henri Ritter Demi Ritter Emmi Ritter Sweet-potato Cream Tartar Caroline Bostwick.[3]

Since the 1920's, literary magazines and magazines of opinion, like the more liberal newspapers, have portrayed Negroes in a more favorable light. The magazines already mentioned muted their acidulous comments; the *Nation* and the *New Republic* became more sturdy, some said

[3] Rayford W. Logan, *The Negro in American Life and Thought: The Nadir, 1877-1901* (New York, 1957), p. 241.

more strident, in their denunciation of Woodrow Wilson's specious "New Freedom." Henry Louis Mencken's pungent and iconoclastic criticisms in the *American Mercury* and other magazines spoofed American prejudices so effectively during the 1920's and the 1930's that subsequent writers have tried in vain to emulate him. *Survey Graphic* published articles that provided the core of Alain Locke's *The New Negro* (1925). *Saturday Review* and the *Reporter* published urbane, scholarly articles and book reviews that educated sophisticated readers. *Crisis, Opportunity, Messenger,* and the *Journal of Negro History* educated readers, largely Negroes, who otherwise would have known little about current issues or the contributions of African and American Negroes to civilization.

Most striking and profound has been the changing character of education provided by national magazines with millions of readers. Gone are the days of Octavus Roy Cohen's stories in the *Saturday Evening Post*, in the *genre* of Amos and Andy on the radio. Unless you are old enough to remember these viciously humorous stereotypes of the American Negro—Stepin Fetchit of the movies was almost a folk hero by contrast—you do not know how damaging Cohen was.

In a special category is the *New Yorker* which, despite a relatively small circulation, has had a great impact on American thought. The *New Yorker*, while still addressing itself largely to the urbane sophisticates so brilliantly described by James Thurber in his book, *The Years with Ross*, has become a most effective crusader for civil rights. Two articles, June 10, 17, 1963, on *Gomillion v. Lightfoot*, the case in which the United States Supreme Court declared unconstitutional the gerrymandering of Tuskegee, Alabama, are almost classics in making understandable to laymen the almost unbelievable, blatant attempts of respectable white citizens to circumvent the Constitution of the United States. Three articles by Calvin Trillin, in the

193

New Yorker July 13, 20, 27, 1963, entitled "A Reporter at Large—An Education in Georgia," gave a remarkably perceptive psychological analysis of the trials and tribulations of Charlayne Hunter, Hamilton Holmes, and other Negro students at the University of Georgia and of the not too laudable performance of the University administration, most professors, white students, and townspeople. Readers of these articles have not been surprised by recent Negro demonstrations in Athens, Georgia.

Even *U. S. News and World Report*, the most conservative of the magazines here analyzed, has "got religion," of a sort.

But it is *Life, Look, Time,* and *Newsweek* that have most effectively championed in recent years the quest of Negroes for equal rights. Many of their editorials, articles, photographs, and photographic essays have rankled segregationists and heartened Negroes and their allies. Their particular importance derives from the fact that they have a readership which, in part, is slightly less conservative than that of *U. S. News and World Report*. Without agreeing with some of the conclusions of the article on the Negro in *Newsweek* for July 29, 1963, I consider it one of the most important single informal educational forces in recent years.

Even the radio must now be included, again on balance, as a positive informal educational force. Gone are the generally unlamented shenanigans of Amos and Andy. National news broadcasts have frequently presented an unemotional narrative of crucial events favorable to the Negro cause. I do not know how many southerners turn off the radio when these broadcasts are scheduled; nor do I know the content of local broadcasts in the South and North. I have been told by southern Negroes, however, that many white southerners listen with avid and perhaps disappointed interest to broadcasts of professional and college sports.

Movies were probably a more powerful informal educational force a few years ago than they are today. Unless you saw "The Birth of a Nation" (1914), one of the most vicious films in the history of American movies, you cannot understand why many Americans, particularly Negroes, wanted it banned. "Gone with the Wind" (1940) was less vicious, but it reached a larger audience, and I suspect that its harmful effects were greater.

On the other hand, some movies began to destroy the myth of the purity of white womanhood before pornographic novels and the recent exposé of London sex scandals interred the myth. Not many of you remember the defiance by the movie heroine that she was "free, white, and twenty-one," but many of you have probably seen the movie, "The Apartment." When I was in Paris, Brussels, West Berlin, Copenhagen, and Stockholm during the summer of 1960, I saw enticing advertisements, "So sexy that it [a movie] has been banned in the United States." In the United States, a movie has sometimes been advertised as "So sexy that it has been banned in Europe." Inadvertently, these silly movies have contributed to the destruction of the myth of "the notorious immorality of Negro women."

Movies have been, however, almost as much of a "vast wasteland" as has television. In "Adult Westerns," the hero must frequently even ride a white horse. Rarely does a Negro have any role except as a menial or villain. Is it not time for a cinematic biography of such Negroes as Alexander Pushkin, Alexandre Dumas *père*, Toussaint L'Ouverture, Frederick Douglass, Harriet Tubman, and Sojourner Truth?

Television, despite Newton Minow's all too accurate description of it as a "vast wasteland," is the most potent informal educational force in America today. One might even contend that television educates more Americans than does formal instruction in schools. I have the firm conviction that the net balance of television promotes the quest of Negroes for equal rights and, hence, the goals of popular education and democratic thought in America. I doubt that any book has taught as enduring lessons as the telecasts of the Arkansas National Guard, bayonets fixed, who barred Elizabeth Eckford from Central High School; of the harridans in New Orleans screaming to their wondering children: "You don't want to go to school with niggers"; of white girls screaming obscenities at James Meredith; of the courageous young Negro confronting the vicious police dogs in Birmingham; of equally courageous girls knocked down by high-pressure fire hose; of Robert Fehsenfeldt in Cambridge, Maryland, twice assaulting a young white man kneeling in front of Fehsenfeldt's segregated restaurant; of Governor George C. Wallace's *opéra bouffe* at the doorway of the University of Alabama.

Some telecasts have revealed that Negroes are human and that they are sometimes not endowed with plain common sense. Many Negroes rejoiced when Governor Wallace permitted millions of viewers to see and hear his not particularly brilliant testimony before the Senate Commerce Committee against the pending civil rights legislation. Alas! Immediately following him on one telecast were shots of a Negro pastor of a large church in an eastern city who was apparently carried away by his own eloquence. He shouted that "We want all our rights now! Now!! Now!!!" Each "now" was louder and longer than the preceding one.

Negro artists and technicians legitimately protest denial of equal opportunities in movies and television. Recently, however, some newspapers and television stations have begun to employ Negro reporters and do not restrict them to news about Negroes. For example, a Negro who participates regularly in a Washington news broadcast was given the assignment of reporting the death of Patrick Bouvier Kennedy.

Obviously, scholars must probe in depth the validity of the conclusions already presented. I would hope that scholars will also consider, dispassionately, the soundness of my views about the educational value of activist movements, particularly of street demonstrations, for Negroes and, hence, for the nation. How much have they taught about the Thirteenth, Fourteenth, and Fifteenth Amendments? I would venture the guess that a small percentage of adult participants and an even smaller percentage of teen-age and younger participants can explain the meaning of the second section of the Fourteenth Amendment and of the practical problems arising from proposals to enforce it. How many have learned from these activist movements the terms of the Civil Rights Laws of 1957 and 1960 or the thrust of *Baker v. Carr*, decided in 1962, which may be more important than the public school decision of 1954 and 1955? How many have learned the value of registering and voting, the ramifications of the power structure, the failure of Big Business, Big Labor, the churches, and universities especially in the South to provide the enlightened leadership that they owe to their communities and to the nation? How much have these activist movements taught about the power of the "traffic cops" in the House Rules Committee, about the inordinate power of southern Congressional committee chairmen by virtue of their seniority based upon "rotten" and "pocket boroughs," about the pros and cons of the Senate cloture rule and about the "Unholy Alliance" between northern economic conservatives and Dixiecrats? It is clear that I have serious doubts about the educational value of activist movements. Their effectiveness on local situations cannot now be accurately assessed, but it can be asserted that they have accelerated action on the national and some state levels for meaningful civil rights legislation and executive orders.

Travel is the last component of informal education that I have time to discuss. Even Soho in London, the *boîtes de nuit* in Paris and the bikinis on the Riviera and the Isle of Capri have value if they are studied for educational purposes. These dividends are meager, however, when compared with those derived from visits to ancient, medieval, and recent monuments. The statues of Alexandre Dumas *père* and Alexandre Dumas *fils* in Paris have impressed me more than have the cafés made famous by Joyce, Hemingway, and Scott Fitzgerald. But the wise traveler observes people particularly.

Allow me to sketch for you one vignette, as an illustration. August, 1960, a few weeks after the independence of the former Belgian Congo. Brussels, where a few days earlier almost any one with a black skin was chased in the streets. Place Bouvier, sometimes called the "Times Square of Brussels." At about four o'clock in the afternoon a tall, dark Negro, dressed in recently washed blue jeans, stands for a half-hour on the corner. Two or three Belgians stop to speak courteously to him. He thanks them and continues to stand there, erect, defiant. To me it seems that he is saying: "If any one wants to try to beat me up or to chase me, dammit, come on." After the half-hour during which I watch him—I do not know how long he has already been there—he nonchalantly lights a cigarette, crosses the street, strolls past a side-walk café and disappears from my view. This vignette will haunt me long after I have forgotten what Notre Dame de Paris, the Brandenburg Gate, the Tivoli Gardens, and Trafalgar Square looked like in the summer of 1960.

Let us now consider some of the more important changes in the character of formal education with special reference to their effect on American Negroes.

The most significant lesson is that changes in formal education have been gradual; they have been gradual because they have been geared to the goals of American society and the changes in these goals have been gradual. Two recently published books illuminate this thesis. Rush

Welter's *Popular Education and Democratic Thought in America* (New York, 1962), according to Professor Merle Curti of the University of Wisconsin, is "one of the more important contributions to the history of ideas in America that the last decade has seen." The provocative sentences from Professor Curti's review of the book are especially relevant to the subject of this essay:

> Under the impact of the unfolding twentieth-century economic revolution with its accompanying changes in social structure, with new emphases on the nonrational aspects of behavior (including preoccupation with and responses to propaganda, advertising, and the concept of myth), reliance on education as the major instrument of realizing the promises of democracy has as Welter shows both cogently and brilliantly, retreated to a near-vanishing point. At the same time faith in education as a means of personal advance and as a mechanism for training leaders has, somewhat paradoxically, made substantive headway.[4]

Professor Curti also points out that "one of the important contributions of the study is the distinction drawn between formal and informal education." Although the expression "required reading" has become a cliché, it aptly describes the value of this book for school administrators, teachers, students, and engineers of social change, despite the fact that relatively little space is devoted to the education of Negroes.

The second recent book that I would particularly commend is Richard Rudolph's *The American College and University: A History* (New York, 1962), although it too has relatively little about Negro education.

The gaps left by these books are filled in some measure by *Negro Education in America: Its Adequacy, Problems, and Needs*, edited by Virgil A. Clift, Archibald W. Ander-

[4] *American Historical Review*, 68 (July 1963), 1080-81.

son and H. Gordon Hullfish, as the Sixteenth Yearbook of the John Dewey Society (New York, 1962).

All of these books emphasize that one of the greatest changes in the character of American public education has been the vast increase in the number of students from nursery schools through graduate schools. You know also that, in general, most Negro students in these schools, North and South, do not enjoy equal educational opportunities; that segregated schools are generally inferior schools, that they damage the personality of teachers and students. In Detroit, of all places, I need not dwell upon the potentially disastrous effects of automation on Negro family life, the Negro community, and Negro students.

I have no panacea for these ills. Permit me, however, as a student for more than fifty years and as a teacher for some thirty-eight years, to present to you some observations on the changing character of formal education with particular emphasis on its effects on Negroes.[5]

The boys and girls of my generation knew practically nothing about the Negro although I was graduated from the best segregated high school in the United States. Our geography text book portrayed the traditional five races of mankind, with the Negro in profile in order to emphasize his dolichocephalic head and his prognathous jaw. It was perhaps from this book that Arnold Toynbee got the idea that "only the black races have contributed nothing to civilization—as yet." In one of the very best ivy-leaf colleges (I was graduated in 1917), I learned very little about the Negro except that he had been a slave. Even in

[5] Limitations of space preclude a discussion of secondary education. Brief mention should be made, however, of courses in remedial reading, remedial English, and remedial arithmetic since a much larger percentage of Negro than of white students benefit from such courses. These courses materially increase the number of Negro students who aspire to move from the fourth track to the third, second, and first tracks and thus to prepare themselves for admission to college.

1930-32, when I was in residence for my graduate work, there were no courses in Negro history or African history. An eminent professor taught Latin American history, but I knew more about Haiti than he did; he introduced his advanced course on Argentina, Brazil, and Chile by saying that he knew so little about Brazil that he would omit it from his lectures. But already Professor Ernest Hooton was teaching a course in physical anthropology which most effectively spoofed concepts of racial characteristics and of inherent racial superiority and inferiority.

During the past half-century, many predominantly Negro colleges and universities have begun to offer courses in Negro history. We certainly owe a salute to Carter G. Woodson, who founded the Association for the Study of Negro Life and History in 1915; who began in 1916 the publication of the *Journal of Negro History* and in 1926 the *Negro History Bulletin*; who inaugurated Negro History Week in 1937; and who published a number of creditable scholarly works and some worthwhile popular books. What a pity it is that Negroes failed to provide the financial support necessary to enable Dr. Woodson to achieve an even more notable place in American historiography!

Most of the reasons for this failure are clear. Some Negro scholars disdained the subject because, they said, there is no such thing as Negro history any more than there is Negro physics, for example; the study of the Negro was inherently less important than the study, for example, of the sources of Chaucer's *Canterbury Tales* or of the *real* author of Shakespeare's plays and sonnets.

Meanwhile white scholars and, of course, white propagandists plowed the field that too many Negroes allowed to remain fallow. These white scholars and propagandists had at least one almost incalculable advantage, namely access to adequate funds. For this reason a nearby "white" university may open its Center of Negro Studies before

Howard University does, although Howard's Center has been in the planning stage for several years.

White scholars and propagandists had other advantages over Negro scholars: more time for research, travel and writing; a larger number of research assistants; greater stature in the academic and publishing worlds.

Today, these reasons have less validity. A few Negro scholars have reduced teaching loads; our better universities provide for sabbatical leave and research grants; some Negro scholars have the advantage of competing with white scholars on the faculties of leading "white" universities.

More important than these reasons is the fact that today Negro scholars who have established reputations in the open market find it impossible to accept firm commitments from reputable publishing firms. One of the most important changes in the character of formal education is the increased opportunity for Negroes to write about Negroes, especially American Negroes.

Three other changes must be considered for the image of Negroes in the United States. Today, so little has been written about Melanesians, Micronesians and Polynesians in the South Pacific that the output has had little influence on the American mind. But a few Negro scholars must soon begin investigations in this fruitful field before propagandists destroy the findings of the few white scholars who have studied the life of peoples almost forgotten until the Second World War.

It is time for more Negro scholars to interest themselves in Latin America, the British, French, and Dutch West Indies, and in Africa. A strange myopia prevails among some white specialists in Latin American history. It is a commonplace for them to refer enthusiastically to the "great revolutionary principles of the revolutions in the Spanish colonies and Brazil." They forget or ignore the fact that the revolution in Saint-Dominigue, later the

Republic of Haiti, had also its great revolutionary principles, Liberty, Equality, Fraternity. Most scholars and
popular writers forget or ignore the fact that Haiti was the
first of the Latin American nations to win independence.
It is therefore incumbent upon Negro scholars to remove
this myopia.

Negro scholars must also take a greater interest in the
British, French, and Dutch West Indies. Is the break-up
of the Federation of the British West Indies due primarily
to the alleged inability of Negroes to work together? Why
is it that color, class, and caste prejudice constitute such
a divisive force in some of the islands? Why is it that
Chinese and East Indians constitute, in some instances, a
disproportionately larger number of the upper classes than
do Negroes? Why have many British and French West
Indians assimilated Western culture more than British and
French, or Belgian and Portuguese, Africans? Why is it
that the Dutch in the Dutch West Indies hold Negroes
there in less contempt than do the Dutch and other Europeans in South Africa? Why is it that oil refineries in Cura-
cao and Aruba pay Negro and colored workers higher
salaries than do sugar companies elsewhere in the Carib-
bean?

The study of African history constitutes one of the most
dramatic changes in American intellectual history and
American historiography. Until recently, African history
was taught as a separate subject only in a few schools such
as Northwestern University and some predominantly
Negro colleges and universities. Today, the competition
among American colleges and universities for competent
Africanists is so keen that these specialists receive some of
the highest salaries paid to faculty members; universities
and foundations award sizable grants for programs of
African studies, including stipends to students engaged in
these studies in the United States and Africa. It is no longer

true that the "only dark thing about the 'Dark Continent' is ignorance about it."

When Woodson and Du Bois described the civilizations of Ghana, Melle, and Songhay, they were accused of writing "propaganda." Now that eminent white scholars are using primarily the same sources that Woodson and Du Bois used, the "discoveries" of white scholars are generally accepted, especially if they advance the thesis that non-Negroes were the rulers of these flourishing kingdoms.

The Pan-African Congresses from 1919 to 1927, once derided as an aberration of Du Bois', are now carefully studied as a necessary background for Pan-Africanism today.

Perhaps the most important of the changes with respect to the history of Africa deals with the problems of the new nations of Africa. Many American Negroes (as well as some American whites and African Negroes) are so thrilled by the winning of independence by these nations that they cannot talk, teach, or write without deep emotion.

I grasp several nettles. One-party states in Africa may be as authoritarian as one-party states in the Deep South of the United States. To me the concept of an "African Personality" is as much of a myth as is the concept of a "European Personality," a "Latin-American Personality," or an "American Personality." "Négritude," which idolizes "Negroness" or "blackness" as a symbol of beauty, purity, intelligence, and other virtues, is in my judgment no more defensible than the association of these attributes with "whiteness."

Pan-Africanism, in the sense of a United States of Africa, may be as hard a row to hoe as a United States of Europe or a United States of Latin America. On the other hand, one should not expect so-called inferior Africans to achieve within a few years what Latin Americans have not been able to achieve in a hundred and fifty years, or Europeans in several centuries.

Our joy over the attainment of independence by the new nations of Africa should not blind us to the dangers of neo-colonialism. Political independence does not necessarily mean economic independence, especially from the former colonial countries. The role of the African nations in the United Nations, their policies *vis-à-vis* the NATO countries, the Soviet bloc, and Nationalist China should also be studied, taught, and written about with scholarly detachment. I have deliberately selected these provocative topics because one of the more frightening changes in the character of education is a revival in some circles of the kind of intellectual black chauvinism that Marcus Garvey preached in the 1920's. Intellectual black chauvinism is as reprehensible as is intellectual white chauvinism.

In passing, I mention briefly a subject that evokes almost as much emotionalism as does black chauvinism, namely, planned parenthood. I have the conviction that, especially as far as Negroes are concerned, the increasing availability of knowledge about planned parenthood constitutes as important a change in education, both informal and formal, as any other topic that I have discussed.

And now to conclude. American Negroes are sociologically rather than biologically identifiable. The acquisition of knowledge through informal education may be more important than the knowledge gained in school. I have devoted more attention to the substantive than to the mechanical and philosophical aspects of knowledge. Changes in the character of education have been gradual because they have been geared to the goals of American society and changes in these goals have been gradual. I have avoided belaboring the obvious and have deliberately endeavored to test your individual and mass reactions to emotion-packed subjects.

By clear implication I have suggested that, in this first

year after the Centennial of the Emancipation Proclamation, scholars—especially Negro scholars—have more opportunities and, hence, more responsibilities than did our revered teachers and those who taught them. Reversing the traditional saying, "We who are about to die, salute you," I venture to suggest: "We who are about to live salute you." Since those who have died for us are members of a countless legion, I do not call the roll of honor. But I hope that we may assure them that we will endeavor to complete the unfinished business of making the goals of American society include equal opportunities for *all* Americans and the promotion of these equal opportunities through education.

This is our pledge, Abraham Lincoln and Frederick Douglass.

III

SOCIAL
MOVEMENTS
AMONG
AMERICAN
NEGROES

Among the forces that have created the social changes examined in the previous portion of the book have been the deliberate efforts of groups of citizens, some organized with exclusively Negro membership and others organized with mixed white and Negro membership. Most of the organizations have followed the successful American tradition that reform organizations should have specific goals, rather than seeking a comprehensive reorganization of the whole society. The Urban League, described in this book by its director, Whitney M. Young, Jr., is one such organization. Its concerns have been primarily those of the professional welfare worker, particularly in the area of housing and employment. There is an informal division of labor with most of the other specialized organizations, such as the National Association for the Advancement of Colored People and the Congress on Racial Equality, both of which were described by their directors *in lectures at the Wayne State University Centennial. In their presentation of their practical philosophies, their strategies of operation, their goals and achievements, all three of these Negro leaders offered a wealth of wisdom and represented American reform associations at their best.*

But the revolutionary social movement, which seeks to change the basic structure of society, is not completely lacking from American society, especially in an area such as the Negro problem where there are such long-standing and deep-seated frustrations. The political scientist C. Eric Lincoln describes one such revolutionary organization that has attracted a good deal of public notice in the past few years—the "Black Muslims." While its goals claim to be revolutionary, it is factually questionable whether the Negro Muslims are much different from other Negro improvement organizations and are merely using a different and unorthodox strategy to achieve the same goals of full equality.

Much, although certainly not all, of the leadership for Negro improvement or civil rights organizations has come from educated Negroes who have an "intellectual's orientation" to their task (using that phrase in its best sense). Yet, the late E. Franklin Frazier told us not so many years ago that the "black bourgeoisie"—by which he meant the educated and well-to-do Negroes—were apathetic toward the Negro problem and toward the strivings of the Negro lower classes to escape their miserable conditions caused by discrimination from the dominant white society. Frazier exaggerated, but he stirred the consciences of some of the intellectuals for whom his description was accurate. Partly because of Frazier, and partly because of the increasing tempo of events, many Negro intellectuals have been "transformed" in their attitude toward participation—which social movement is described for us by John Hope Franklin in the closing chapter of this book.

209

CIVIL RIGHTS ACTION
AND THE URBAN LEAGUE

Whitney M. Young, Jr.

Briefly and simply, the Urban League is a professional community-service agency, founded in 1910 to secure equal opportunity for Negro citizens. It is nonprofit and nonpartisan, and interracial in its leadership and staff. The Urban League's goal is to eliminate racial segregation and discrimination in American life, and to give guidance and help to Negroes so that they may share equally the responsibilities and rewards of citizenship.

One of the major problems of public interpretation and public relations which have plagued the Urban League throughout its history is the fact that the organization is not a "civil rights agency," as the term is usually defined by the general public, both white and Negro. To most people it is more convenient and less complicated to think of civil rights activities always as the overt, visible protest —law suits, demonstrations, and political lobbying. This is characteristic of America and Americans. We like things that are simple and easy to label, to judge, to characterize, to pigeonhole and file away. We like our answers to come quickly and easily, our reading and culture to be condensed and capsuled. We want to be briefed, not taught, and many Americans make a god of veneer and surface image while nervously ridiculing the depth-seeker.

And so it is in the field of civil rights. We prefer clean-cut problems and equally clean-cut solutions. We want our heroes as well as our villains to play their roles by the books, and when they do not we are understandably annoyed. We wish that Senators Ervin and Russell would act like Governors Barnett and Wallace, for then we could handle them more easily. The Ku Klux Klan wishes this, too, but for a different reason.

Similarly, most advocates of civil rights wish that Whitney Young, Roy Wilkins, and Jim Farmer were utilizing identical methods to achieve a common goal. Here, again, the Ku Klux Klan would like the same thing, but for a different reason. The civil rights battle would have been won long ago if all the southern opposition had modeled their maneuvers after Senator Bilbo's, and all the northern opposition after Gerald L. K. Smith's; and the Negro today would have been much further behind in the struggle for civil rights if only the NAACP method—or only the Urban League method—or only the CORE method—had been used.

However disconcerting it may be to our conventional thinking, reality forces us to concede that civil rights is no single-faceted problem, nor is there any monolithic solution. The Urban League recognized this fact of life some fifty-two years ago, when it was first founded by a group of prominent white and Negro citizens in New York City. The value of interracial teamwork, and the need to elevate the problem from a condescending and missionary concept was best expressed by Mrs. Ruth Standish Baldwin, who said at that time, "Let us work not as colored people nor as white people for the narrow benefit of any group alone, but together as American citizens for our common good, our common country."

This aspect of interracial teamwork has remained complete and universal throughout Urban League history, even to the point of writing into our Terms of Affiliation the provision that boards and committees must always reflect as close to a 50 per cent Negro-white ratio as possible. Our staffs throughout the country have shown increasing racial diversity.

The early history of the Urban League reflects a concern for the adjustment of Negro citizens who were migrating from the rural and urban South to the urban North. These citizens were experiencing a social and economic exploitation by unscrupulous employers, businessmen, landlords, and others, which made their previous conditions in the South worse only in degree, and that only slightly. The Urban League, therefore, became in effect a Travelers Aid, directing people to housing, to jobs, and to educational resources, and warning them of the dangers and the exploiters lurking in the urban setting.

But the Urban League did even more; it followed these people within the cities; and working through the churches, schools, and other social agencies, the League received complaints, exposed intolerable discrimination, and fought for changes in policies. Gradually the League grew—through the organization of affiliates in many cities —with the result that by the Great Depression some thirty-seven Urban Leagues had been formed. It was largely the Urban League that insisted, and to which the government turned, to assure that Negro citizens were involved in the major remedial and emergency programs such as the Works Project Administration, the Federal Emergency Relief Act, the National Youth Administration, the Civilian Conservation Corps, and, later, the various programs under the Social Security Act.

It must also be remembered that during the early period there were few agencies like the public employment service, and few private health, welfare, recreational, and employment services. Of these, few, if any, sought out the Negro citizen or made him feel comfortable as a client. The settlement house movement was one of the exceptions. This meant that for many years the Urban League was the only agency to which Negro citizens could turn for many of the direct services white citizens were receiving from a multitude of agencies. But while the League made an effort to render these direct services, it recognized its great limitations and, therefore, made a pointed effort to get existing public and private agencies to open their doors and accept their responsibility to these citizens.

The League's tools were those that today many people ridicule and sometimes properly reject, but they were all that were available at that time. They were negotiation, persuasion, education, exposure, and in some cases simply a shaming of people. But, little by little, cracks were made in the wall. Other health and welfare agencies began to provide services; a cooperative plan was developed with the United States Employment Service; a builder or an employer here and there would establish a housing development or hire a qualified Negro for an unusual job. Many hours were spent pleading with employers, with only limited results. But the League, using all of its creativity, and identifying nationwide objectives, made some qualitative if not quantitative breakthroughs. Examples: Negroes employed as telephone operators, sales clerks, street-car conductors, and taxi-drivers—and later engineers, draftsmen, etc.

By 1945 some fifty-four cities had Urban Leagues, all professionally staffed and for the most part all members of the social work family and supported by local community chests. By now the unceasing and brilliant efforts of the NAACP to make segregation and discrimination illegal began to pay off. Other forces stirred to action following the Second World War—industrialization, unionism, urbanization, the cold war, a changed political climate— these and other factors contributed to a changed status for the Negro in America. At least, he could no longer be ignored. Some concessions were obvious and indicated as necessary for the enlightened self-interest of all Americans.

The Urban League during this period began to give top priority to education and motivation of youth. Career conferences at schools, colleges, churches, and settlement houses became a weekly program. Extensive work with school counselors became a must. Employment efforts shifted from direct service to the masses to pilot placement in pioneering jobs and work with top management to modify patterns of employment. Housing efforts were limited to improving the facilities and services in the Negro community, fighting for public housing, and occasionally securing a new, small, private subdevelopment. Health and welfare agencies were urged with some success to employ Negro workers, to eliminate segregated services, to add Negro citizens to their boards, and in general to view the minority client as the greatest challenge to their professional training and dedication.

The last fifteen years have witnessed great changes in race relations. An acceleration of all the forces mentioned earlier, plus legal victories, the Montgomery bus boycott, the "sit-ins," "freedom rides," federal executive orders, consumer boycotts and greater political sophistication, have all set the stage for a significant change in the status of the American Negro. You will note I said "set the stage for change." That change is far from being here. The Negro still stands on the periphery of American democracy. He has established only a beachhead.

In the last two years the Urban League has undergone major reorganization and expansion. To some degree it has a new philosophy. At present we have over five hundred full-time professional and technical staff members, most of them with their master's degrees acquired in a variety of fields. They are located in 65 strategic American cities, where 77 per cent of the urban Negroes live (cities with 100,000 or more). Our aggregate budgets for these 65 affiliates and the National Office come close to four million dollars a year. Thousands of volunteers serve on boards and committees to reinforce the professional staff.

We have made it clear that we are not competitive with nor rejecting of the legal and responsible methods of other organizations. Our ultimate goal is the same as that of the NAACP, or of CORE, and we feel that organizations such as these have a great past and a great future. But after months of serious consideration of the nature of the current problem of race relations, the Urban League's role is clear. We in the Urban League are concerned not solely with new laws and new programs, but with all laws and with all who are responsible for their implementation. As Negro citizens for generations have not benefited equitably from the billions of dollars of public funds spent for federal, state, and local programs in employment, housing, health, welfare, and education, the same holds true today and will continue to hold true unless we are both vigilant and determined. This we intend to be, and no amount of tokenism or pious platitudes will prevent us from exposing the areas from which Negro citizens are excluded, whether this exclusion be due to the timidity of policy-makers or apathy on the part of the Negro community itself.

One of our concerns must be the fact that there has been very little progress in these areas in the last ten years, when the Negro is compared to other Americans. For example, the average Negro family income today is $3,233 —54 per cent or a little better than half of the white family income, which is $5,835. In 1952 it was 57 per cent.

From here on, our measuring rod must be progress, not as determined by the previous conditions of Negro citizens, but progress in the degree to which we close the gap between the Negro and his fellow-citizens. What are some of the characteristics of this gap?

1) *Continued migration and urbanization*, that will find a steadily increasing number of Negro citizens residing in large urban centers where technically or legally they will not face visible barriers to jobs, housing, education or other facilities, but where, due to historical deprivation and injustice, they will be handicapped economically and socially in their efforts to realize the better life they seek;

2) *Industrialization and automation*, which will continue to make expendable large numbers of unskilled and semiskilled employees, including a disproportionately high number of Negro workers;

3) *Urban renewal, slum clearance, and superhighway construction*, which will continue to disrupt and dislocate Negro families who, because of subtle, extralegal maneuvers and low incomes will find themselves not less segregated, but more segregated in the unattractive areas of the city, which remain educationally, culturally and socially substandard.

You might rightfully ask: What successes have we recorded in our efforts to close this gap? Time will not permit a full recital, but here are a few which bear mentioning and which might be duplicated in most of our cities.

In *Atlanta*, Urban League "know-how" in housing and urban renewal was the primer that set into motion a chain of community actions. Guidance was given to a church in the complexities of FHA application; the church successfully won its bid for urban redevelopment land, an insurance company supplied $450,000 for the purchase, and the League continues to give advice and assistance toward bringing to fruition the four-million-dollar plan for 520 units in Atlanta's Northeast to answer the cry of moderate-income Negro families for decent homes.

In *Los Angeles,* junior high school youngsters in one of the ghetto-ized schools of the city are beginning now to dream of what they might become some day, just because concerned teachers turned to the Urban League for help. Volunteers—this time a local chapter of The Links—cooperated with the Urban League's staff, with faculty and counselors, and worked out a youth incentives program modeled after our national plan, thus broadening the horizons of boys and girls who are not working up to their capacity.

In *New Orleans,* a day-long conference organized by the League transmitted the idea of "responsible migration" to civic, church, fraternal, club, social work, and other responsible leaders from forty communities in Alabama, Arkansas, Louisiana and Mississippi. Going back to their grass-roots fellowship, these leaders were committed to a continuing effort to stamp out the cheap publicity stunt which we know as "Freedom Rides North." Under the theme "Before You Migrate—Investigate" the conference climaxed an Urban League campaign to acquaint Negro citizens with the facts to be considered before leaving their home communities for the supposedly greener pastures far away.

In *New York City,* the local League converted despair into hope for dozens of Negro youth whom they channeled into apprenticeship opportunities made possible by a League Board member who heads an enlightened union.

In *Omaha,* over half the large number of Negro workers facing unemployment after automation of the meat packing plants have now been retrained and rehired because of the local Urban League.

In *St. Louis,* after months of negotiations between League staff and union and management officers, a nineteen-year-old technical-high-school graduate, employed as a porter in the county hospital, yet described by his principal as "one of the finest students ever to graduate from the drafting department," was accepted as the first Negro youth in the Carpenters Apprenticeship Training Program.

In *Westchester County*, in a special teacher recruitment program, twenty-nine superior Negro teachers were placed in Westchester school districts, not only adding approximately $270,000 to the income of the community's Negro citizens, but broadening the experience of school children and their parents.

In *Washington, D. C.*, in an exciting Friends and Neighbors project, twenty newcomer families from the South have been recruited, helped by twenty resident established families to sustain the buffeting and neglect of a strange new environment. In such a program these families are helped to find housing and learn urban home-making patterns; to spend their dollars wisely in purchases of food and clothing; to find new church homes, and thus realize their hopes and aspirations for security and happiness.

In *Seattle, St. Paul, Winston-Salem, Newark,* and elsewhere, because of Urban League programs or projects hundreds of Negro babies now have adopted homes with loving parents instead of institutions and custodians to care for them.

And, finally, in capsule, only two items from the many that form the overall picture of national headquarters operation:

(1) In our nation's capital, conferences early in the year with President Kennedy and later with Vice-President Johnson; a conference with officials of local Urban Leagues and departmental heads to discuss problems in which the government and the League have parallel concerns; the opening last year of our Washington Bureau to maintain liaison with government agencies and private organizations in the health and welfare field headquartered in Washington—all have set the stage for continuing and mutual sound planning and programming.

(2) In New York, the enthusiastic response of the nation's major corporations to our new job development thrusts as we move with greater speed to expand and broaden employment opportunities for qualified Negro youth and adults in the great array of professional and technical jobs exploding daily in our midst.

These are simply smatterings of League approaches to the areas of our special concern. I can say this with reference to future directions for the League: I think that all need to recognize that as a movement we will be at war—at war against prejudice and discrimination, against apathy and indifference, against rationalization, greed, selfishness, and ignorance—and we will not hesitate to identify our enemies in this war, whether they be Negro or white, confident that by rendering this service to our communities our financial support will be increased, not diminished.

Ours is a crusade for justice, for decency, morality, honesty, and frankness. It is a crusade to put into operational framework on a day-to-day, person-to-person basis the American creed and democratic promise. Ours is an obligation, most immediate to the Negro citizen or other minorities whom we serve, but in the final analysis it is a responsibility to America as it faces its greatest hour of challenge.

We cannot allow this nation to lull itself into a false sense of security about the status or progress of its race relations, only to be rudely awakened by a violent explosion. Benjamin Segal, writing on the American character in a recent pamphlet from the Center for the Study of Democratic Institutions, tells of the ancient Greek scholar who was asked "Will we ever achieve justice in Athens?" and who replied, "We will achieve justice when those who are not injured are as indignant as those who are."

THE BLACK MUSLIMS
AS A PROTEST MOVEMENT

C. Eric Lincoln

The social movement called the "Black Muslims" is symptomatic of the anxiety and unrest which characterizes the contemporary world situation. It is not an isolated phenomenon; for it has its counterparts in Asia, in Africa, in South America, in Europe, and wherever the peoples of the world are striving for a realignment of power and position. Such conditions of social anxiety generally follow in the wake of major disturbances in the power equilibrium, or in anticipation of such disturbances. Wars ("hot" or "cold"), major political changes, in short, whatever is perceived as a threat to the continued existence of the group, or the values without which existence would be interpreted (by the group) as meaningless, contributes to a condition of anxiety which may well be reflected in various forms of conflict—of which the protest movement is one.

We may restate our thesis in another way: Whenever

there is an actual or a felt discrepancy in the power relations of discrete systems or subsystems, a condition of social anxiety will emerge.

A protest movement is an expression of the pervasive anxiety and discontent of a group in negative reaction to what is perceived as a discrepancy of power. Power is the control over decisions. The protest movement is a reaction protesting that control, or the character of its expression.

Conflict may also derive from a persistent inequity in the distribution of scarce values within a society. By scarce values I mean such tangibles as jobs, food, houses, and recreational facilities (*resource scarcity*); and such intangibles as status, recognition, respect, and acceptance (*position scarcity*).[1]

Such conflict may exist at one of several possible levels: It may be (1) *latent*, with the subordinated group unorganized in the recognized presence of a vastly superior power. The conflict may be (2) *nascent*, a situation in which an organization for conflict is in existence or under development, but the conflict has not yet become overt. Again, conflict may be (3) *ritualized* by the contending parties, thereby assuming a nonviolent expression. Very often conflict is (4) *suppressed*, by proscription of the organizations of the subordinated group, or by force or the threat of force. In extreme circumstances conflict becomes (5) *violent*, resulting in the destruction of life and property.[2]

---

[1] " 'Resource scarcity' is a condition in which the supply of desired objects (or states of affairs) is limited so that parties may not have *all* they want of anything." " 'Position scarcity' is a condition in which . . . a role cannot be simultaneously occupied or performed by two or more actors, and different prescribed behavior cannot be carried out simultaneously." Raymond W. Mack and Richard C. Snyder, "The Analysis of Social Conflict—Toward an Overview and Synthesis," *Conflict Resolution*, I, No. 2 (1957), 218.

[2] See St. Clair Drake, "Some Observations on Interethnic Conflict as One Type of Intergroup Conflict," *op. cit.*, p. 162.

The Black Muslims are a symbol and a product of social conflict. They represent a point at the extreme edge of a spectrum of protest organizations and movements which involves, directly or indirectly, probably every Negro in America. The spectrum of protest begins on the near side with the conservative churches, then shades progressively into the relatively more militant congregations, the Urban League, the NAACP, the SCLC, the SNCC, CORE, and finally the unknown number of black nationalist organizations of which the Black Muslim movement is the largest and the best known. The organizations mentioned do not exhaust the roster of protest by any means. Some of the protest movements have sizeable memberships in spite of their amorphous character. Some have no more than ten or twelve members. Some do not even have names.

But almost every church, every social club, sorority, or fraternity, every business or civic association doubles as a protest organization. The effort is total, or very nearly total. In some cities the protest membership is quite fluid, with individuals moving freely from group to group within a defined range as they become more activist-oriented, or perhaps less certain of the final efficacy of the action groups. The wide range of affiliative possibilities is both functional and dysfunctional to the protest interests. Because there are many organizations, there is greater opportunity for a wider variety of personal expression than was possible when the Urban League and the NAACP had the field to themselves. However, the supply of leadership material has not kept pace with the proliferation of movements and organizations. The most effective leadership remains concentrated in a few organizations, while the energies and enthusiasms of a good number of the lesser-known protest groups are dissipated for want of planning and direction. Theirs is an inarticulate protest—unknown and ineffective.

The Black Muslims are among the best organized and most articulate of the protest movements. In terms of their immediate internal objectives, they have a highly effective leadership, some of which has been recruited from the Christian churches and retrained by Elijah Muhammad to serve the cause of Black Islam. Their newspapers and magazines are superior in layout and technical quality to much of the Negro press; and their financial support of the movement is probably higher in proportion to income than that of any similar group. Yet, the Black Muslims are not generally acceptable to the spirit of protest which has won universal respect and frequent admiration for some other members of the Negro's spectrum of protest. To understand why this is so, it will be fruitful to offer some analysis of the circumstances out of which the movement was born, the character of its membership, and the nature of its goals.

The psychological heritage of the Black Muslim movement, in common with that of all other Negro protest organizations, is at least as old as the institution of slavery in America. Protest has been a distinctive although frequently a subdued thread widely distributed across the whole fabric of white-black relations throughout the history of white and Negro contact in America. The successive roles of masters and bondsmen, masters and slaves, white men and freedmen, majority and minority groups, have been successive arrangements of hegemony and subordination in which the Negro's role *vis à vis* that of the white man has not changed. From time to time, especially since the Second World War, there have been varying degrees of adjustment *within the system of arrangements*, but the power relationship has remained constant. Hence, the capacity of Negroes to affect decisions relating to themselves and the system of values they hold to be important is not appreciable.

Even the Negro's limited capacity to affect decisions

and produce change depends primarily upon the conscience and the convenience of the white man, rather than upon any existing corpus of power possessed by Negroes. Indeed, it is unlikely that the Negro will ever have a dependable share in the control of the decision-making apparatus of his country until he either controls a significant segment of the economy, or a much larger percentage of the vote than he does at present. His inordinate dependence upon "protest" derives precisely from his failure to achieve the more dependable protection for his interests that comes from sharing the white man's power rather than appealing to the white man's conscience.

A protest movement is an aggressive expression of a subordinated group. It is the organization of the resources of the subordinated group to resist the coercive power of the dominant group, or to challenge the morality or the justice of the expression of that power. The Negro did not wait until he was delivered in America to begin his protestation of the white man's concept of the black man's "place" in the caste system to be established here. Available records show that no fewer than fifty-five slave revolts occurred at sea between 1700 and 1845. During the height of the slave period—the two hundred years from 1664 to 1864, there are recorded accounts of at least 109 slave insurrections which occurred within the continental United States. Since it was customary to suppress all news and information concerning revolts lest they become infectious, it is reasonable to assume that the reported cases were of some magnitude, that very many cases were not reported, and that some cases which were reported have not yet been made available to research.

Protest was not limited to armed insurrection. The rate of infanticide was high. Suicide became a problem of such magnitude as to require the slave owners to devise "the strongest arguments possible," (supported by religious and social taboos) to reduce the rate of self-destruction. Sabotage of livestock, machinery, and agricultural produce was not unknown. "Taking" (from the white man, as distinct from "stealing" from each other) was routine. Running away was a form of protest so common as to have been considered a disease. Southern physicians described its symptoms in the journals of the period and gave it the name monomania—"a disease [it was said] to which the Negro is peculiarly subject."[3]

As slavery became increasingly profitable, the slavocracy became concerned to offer a moral justification for its peculiar institution. At the same time, it sought to inculcate the illiterate slaves (as it sought later to indoctrinate the freedmen and their abolitionist friends), with an image of the Negro shrewdly designed to discourage protest and to encourage resignation and accommodation. This was the "Myth of the Magnolias," so called because it was usually accompanied by a fantasy of banjo-strumming darkies lounging peacefully under the sweet-scented magnolias behind the big house—happy and contented in their station, and forever loyal to the kindhearted master and his arrangements for their mutual felicities. The Magnolia myth explained the Negro's condition in terms of "his *natural docility*, his *instinctive servility*, and his *inherent imbecility*." It alleged that the Negro's "docile nature" led to his willing acceptance of his condition of bondage, and that his "instinctive servility" made him an ideal slave—a being equipped psychologically to submit his will completely to that of another; who sensed his own inferiority, and who willed that his body be at the complete disposal of the more sophisticated will of his master. His alleged "imbecility" derived, it was argued, from an inherent incapacity to be creative, or to learn at a level beyond the simple abilities of a child. This was a principal

[3] See Melville J. Herskovits, *The Myth of the Negro Past* (Boston: Beacon Press, 1941), pp. 86-109.

intent of the Magnolia myth—to perpetuate an image of the Negro as being inherently intellectually inferior, and therefore incapable of mastering the complex requirements of adult citizenship and self-determination. The Negro was a child who could never grow up. He would never be "ready." This was the image he was required to accept of himself. This was the image the world was asked to accept.

The historians, the novelists, the politicians, and a varied assortment of other myth-makers have done America a great disservice. Each repetition of the myth makes it more difficult for those segments of the white majority who believe it, to understand the behavior of Negroes; and each repetition of the myth increases the determination of the Negro minority to belie it. Both science and history have discredited the Magnolia Myth, but the protest movements provide the most dramatic refutation. There are, for example, no docile Muslims. There are no servile students participating in the sit-ins. And considering its success before our highest tribunal, it is hard to believe that the legal staff of the NAACP is a council of imbeciles.

The Magnolia Myth with local modifications remains a pervasive influence in our society. Our information media have done little to refute it. The editors of the texts we use to educate our children have done even less. It has remained then to the Negro to destroy the myth himself. The Black Muslims have gone a step further and have created for themselves a counter-myth, *the myth of black supremacy*.

The Black Muslim movement had its beginning in the black ghetto of Detroit. The time was 1930. It was the first year of the Great Depression—a time of hunger, confusion, disillusionment, despair, and discontent. It was a period of widespread fear and anxiety. Between 1900 and 1930 two-and-a-quarter-million Negroes left the farms and plantations of the South. Most of them emigrated to selected urban areas of the North—New York, Philadelphia, Chicago, and Detroit being among the most popular destinations. The Negro population of Detroit, for example, increased 611 per cent during the ten years of 1910 to 1920. During the same period, the total Negro population in the North increased from a mere 75,000 to 300,000, an increase of 400 per cent.

Floods, crop failures, boll weevils, and the revival of the Ku Klux Klan all served to hasten the Negro's departure from the South. One hundred Negroes were lynched during the first year of the twentieth century. By the outbreak of the First World War in 1914, the number stood at 1,100. When the war was over, the practice was resumed—28 Negroes being burned alive between 1918 and 1921. Scores of others were hanged, dragged behind automobiles, shot, drowned, or hacked to death.

The Negroes who left the South were temporarily welcomed in the North, although the congenialities of the North have always been of a most impersonal sort. Many industries sent agents into the South to lure the Negroes north with promises of good jobs. But the Negro was soon to find that it was his labor, not his presence, that was wanted. It was a common practice for the agents to purchase tickets for whole families and to move them *en masse* for resettlement in the great industrial cities. The war had drained away the white manpower needed to build the ships, work the steel, pack the meat, and man the machines; and it had also cut off the normal supply of immigrant labor from Europe.

After the war was over, the Negro's welcome wore thin. It became increasingly hard for Negroes to get jobs except as strike-breakers. Soon there were not enough jobs to go around, and thousands of Negroes were fired and replaced with white men. There was not enough housing, and most Negroes were crowded into the black ghettos in the most deteriorated part of the inner city. Landlords and law-enforcement agencies alike were unsympathetic. But still the Negroes came out of the South. Few had skills; many were illiterate. All were filled with hope for something better than what they had left. Soon there was hunger and crime and delinquency—and trouble with the police. The bright promise of the North had failed. Hope turned to desperation. In desperation is the onset of anxiety.

It is an interesting historical phenomenon that when a people reach the precipice of despair, there is so often waiting in the wings a savior—a messiah to snatch them back from the edge of the abyss. So it was that in Detroit there appeared in the black ghetto a mysterious Mullah who called himself W. D. Farad Muhammad. He had come, he told the handful of Negroes who gathered to hear him, from the holy city of Mecca. His mission, as he described it, was "to wake the 'Dead Nation in the West';[4] to teach [them] the truth about the white man, and to prepare [them] for the Armageddon." The Armageddon? What did this apocalyptic concept have to do with the problems of the Negro in America? Farad was explicit on the point: In the Book of Revelation it is promised that there will be a final battle between good and evil, and that this decisive battle will take place at Har-Magedon, "the Mountain of Megiddo," in the Great Plain of Esdraelon in Asia Minor.[5] But the Bible has a cryptic message for the initiated of Black Islam (even as it has for more familiar sects). The forces of "good and evil" are the forces of "black and white." "The Valley of Esdraelon" symbolizes "the Wilderness of North America." The Battle of Armageddon is to be the Black Man's final confrontation of the race which has so long oppressed him.

At first Farad (who was at the time thought to be a

[4] I.e., American Negroes.
[5] "Armageddon" is Greek transliteration from the Hebrew "Har-Magedon."

228

prophet, but who was after his departure recognized as Allah himself) met from house to house with small groups of Negroes. He went about his mission as unobtrusively as possible, listening to the problems of the destitute Negroes, sharing whatever they had to offer him. A contemporary convert recalls his *modus operandi*:

> He came first to our house selling raincoats, and afterwards silks. In this way he could get into the people's houses. . . . If we asked him to eat with us, he would eat whatever we had on the table, but after the meal he began to talk. . . .[6]

What he had to say must have been electrifying. Another Muslim describes his first encounter with the Prophet as follows:

> Up to that time I always went to the Baptist church. After I heard that sermon from the Prophet, I was turned around completely. When I went home and heard that dinner was ready, I said: "I don't want any dinner, I just want to go back to the meetings." I wouldn't eat my meals but I [went] back that night and I [went] to every meeting after that. . . . That changed everything for me.[7]

The fame of the Prophet spread and he soon established in Detroit the first of the Temples of Islam. As his following increased he grew more bold in his attacks upon the habits and the culture symbols the Negroes had always taken for granted. In the first place, he taught his followers that they were not "Negroes," but "Black Men." The word "Negro" was alleged to be an invention of the white man designed to identify his victims better and to separate them from their Asian and African brothers. Further, the

[6] Eradmann Beynon, "The Voodoo Cult Among Negro Migrants in Detroit," *The American Journal of Sociology*, XLIII (July 1937-May 1938), 895.
[7] *Ibid*, p. 896.

so-called Negro was not an American, but an "Asiatic," for his forefathers had been stolen from the Afro-Asian continent by the white slavemasters who came in the name of Jesus. Christianity, the Prophet taught, was a white man's religion, a contrivance designed for the enslavement of nonwhite peoples. Wherever Christianity has gone, he declared, men have lost their liberty and their freedom. Islam was declared to be "the natural religion of the Black Man." Only in Islam could the so-called Negroes find freedom, justice, and equality.

Little by little the Prophet began to enlighten these disillusioned migrants from the South about their true history and their place in the future. Black Man was the "Original Man," he taught. On the continent of Afro-Asia black civilizations flourished "long before the white man stood up on his hind legs and crept out of the caves of Europe." Further, the white man was pictured as "a devil by nature." He is, the Prophet taught, the physical embodiment of the principle of evil, and he is incapable of doing good. Further, said Farad, "the white man is the eternal adversary of the one true God whose right and proper name is Allah."

By "tricknology" the blue-eyed devils had enslaved the Black Man, the chosen people of Allah. The devils had taken away the slaves' native language (which was Arabic), and forced them to speak a foreign tongue. The white devils had taken away their names (i.e. their identity), and given them European names (which are to be hated as badges of slavery). Above all, the cruel slavemasters took away their natural religion (which is Islam) and made them worship a blue-eyed Jesus with blond hair, telling them that this was their God.

The so-called Negroes, although unknown to themselves, comprised "The Nation of Islam in the West." They had been brainwashed and given a false image of themselves by their white teachers, especially the Christian preachers who lulled them into submission by promising them a home "over Jordan" when they would no longer hew the wood and draw the water for the white man's comfort.

"The wheel must turn," the Prophet insisted. The Nation of Islam had a manifest destiny. The Armageddon must come. It would come as soon as the Black Man in America learned who he himself was, and accepted the truth about the white man, which the Prophet had been sent to declare.

Not all of Farad's energies were spent in attacking the white man. He taught his followers cleanliness and thrift. He persuaded them to give up liquor and such "unclean" foods as pork, cornbread, peas, possums, and catfish, bidding them to separate themselves from the habits they acquired in slavery. He established a school where homemaking, Negro history, Arabic, and other subjects of interest to the Muslims were taught. He demanded that his followers be clean at all times, bathing at least once each day. He taught them to give an honest day's work for an honest day's pay. He taught them to be respectful of others, and above all, to respect themselves. They must obey "all constituted authority," but they must require an eye for an eye and a tooth for a tooth. The *lex talionis* was the law of survival.

The Prophet's first appearance in Detroit is dated as July 4, 1930, and no one remembers seeing him after June 30, 1934. There are many legends, but no authentic information on where he came from, or where he went. But four years of preaching left a legacy of good and evil for eight thousand Negroes who had come to call themselves Muslims.

In the troubled times of the early 1930's, men and women everywhere were looking for some panacea to save them from the desperate circumstances of the Depression.

Large numbers of people found that they could not cope rationally with the excruciating anxiety—the uncertainties with which they were confronted from day to day. Some escapists leaped from the roof-tops of the very buildings which were symbols of more stable times. Some clairvoyants, who thought they could discern the wave of the future in Marxist philosophy, found their panacea in the Communist party. The Negro's ecapism tended to be of a more practical nature. Instead of taking the long route to heaven, he built himself "heavens" here on earth in the cults of Father Divine and Daddy Grace.

The followers of Farad were both escapists and clairvoyants. Farad himself was the messiah who had come to lead the so-called Negroes into the millennium which was to follow the Battle of Armageddon. He was the Prophet who had foreseen and foretold the Golden Age that would be theirs when the Black Nation in the West had thrown off the yoke of the white slavemasters. But Farad had disappeared.

The Prophet had not left himself without a witness. Very early in his brief ministry in Detroit he had attracted the admiration and the loyalty of a young Negro from the town of Sandersville, Georgia. Elijah Poole, son of a Baptist minister, was already embittered by the harshness of race relations in the South when he left Georgia and migrated to Detroit with his family in the early 1920's. In Detroit, his disillusionment with the "promised land" was almost immediate, for he soon discovered that the limitations which prescribed his place in the North differed only in degree from the familiar pattern of circumscription in the South. For a time, better jobs were available in the North, but Poole was soon to discover that job security operated on a racial basis. Housing was more strictly segregated than in the South, and living conditions in the black ghetto were often worse than they had been in the sharecropper's cabin. The lynchings in the South had their counterparts in the race riots of the North. There seemed to exist a universal conspiracy to make life in America as untenable as possible for Negroes.

The belittling paternalism of the South had been replaced by the cold indifference of the North, and Elijah Poole found himself and his family with no better chance of assimilation in the great "melting pot" of the North than he had left in the South. As a matter of fact, his daily contact with foreign-born elements speaking in strange "un-American" accents and wearing "foreign" clothes increased his feelings of isolation and resentment. He saw the jobs of Negroes taken from them and given to white men who had not fought for this country, and who in some cases had fought against it. Inevitably, the Georgia-born Poole arrived at the conclusion that even in the North the color of a man's skin, not the fact of his citizenship nor the quality of his intrinsic worth, was the determining factor in all his social relationships.

Elijah was now ready for the racist doctrines of Wali Farad. From their first meeting he became the Prophet's most dedicated apostle and his chief amanuensis. Farad had identified the Black Man's oppressor in terms never before heard in the Negro community. He had exposed the white man as a devil—a *literal* devil, created on the Isle of Patmos by a mad scientist whose name was Yakub. This was the secret of the white man's power, his cruelty, *and* his vulnerability. Allah had given the devil a certain time to rule, and the time of the devil was up. *The Black Man must prepare himself for the Armageddon!* Poole was impressed. Farad had the explanation of the white man's cruelty as well as the key to his power. Eventually, Farad entrusted his mantle and his mission to Elijah. He made Poole First Minister of Islam and put the Muslim school, the training of ministers, and the highly secret FOI (the Fruit of Islam, the leadership training corps "for the coming Armageddon") under his direction. Later, Poole was

sent to Chicago to found Temple No. 2, the present headquarters of the movement.

In recognition of Poole's dedicated leadership, Farad
relieved him of his "slave-name" (i.e. "Poole") and honored
him with the Muslim name "Muhammad." Thereafter,
Farad's public appearances were progressively less frequent until the day of his final disappearance.

Under Elijah Muhammad, the new "Messenger of
Islam," the movement spread from the initial temple in
Detroit to almost every major city in the country where
there is a sizable Negro population. In most of these cities
there is a temple; in others, where the movement is less
strong, there are missions. Where there are no missions
there are likely to be representatives of the movement who
are in contact with the Muslim leadership in nearby cities.

The black ghetto is the principal source of Muslim recruitment. There, in the dirty streets and crowded tene-
ments where life is cheap and hope is minimal, where isolation from the common values of society and from the
common privileges of citizenship is most acute, the voice
of the Messenger does not fall upon deaf ears. So often, his
is the only message directed to the pimps, the prostitutes,
the con-men, the prisoners, the ex-cons, the alcoholics, the
addicts, the unemployed, whom the responsible society
has forgotten. It is a voice challenging them to recover
their self-respect, urging them to repudiate the white
man's religion and the white man's culture, daring them
to believe in black supremacy, offering them a Black God
and a Black Nation, promising them that the day will come
when "we will be masters . . . and we are going to treat
the white man the way he should be treated,"[8] demanding
of them that "if anyone comes to take advantage of you,
lay down your life! and the Black Man will be respected
all over the Planet Earth."[9]

[8] *Chicago's American*, February 22, 1960.
[9] See "Tensions Outside the Movement," C. Eric Lincoln, *The
Black Muslims in America* (Boston: Beacon Press, 1961), pp. 135-78.

"Never be the aggressor," the voice proclaims, "never look for trouble. But if any man molests you, may Allah bless you."[10]

"We must take things into our own hands," the Messenger insists. "We must return to the Mosaic law of an eye for an eye and a tooth for a tooth. What does it matter if 10 million of us die? There will be 7 million of us left and they will enjoy justice and freedom."[11]

Such is the challenge of Elijah Muhammad who is hailed by his ministers as "the most fearless black man in America." His followers are, with few exceptions, from America's most underprivileged class. They are denizens of the black ghetto. To them, the voice of Elijah Muhammad is a voice raised against injustice—real or imagined. Muhammad is a paladin who has taken up the cudgel against the "devil" responsible for all of their miseries and their failures. The resentments and the hostilities that breed in the ghetto are finally brought to focus upon a single object—*the white man*. Outside the black ghetto there are Muslim units in many of the state and federal prisons across the country. Here the movement finds its prison audiences to be ready made and highly receptive, for the racial character of the law-enforcement agencies, the courts and the custodial personnel, is a key factor in sharpening the Negro prisoner's resentments and his sense of persecution.

I have tried to present a developmental background for the Black Muslim movement against which we may now more profitably examine their demands as a protest group. Generally speaking, the movement has been a protest directed at the whole value-construct of the white Christian society of which the Black Muslims feel themselves (as Negroes) to be an isolated and unappreciated

[10] *Op. cit.*, p. 5.
[11] *Chicago's American*, February 23, 1960.

appendage. Hence, the burden of their protest is against their "retention" in a society where they are not wanted. This is the soft side of the "Armageddon complex" which looks to the removal of the source of their discomfiture rather than to going anywhere themselves. Mr. Muhammad teaches that "the white man's home is in Europe," and that "there will be no peace until every man is in his own country."

In a recent issue of the official Muslim newspaper, *Mr. Muhammad Speaks*, the Muslims stated their protest in the form of the following ten propositions:

1. We want freedom. We want a full and complete freedom.
2. We want justice. Equal justice under the law. We want justice applied equally to all, regardless of creed or class or color.
3. We want equality of opportunity. We want equal membership in society with the best in civilized society.
4. We want our people in America whose parents or grandparents were descendants from slaves, to be allowed to establish a separate state or territory of their own. . . .
5. We want freedom for all Believers of Islam now held in federal prisons. We want freedom for all black men and women now under death sentence in innumerable prisons in the North as well as the South.
   We want every black man and woman to have the freedom to accept or reject being separated from the slave master's children and establish a land of their own. . . .
6. We want an immediate end to the police brutality and mob attacks against the so-called Negro throughout the United States.
7. As long as we are not allowed to establish a state or territory of our own, we demand not only equal

justice under the laws of the United States, but equal employment opportunities—NOW! . . . .

8. We want the government of the United States to exempt our people from ALL taxation as long as we are deprived of equal justice under the laws of the land.

9. We want equal education—but separate schools up to 16 for boys and 18 for girls on the condition that the girls be sent to women's colleges and universities. We want all black children educated, taught without hindrance or suppression.

10. We believe that intermarriage or race mixing should be prohibited. We want the religion of Islam taught without hindrance or suppression.

These are some of the things that we, the Muslims, want for our people in North America.[12]

Some of the proposals of the Muslims are obviously unrealistic, and we need not discuss them here. Other tests and demands of the Black Muslims as stated in the foregoing propositions do not seem unreasonable. I do not know any Americans who do not "want freedom," for example. Justice under the law, equality of opportunity, and freedom of worship are all "approved values" in our society, and they find their sanctions in the American creed. Further, they are objectives which are implicit in the programs of all other movements within the Negro spectrum of protest. What, then, are the factors which qualify the Muslim protest movement and make it unacceptable to the general American public?

The fundamental differences between the attitudes, the behavior, and the goals of the Black Muslims as compared to other Negro protest organizations may be explained in terms of their differing degrees of dissociation deriving from the unusual anxiety and frustration incident to their status in the American social arrangement. Ne-

[12] July 31, 1962.

groes, as a caste, are *all* outside the assimilative process, and they exhibit from time to time the frustrations which are the corollaries of their marginality. However, the dissociation of the Muslim membership from the larger society, and even from the general Negro subgroup (which ordinarily seeks to identify itself with the American mainstream), may be considered extreme. In reacting to the unique pressures of their day-to-day experiences as low-caste Negroes in a white-oriented society, the Muslims have abandoned the fundamental principles of the American creed and have substituted in its place a new system of values perceived as more consistent with the realities of their circumstances.

It is meaningless to label the Muslims as "unAmerican," for the American creed is not a legal or constitutional document against which the political loyalty of a group may be measured.[13] The American creed is a common set of beliefs and values in which all Americans have normally found consensus. It is a body of ideals, a social philosophy which affirms the basic dignity of every individual and the existence of certain inalienable rights without reference to race, creed, or color. The roots of the American creed are deep in the equalitarian doctrines of the eighteenth-century Enlightenment, Protestant Christianity and English law. For most of us, it has been the cultural matrix within which all discordant socio-political attitudes converge, and from which derives the great diversity of social and political interpretations which makes democracy possible in a society of widely variant populations.

The Black Muslims, by the nature of certain of their goals and institutions, have excepted themselves from the aegis of the American creed. The Black Muslims repudiate American citizenship in favor of a somewhat dubious

[13] For an excellent interpretation of the American creed see Arnold Rose, *The Negro in America* (Boston: Beacon Press, 1957), pp. 1 ff.

membership in a mystical "Asiatic" confraternity, and they are violently opposed to Christianity, the principles of which are fundamental to our understanding of the democratic ideal. Not only do they resist assimilation and avoid interracial participation in the life of the community, but the Muslim creed assigns all nonblacks to the subhuman status of "devils" (and promises to treat them as such); the sustaining philosophy is one of black supremacy nurtured by a careful inculcation of hatred for the white man and his characteristic institutions. By their own choice the Black Muslims exclude themselves from the body of principles and the system of values within the framework of which Americans have customarily sought to negotiate their grievances.

Other groups advocate white supremacy, resist the assimilation of Negroes and others, and practice hatred rather than love, yet they retain an idealistic loyalty to the principles of the American creed. The point is that although the creed is violated constantly in practice, it remains an *ideal* to which all give their asseveration—in which all believe, and from which we continue to derive our laws and our moral values in spite of our failures to honor them completely.

The Black Muslim movement does not conceive itself to be in violation of the principles and values of the American creed. Rather, the movement views itself as having substituted new principles, new values, and a new creed based on a radically different interpretation of history from that expressed in the American creed. Muhammad promises a new order based on the primacy of a nation of Black Men with a manifest destiny under a Black God. His is a nation radically different from those now shaping the existing American society. In spite of the fact that the Black Muslim movement shares at some points the immediate goals of the lesser Negro protest movements, its oppugnance to traditional values limits its general acceptability as a protest organization. The action impact of the movement on the general Negro community has been negligible considering the fact that most of America's twenty million black citizens live under conditions considerably more iniquitous than those which at other times and places have been productive of the gravest social consequences. This is not to suggest that Negroes are not aware of the movement. They are. And there are important pockets of sympathy among Negroes for the Muslims as a class more oppressed than other Negro classes, and a certain covert admiration for their militant, nonaccommodative stance against the traditional aggressions of the white man.

Nevertheless, the depth of the Negro's commitment *as a class* to the democratic procedures implicit in the American creed has operated successfully to contain the Muslim movement—eliminating it as a serious threat to racial peace or national security. But the Black Muslims remain a somber symbol of the social callousness that is possible even in an equalitarian democracy. Such movements do not "just happen." The Muslims are the most insistent symptoms of the failure of this society to meet effectively the minimum needs of one-tenth of its population to find a meaningful level of participation in the significant social values most Americans take for granted.

The Muslims represent that segment of the Negro subgroup who, being most deprived of traditional incentives, have finally turned to search for alternatives outside the commonly accepted value structure. They are the products of social anxiety—people who are repeatedly frustrated in their attempts to make satisfactory adjustments in a society unaware of their existence except as the faceless subjects of statistical data. As Negroes, their future was unpromising. As Muslims, theirs is a creed of futility. As Americans, the responsibility for what they are, or what they will become, is our own.

THE TRANSFORMATION OF
THE NEGRO INTELLECTUAL

John Hope Franklin

Every society, however backward or advanced, has within it some members who are engaged in, or have the capacity to engage in, the task of examining and criticizing the human condition—the structure of society, the economic order, the role of government, and the morale of the human spirit. The approach and technique of such persons are naturally more sophisticated and advanced in some societies than in others. But one woud be lacking in perception if he concluded that the capacity to exercise these functions was limited to those societies possessing a full complement of advanced educational institutions and highly developed intellectual traditions. A sure sign of complacency and parochialism is manifested when people of a given society insist that they have a monopoly or even a superiority in the intellectual resources of mankind. Throughout the ages, those who have provided searching examinations of the past and constructive criticisms of the present have contributed to the advancement of their own societies. Those who have resisted empty and meaningless slogans, rejected blind loyalties, and spoken fearlessly to the problems at hand have done much to move the backward, undeveloped social order toward a more civilized state of human existence. In a very real sense, they are intellectuals—wielding an influence on society through the power of their minds.

Happily, for the sake of human improvement, one can find scattered through the centuries persons who wielded such influence. John Locke, England's great philosopher of the seventeenth century, provides a telling example of how an independent line of thought can strike powerful blows against faulty political institutions. Rulers, he said, who usurp and abuse power and invade the rights and properties of their subjects convict themselves of breach of trust. Where such usurpations and abuses are practiced, the victims are fully justified in resorting to drastic means to put an end to them. Rulers have only themselves to blame if "a long train of abuses, prevarications, and artifices, all tending the same way" finally drive their subjects to resistance and revolution. In taking such a stand, Locke was not restrained either by convention or tradition in his determination to improve the social and political order. And the impact of his reason and his wisdom is still being felt throughout the world. But he was merely one of many hard and straight thinkers, to which group also belonged men like Diderot, Voltaire, Rousseau, and Montesquieu.

Nothng is clearer than the fact that the great resources of man's mind are not always used for the advancement of man's freedom. One of the tragedies of the human intellect is its capacity for perversion and its consequent employment for the degradation of mankind. Look, for example, at the argument of Locke's near-contemporary and great thinker, Thomas Hobbes. In his *Leviathan*, Hobbes said that every man was the enemy of every other man. There was no hope, therefore, that man could ever achieve peaceful and constructive self-government. Since this was the case, he argued, man should agree to the establishment of a government that would be unlimited in its power and authority and responsible to no one. It seems incredible that a person could thus use his enormous intellectual gifts to deprecate the intellectual capacities of mankind. But we have witnessed enough of this in our own day to know that it is entirely possible. We have seen so-called intellectual giants register votes of no-confidence in the human race. We have seen them use all their powers in the interest of preserving the *status quo*, even when it meant untold human misery and suffering. And we have reluctantly reached the inescapable conclusion that the intellectual resource is not always a power for good in the affairs of men.

In the United States, the intellectual has had an interesting, if not always savory, history. It was the nature of the American experience to give a minimum of attention to the life of the mind. Intellectual prowess and mental acumen, it was argued almost from the beginning, could make no substantial contribution to solving the major problems confronting the settlers in the New World: clearing the forests, making pathways to new frontiers, and surviving in the hostile wilderness. The doer—the one whose achievements were tangible and measurable—was exalted; and early America claimed that it had no time for the abstract thinker or theoretician. This was never entirely true, however. For, even in the earliest stages of the history of the New World, those who devoted themselves to intellectual pursuits became pillars of strength in the community, both good and bad, in spite of the community itself.

The lack of respect for learning, or the lack of concern for it, in early America melted before the exigencies of conflict, when ideological justifications and rationalizations were needed for decisions already made and actions already taken. Thus, when the patriots were fighting for independence, the intellectuals came to the rescue of the polemicists and agitators; Locke and Hume and Dickinson and Jefferson became household words among groups considerably larger than those who could be described as intellectuals. It was at this juncture that the peculiar ambivalence that was to characterize American attitudes became so evident. On the one hand, there was little regard, if not downright contempt, for the serious thinker. On the other hand, there was the acknowledged need for the talents and resources of the intellectual. And there was the willingness to call upon him to strengthen the hand of those who had decided upon a particular course of action.

From that day to this there has always been some recognition of the importance of the intellectual in American life. Too often, it has been begrudgingly conceded; and too often the pervasive influence of the intellectual has provoked adverse reaction that has ranged from cool scorn to scathing attack. But the influence of the intellectuals has persisted. They were often enlisted on the side of change. On occasion one can hear their voices loud and clear, as when Emerson called in 1837 for an American declaration of intellectual independence, or when Whittier and Bryant and Sumner and Phillips condemned slavery with a fury and an eloquence that left no doubt that the intellectual could be a powerful and passionate advocate. Their righteous indignation over the barbarism of slavery and their advocacy of its abolition served notice on all America that the intellectual life was not necessarily a sterile, ivory-tower existence, but could be one full of involvement and commitment, one dedicated to the rectification and, indeed, the transformation of the social order.

But intellectual pursuits in America, as elsewhere, could be employed to destroy legitimate aspirations and oppose change, when it was in the interest of the entrenched group to do so. In the late nineteenth century the so-called social Darwinists were particularly anxious to justify the actions of those who had taken unfair advantage of their fellows, and they brought forth a fully developed body of arguments that claimed that it was in the interest of social advancement that certain elements in society should dominate others. Whites were in a dominant position because they were the superior race. They were the fittest. If, as such theorists assumed, the development of the individual is a recapitulation of the race, "primitives" such as Negroes must be considered to be in the arrested stages of childhood or adolescence. Laws, therefore, should not be passed that seek to reverse the "natural order" of things, as the Reconstruction laws had attempted to do. These arguments were both unwise and futile, as subsequent developments proved. That such outstanding intellectuals as Herbert Spencer, Franklin H. Giddings, and William Graham Sumner supported them and lent the weight of their prestige to the dissemination of them is clear proof that virtually any position on the intellectual spectrum can find some supporters among those who claim to be committed to the search for truth.

Thus, the vagaries of the intellectuals who have no particular obstacles to overcome in their effort to achieve acceptance among thoughtful men and women are often inexplicable. One wonders how they can entertain and promulgate views that can bear the scrutiny of neither logic nor science. For groups in special circumstances and conditions, such as Negroes whose very capacities to function effectively and responsibly on an intellectual plane have often been seriously challenged, the struggle to gain acceptance renders somewhat difficult the task of avoiding whimsicalities and illogicalities while functioning on that plane. For centuries Negroes have had the task of trying to gain acceptance of the fact that they had brains that could be employed in the area that many whites had arrogated to themselves as their exclusive domain; and during those same centuries, many of those same whites have argued vehemently that Negroes had no such brains. The ingenuity that the whites displayed in such efforts proved that at least *they* had brains. In the view of Dr. S. C. Cartwright of the University of Louisiana, for example, the capacities of a Negro adult for learning were equal to those of a white infant; and the Negro could properly perform certain physiological functions only when under the control of white men:

> [Negroes] under the compulsive power of the white man . . . are made to labor or exercise, which makes the lungs perform the duty of vitalizing the blood more perfectly than is done when they are left free to indulge in idleness. It is the red, vital blood sent to the brain that liberates their mind when under the white man's control; and it is the want of a sufficiency of red, vital blood that chains their mind to ignorance and barbarism when in freedom.

Such so-called scientific arguments and the consequent subordination and degradation of the Negro stood firmly in the way of his enjoying the opportunity to develop his mind and refute the arguments. But not all were convinced that the Negro was incapable of intellectual attainments. In the 1790's James McHenry, the future Secretary of War, said that the remarkable work of Benjamin Banneker, the Negro mathematician and astronomer, was "fresh proof that the powers of the mind are disconnected with the color of the skin," and "a striking contradiction to Mr. Hume's doctrine, that the Negroes are naturally inferior to the whites, and unsusceptible of attainments in arts and sciences." While Banneker's work convinced some whites, there were some Negroes who argued with great force that the very basis for judging Negro intellectual capacities was palpably fallacious. "It is not necessary," said Frederick Douglass in 1854,

> in order to establish the manhood of any one making the claim, to prove that such an one equals Clay in eloquence, or Webster and Calhoun in logical force and directness; for, tried by such standards of mental power as these, it is apprehended that very few could claim the high designation of *man*. Yet something like this folly is seen in the arguments directed against the humanity of the negro. His faculties and powers, uneducated and unimproved, have been contrasted with those of the highest cultivation; and the world has then been called upon to behold the immense and amazing difference between the man admitted, and the man disputed.

But the time was approaching when a small, but steadily increasing number of Negroes succeeded in gaining sufficient education to make a claim to be considered as intellectuals. In the years following emancipation, they were securing a formal education in some of the best colleges and universities in their own country and abroad as well as in the segregated institutions of the South. It must have been a shattering experience for aspiring Negro intellectuals to survey the American scene and discover the low esteem in which they were held solely because of their race or color. These were the years when some of America's great intellectual giants strode across the stage and gave real meaning to the nation's claim to intellectual independence. Their very names arouse an appreciation for what they meant to the growth of American thought: Henry James, William Dean Howells, and Mark Twain in belles lettres; Henry Adams and Herbert Baxter Adams in history; William James and Josiah Royce in philosophy; Washington Gladden and Walter Rauschenbusch in religion; Louis Agassiz and Asa Gray in science. At last America knew, through first-hand experience and observation, what an intellectual was.

But the Negro intellectuals received little encouragement and scarcely an approving nod from America's intellectual giants. For the most part they functioned in a world apart from America's most pressing social problem; and they were as untouched by it as one living on another planet. Some of them were disdainful of their Negro would-be counterparts; some were openly hostile; most seemed to care not at all. And if they did not care—those who were the keepers and arbiters of the nation's intellectual predilections and tastes—then, who would? No one! Small wonder that any efforts Negro intellectuals dared to make to indicate that they possessed even normal mental powers were met with cold incredulity and disdain. Small wonder that any contribution they dared to offer to the general discussion of the condition of man or the improvement of the social order was rejected out of hand, not because it had no merit but because the white community had pronounced the Negro intellectual disfranchised as a thinker as he had been disfranchised as a voter.

In the press the Negro saw himself abused and ridiculed. In the national literature he read with utter amazement and dismay how those with whom he sought to make common cause had cast him away from them as an intellectual untouchable. One of them said, "The Negro has not progressed, not because he was a slave, but because he does not possess the faculties to raise himself above slavery. He has not yet exhibited the qualities of any race which has advanced civilization or shown capacity to be greatly advanced." On the platform he heard himself described in the most revolting language. He was a brute, a beast, unworthy to be in the company of civilized society, incapable of tasting, feeling, thinking, writing. Any contribution that the Negro intellectual would make to the understanding of the problems of American society would be made in an atmosphere of utter hostility on the part of that society itself.

But the aspiring Negro intellectual was undaunted. If he ever doubted himself, he displayed neither fear nor panic. With his newly found weapon of mind and word he not only went about the business of trying to solve some of the fundamental problems that beset American society, but he also turned on his detractors with all the resources and power that he could command. In reply to those who said that Negroes had achieved little or nothing as individuals or as a group, George Washington Williams wrote his *History of the Negro People* in which he pointed to the achievements of early Negro civilizations and to the significant contributions that Negroes had made to the development of American civilization. With a methodological approach in keeping with the best American historical traditions and in quite felicitous language, he eloquently defended the right of Negroes to a place of equality in American life.

Nor was Williams alone. Kelley Miller, the distinguished Howard University professor, addressing himself to the assertion that there were no Negro counterparts to the great white men that America had produced, exposed the sophistry and absurdity of such reasoning. "The white people of the South," he asserted, "claim, or rather boast of, a race prepotency and inheritance as great as that of any breed of men in the world. But they clearly fail to show like attainment." He asked southerners,

Has it ever occurred to you that the people of New England blood, who have done and are doing most to make the white race great and glorious in this land, are the most reticent about extravagant claims to everlasting superiority? You protest too much. Your loud pretensions, backed up by such exclamatory outburst of passion, make upon the reflecting mind the impression that you entertain a sneaking suspicion of their validity.

Toward the turn of the century Negro writers, by way

of sanctioning and underwriting the arguments advanced by Williams and Miller, produced a veritable spate of histories and essays having to do with the life of the Negro in America and elsewhere. In 1888 William T. Alexander published a volume to establish the claims of the Negro's mental and intellectual equality with others. "By the closest analysis of the blood of each race," he argued,

> the slightest difference cannot be detected; and so, in the aspirations of the mind, or the impulses of the heart, we are all one common family, with nothing but the development of the mind through the channel of education to raise one man, or one people above another. . . . So far as noble characteristics are concerned, the colored race possess those traits to fully as great a degree as do the white.

W. H. Crogman, teaching Greek in Atlanta, paused long enough to write a book entitled, *The Progress of a Race*. The distinguished Negro physician, C. V. Roman, gave in his *American Civilization and the Negro* a striking argument in support of the biological equality of whites and Negroes. Benjamin Brawley, a student of English literature, forsook his field to write *The Negro Genius* and other works underscoring the intellectual powers of the Negro.

Other Negro intellectuals, from the beginning, were drawn into the field of what came to be known as Negro studies. Such Negro scholars as W.E.B. Du Bois and Carter G. Woodson established their standing in the field of American scholarship by dealing objectively and in a scholarly fashion with the problems related to the place of the Negro in American life. In pioneer sociological studies, definitive historical monographs, and trenchant essays they made a case not only for the Negro as a human being but also for the study of the Negro as a respectable field of inquiry by intellectuals regardless of race.

It soon became clear to many thoughtful Negroes that it was not enough to refute those who argued that the

Negro had no place in American life. It was necessary, they concluded, to become more active and more aggressive in the struggle to gain equality for all Negroes as well as for themselves. These Negroes had become alarmed at the increasing hostility that was everywhere evident at the turn of the century. The "legal" disfranchisement of the Negro was being written into the constitutions of the southern states in the 1890's and in the first decade of the twentieth century. Lynchings were on the increase—2,500 in the last sixteen years of the nineteenth century. A new form of terror, the urban race riot, had come into prominence— one in 1898, two in 1905, two in 1906, and several in 1908. This was enough to disturb even the more complacent of humans.

Negroes were also alarmed by the complacency that was being induced by the arguments of Booker T. Washington and his white supporters who insisted that if the Negroes were patient and worked hard, they would enjoy the respect and good will of the dominant elements of American society. Washington preached a gospel of "work and money" and subscribed to the view that the same qualities that made it possible for whites to rise in America would, when possessed by Negroes, cause them to rise likewise. The facts did not support this view, and thoughtful Negroes rejected it for the naïve reasoning that it obviously was. They had lost faith in such arguments as Washington advanced, and they began to demand their rights as citizens and as human beings.

The most articulate spokesman of the new, aggressive Negro was William E. B. Du Bois, who believed that the Negro could move toward equality only by expressing righteous indignation regarding his treatment and demanding his rights as a citizen. In 1904 he published his "Credo":

I believe that all men, black and brown, and white, are

brothers, varying through Time and Opportunity, in form and gift and feature, but differing in no essential particular, and alike in soul and in the possibility of infinite development.... I believe in Liberty for all men; the space to stretch their arms and their souls; the right to breathe and the right to vote, the freedom to choose their friends, enjoy the sunshine and ride on railroads, uncursed by color; thinking, dreaming, working as they will in a kingdom of God and love. . . .

It was the spirit expressed in the Credo that led to the calling of a conference of Negro leaders, under Du Bois' guidance, to meet in Niagara Falls, Canada, in June 1905.

The Niagara meeting, and the movement that grew out of it, was essentially the creation of the Negro intellectual. Those who met at Niagara Falls were among the best educated, most articulate, and most courageous Americans to be found anywhere. In the "Declaration of Principles" which they drew up, they insisted that Negroes should "protest emphatically and continually against the curtailment of their political rights . . . the denial of equal opportunities . . . in economic life" and discrimination in the public schools. They demanded "upright judges in courts, juries selected without discrimination on account of color and the same measure of punishment . . . for black as for white offenders." They denounced segregation in all its aspects and asserted that "any discrimination based simply on race or color is barbarous." In succeeding years the group organized a Department of Civil Rights which urged civil rights legislation in each northern state, an organization of state units to press for action, the repeal of segregation statutes, and the inclusion of Negroes on juries in southern states.

For the next two decades Negro intellectuals worked on a variety of fronts, but usually in the uncompromising spirit of the Niagara Movement. Many of them joined the National Association for the Advancement of Colored

People, when it was organized in 1909; and one of them, Du Bois, became editor of the *Crisis* and director of research. The fact that by 1914 most of the thirteen Negro members of the Board of Directors had been in the Niagara Movement indicates the extent to which the NAACP had a program that was consonant with the principles of the Niagara Movement. They joined in the organization's struggle in the courts to restore the vote to the Negro and to secure a fairer administration of justice. They also supported the organization's futile effort to secure federal legislation against lynching and in support of civil rights for all citizens.

Negro intellectuals were also sensitive to political currents and sought to force major parties to give some attention to the plight of the Negro. But they were neither naïve nor gullible. As early as the 1880's T. Thomas Fortune, the Negro editor and essayist, disillusioned by the betrayal of the Republican party, had urged Negroes to steer a course of political independence. Rejecting Booker T. Washington's policy of indifference to political activity, they criticized Presidents Roosevelt and Taft for their racial policies; and they demanded that President Wilson take a stand in support of decency in human relations. They urged Negroes to vote, wherever possible; and they helped launch the assault on the white Democratic primary, that was not to achieve complete victory until after the Second World War.

Most articulate Negro leaders enthusiastically supported their country in the great war that President Wilson described as one to save the world for democracy. But they had few illusions, particularly when segregation and discrimination in the army of democracy and when rioting against Negroes in defense industries indicated the nation's lack of commitment to democratic principles. Du Bois urged Negroes to "close ranks" behind their government; but this did not prevent him and others from pressing for equal treatment for Negro soldiers and urging the government to commission Negro officers. Negro lawyers, writers, doctors, teachers, and preachers participated in the New York protest parade against the terrorizing and murder of Negroes in East St. Louis in 1917. The Negro press roundly criticized the American government's treatment of Negro soldiers and its failure to protect Negroes on the home front. One of them, A. Philip Randolph's *Messenger*, even criticized Negroes for supporting the war effort. There can be no doubt that America's failure to maintain even a semblance of consistency between its profession and practice of democracy plunged Negro intellectuals into a mood of disillusionment and despair, from which they were to emerge only quite slowly in the postwar years.

When Du Bois assumed the role of leadership among Negro intellectuals at the beginning of the century, he recognized the obvious fact that their numbers were small and their burdens staggering. In 1903 he said, "The Talented Tenth of the Negro race must be made leaders of the thought and missionaries of culture among their people. No others can do this work and Negro colleges must train men for it. The Negro race, like all other races, is going to be saved by its exceptional men." It was a task that was all but impossible, not only because of the unceasing efforts of those who were determined that the Negro race was not to be saved, but also because the "Talented Tenth" was actually only a fraction of one-tenth of the Negro population. The number of Negroes obtaining a college and university education remained pitifully small; and most of those who were involved in higher education were securing their training in institutions that were often deficient in equipment and staff. Once out of the college or university the major task of these Negro graduates, as "leaders of thought and missionaries of culture," was not so much to think deeply about the major problems

confronting them and their country as to teach the funda-
mentals to unlettered Negroes. For decades, therefore, the
small group of would-be Negro intellectuals had little
opportunity to function as intellectuals, even when they
were prepared by virtue of training and interests to do so.

By the end of World War I, however, there emerged a
group of able, thoughtful, and articulate Negroes who
could claim the attention of their white counterparts and
contribute to the several fields of human enterprise. Perhaps they were not yet a tenth of the Negro population,
but that they were talented seems beyond question. Conditions favored their emergence. For two generations some
kind of educational opportunity, however limited, had
existed; and an increasing number had benefited from
higher education. More and more Negroes were moving
into northern communities, where educational and cultural opportunities were greater and where the old, nag-
ging fear gave way to a new sense of confidence and even
of importance. If northern whites succeeded in relegating
most Negroes to a ghetto existence, they utterly failed to
keep the masses subordinated or the more talented intimi-
dated and silent.

As Negro intellectuals surveyed the condition of
American life they could scarcely contain their bitterness
over what was happening to them and, indeed, to their
country. As they became more capable of discharging the
responsibilities of full citizenship, they were rejected even
more unequivocally than ever before by their white compatriots. They recalled the segregation and discrimination
in the army of the United States, as it fought to save the
world for democracy. They witnessed the craven and barbaric treatment of Negro soldiers as they returned to take
their places in a segregated society. Small wonder that
they became bitter and defiant and impatient; and in their
despair they cried out against social and economic wrongs,
against segregation and lynching. In poetry, prose, and

song they denounced the injustices and imperfections of the American democratic system.

While it cannot be said that Negro intellectuals retreated into a shell after World War I, their activities did suggest a frustration and a pessimism that expressed little hope for the future. Theirs was a bitter cry, no less anguished than that of their predecessors, but without the specific programs that characterized the intellectuals of an earlier generation. The tone had been set by James Weldon Johnson in 1913 when, in his poem celebrating the fiftieth anniversary of the Emancipation Proclamation, he declared that

> This land is ours by right of birth,
> This land is ours by right of toil;
> We helped to turn its virgin earth,
> Our sweat is in its fruitful soil.

Later, in 1922, Claude McKay went a step beyond Johnson by declaring that if Negroes must die they should not die like hogs, "hunted and penned in an inglorious spot," but like men, facing "the murderous, cowardly pack, pressed to the wall, dying but fighting back!"

The bitter criticism of the American social order was expressed in 1927 by E. Franklin Frazier in a remarkable article entitled, "The Pathology of Race Prejudice." In it Frazier declared that "The Negro-in-America is a form of insanity that overtakes white men." He went on to describe southern white people as afflicted with a Negro complex that made them incapable of rendering just decisions where whites and Negroes were concerned, although in other connections they could speak with all sincerity regarding "the majesty of the law, the sacredness of human rights, and the advantages of democracy." The depth of the despair of Negro intellectuals was symbolized by the decision of Du Bois in 1933 that it would be best for Negroes to turn their backs on efforts to integrate into American society and, instead, to cultivate a Negro social order completely apart from that of the whites.

What McKay, Frazier, and Du Bois were reflecting was a frustration that was typical of the Negro intellectuals of the post-war period. This frustration was seen in the writings of Countee Cullen, Jessie Fauset, Jean Toomer, and numerous others. Its expression was eloquent but rather lofty, harsh, but hardly constructive. James Weldon Johnson remained with the NAACP, and the organization recruited some new, able talent. But Du Bois drifted away; and his going symbolized, in a sense, the lack of a viable program for America on the part of Negro intellectuals. This fact is not in derogation of them, for persons dedicated to the life of the mind must follow their interests and predilections; and it can be said that as Negroes grew in intellectual stature they developed numerous interests that, in one way or another, indicated their own intellectual emancipation. They became scientists, political scientists, social scientists, novelists, essayists, journalists. To some of them the Negro problem became a matter of intellectual if not merely academic interest.

Understandably, Negro intellectuals, whose main interests were in the larger fields of knowledge, found it difficult to pursue abstruse problems in mathematics or physics in terms of their status as Negroes. Those who were concerned with French foreign policy in Turkey or with the finer points of classical archaeology or even with the partition of Africa had more than a full-time job before them if they would attain success in their chosen field. This, too, was a most important approach to the solution of the most pressing social problem that the United States faced in the twentieth century. In a sense, the Negro intellectual became somewhat estranged from the everyday task of coping with the problem of being a Negro in America. It was not that the problem ceased, but that he tended to live above it or apart from it as he sought to live merely as a human being.

But he was soon to learn that any belief that he could live above the problem or apart from it was only an illusion; and soon enough he came to realize it. If Booker T. Washington's view that Negroes could solve their problems merely by being constructive, law-abiding citizens was erroneous, equally so was the Negro intellectual's view that he could live above or apart from the problem of being a Negro in the United States. Negro historians, whatever their attainments, were still subjected to as much discrimination and segregation as the humblest of their black brothers; and Negro scientists, even as they uncovered the hidden mysteries of the universe, were still unable to vote in the South or to secure decent housing in the North.

Aside from the cruel facts of life that were daily revealed even to the most insensitive of Negroes, the experiences of the Second World War had much to do with transforming the lofty Negro intellectual of the 1920's and 1930's into an active, vigorous protagonist for the improvement of all conditions of American life. Already, the favorable climate for an expanded role of the intellectual in American life had been created by Franklin D. Roosevelt and his New Deal. President Roosevelt drew large numbers of America's intellectual elite into the government, and even a considerable number of highly trained Negroes were given an opportunity to serve in rather carefully limited roles as advisors. When the war came, the waste of Negro manpower on the home front as well as on the fighting front, the widespread segregation and discrimination in and out of the armed services, and the untold indignities to which even the Negro intellectual elite was subjected were enough to convince any Negro that there was a basic battle for human decency to be fought and won in the arena of the American social order.

In the 1930's some Negro intellectuals had entertained the notion of joining forces with one or another of the left-wing radical movements to remake the United States in the image of a preconceived revolutionary utopia. Few of them, however, actually made the move, perhaps because it seemed both impracticable and, indeed, no solution at all. Others had thought in terms of forming a united front with labor, but for the moment little came of this as a technique for remaking American society. By the time that Negro intellectuals had experienced the searing effects of the Second World War, they came to believe that no single or simple solution to the vastly complex problem of improving the relations of America's citizens was possible. They had become convinced that, as Myrdal put it, "the vicious circle of keeping Negroes down is so perfected by such interlocking caste controls that the Negroes must attempt to move the whole system by attacking as many points as possible." It was this conviction that swept them out into the field of active, practical endeavor, characterized by countless approaches and techniques.

Taking their cue from the successful threat of Negroes to march on Washington in 1940 to secure their rights, post-war Negro intellectuals became more activist than ever. They were in the crusade for a permanent Fair Employment Practices Committee, that captured the imagination of President Truman in 1947 and 1948. They participated in the rallies to save the FEPC, writing and speaking about the desirability of improving the economic conditions among Negroes. They were active in the effort of the Legal Defense and Educational Fund of the NAACP to break down segregation in the public schools and elsewhere. More than a score of Negro social scientists worked on the nonlegal research staff of the fund and contributed significantly to the writing of the briefs in the school desegregation cases. Negro college men and women in their American Council on Human Rights formulated new, imaginative programs to carry through the struggle for equality to a successful conclusion. Later, Negro intellectuals joined their fellows in contributing ideas and techniques for boycotting the buses in Montgomery and segregated white business establishments in many parts of the South and North. They joined new direct action organizations, sat in lunch rooms, rode to freedom on desegregated interstate carriers.

Nowhere was the new power and drive of the Negro intellectual more clearly manifested than in the writer—historian, sociologist, novelist, playwright, essayist, and others. Negro historians like Carter G. Woodson with all the objectivity that they could muster, increased the tempo of their delineation of the American Negro as an integral part of the history of his country. Negro sociologists, like E. Franklin Frazier, identified and analyzed numerous problems that continued to confound and divide the country along specious racial lines. Novelists like Ralph Ellison and playwrights like Lorraine Hansberry effectively employed their talents to describe the tragedy of American race relations in plots that were merely thinly disguised real life situations. Essayists like James Baldwin couched the great American moral dilemma in a new and moving eloquence. And one of the truly great triumphs of the Negro intellectual was the increasing association with him of the white intellectual in a cause that was, indeed, a common cause for all America. In words and deeds—in powerful literary tracts and in sit-in demonstrations—some white intellectuals have moved ahead of their compatriots, because they have caught the vision of the vast and significant implications of the American race problem for the survival of decency in their country.

No one could wisely claim for the Negro intellectual, any more than for the white intellectual, that his transformation has been either complete or altogether in one direction. It is the very essence of the intellectual life that it must be free to follow the path dictated by its insights, skills, and conscience. The experiences and influences bearing on an individual are so numerous and varied that it is inconceivable that they could produce unanimity regarding either goals or approaches. What we have seen during the past generation has been the gradual awakening of an increasing number of thoughtful Americans to the urgency of doing something about a fundamental American social problem. That Negroes have been more sensitive to the urgency is understandable, in view of their own plight. That whites in increasing numbers have eventually become aware of it was inevitable, as they came to it in terms of their own involvement and responsibility.

Meanwhile, others—Negroes and whites—have moved in utterly different directions. Some of them, preoccupied with work unrelated to this central problem, have had neither the interest nor the inclination to become personally involved in it. Others, without any immediate stimulus, have remained indifferent and even uncommitted. Still others, with interests tied up with maintaining the *status quo*, have used their talents to prevent any significant changes. Even now, as in the eighteenth and nineteenth centuries, no one side of an argument enjoys a monopoly of all the available talent.

This discussion of the Negro intellectual has been necessarily concerned largely with the problem of race that confronts him. That is because, for the most part, he has been unable to escape the problem of race; and much of his talent has inevitably been utilized in the effort to cope with the problem. Surely, one of the great tragedies of American life has been the manner in which one's intellectual resources, whether they be of the order of a moron or of a genius, have been used up in the effort to survive as a decent, self-respecting human being. Negro intellectuals in increasing numbers have come to appreciate this as one of the stark, grimly tragic facts of life. In increasing numbers they have come to regard this fact as a challenge which they would not escape, even if they could. Until they can live as other human beings—pushing back the frontiers of knowledge, writing a great novel, composing a beautiful symphony—Negro intellectuals have come to realize that they must carry on the fight, in concert with others, to make America true to her own ideals of equality and democracy. The realization of this fact and the continued preoccupation with a program to achieve success constitute the transformation of the Negro intellectual.

POSTSCRIPT*

Clarence B. Hilberry
President of Wayne State University

At Wayne State University we have always tried to keep the graduates at the center of the commencement ceremonies. From time to time we have found a man with something to say of particular importance to you who are graduating and then we have had a commencement speaker. But in general we like to think of this as an occasion for a summing up, a moment for a restatement of faith.

This year we have dedicated ourselves to the formal recognition of the centennial of President Lincoln's proclamation that ended slavery, and to the study of American life and the place of the Negro in it in these last one hundred years. We began planning this program on a national, and indeed an international scale, twelve months ago, because to us the recognition of human dignity and the pro-

*An informal address by President Hilberry given at Commencement, June 20, 1963.

263

vision of equal opportunity is not a sudden crisis. It is deeply imbedded in the daily life of your university as anyone who looks about at the faculty and student body will see.

As Americans we have been—all of us—a free people for one hundred years, but we have been very slow in developing social equality. The slowness of this process has always been a matter of great concern to this student body, to the faculty, to the Board of Governors and to myself, speaking to you as I do out of thirty-three years of association with Wayne. As its president, I want to sketch the tradition of concern for human rights at this university so that you may understand its character, a character that you, too, have helped to shape during your years here and which you pass tonight to a new generation of students; and I want to speak particularly about the moral crisis in which we find ourselves today.

One hundred years ago, the United States was locked in a struggle to see whether any nation, "conceived in liberty and dedicated to the proposition that all men are created equal," could survive. At that time President Lincoln issued a rather simple Proclamation giving notice that on January 1, 1863, "all persons held as slaves" within the United States, "shall be then, thenceforward and forever free." It is good for us to remember that there were many leaders who counselled President Lincoln against taking this action—just as Senator Thurmond today is violently opposing President Kennedy's civil rights program.

Five years after the Emancipation Proclamation our College of Medicine was founded, the first unit of what we now know as Wayne State University. Two years later, in 1870, the first Negro enrolled in the college. He was a Canadian from just across the river at Amherstburg, and he went out from this university to found and become Dean of a Negro medical school in Louisville, Kentucky.

A few years later another Negro, this time a freedman from Georgia, reached Detroit, went through our schools, and entered the College of Medicine. He graduated in 1883 and returned to the South to practice medicine.

In January of this year, 1963, the Vice-President of the United States, Mr. Lyndon B. Johnson, came here to address the student body and leaders of this community and to receive an honorary degree in a special convocation launching the celebration of the Centennial of the Emancipation Proclamation. At the January commencement ceremonies we recognized the courage and integrity of Mr. Thurgood Marshall and Mr. Ralph McGill in the field of civil rights, and we conferred your university's honorary degree upon them. Most recently we have had a special convocation for Professor Gunnar Myrdal, the world's leading scholar in the field whose book *An American Dilemma* is the best statement yet made of the problems of freedom and equality still facing us as American citizens. Professor Myrdal came all the way from Stockholm, Sweden, to join us in this celebration, spending several days in this community. On the night before he left the campus for home he spoke publicly about this university and about the joining together here throughout a whole year of the country's leading men in the field of human rights. About each of you, as he had seen you during his days here, he said: "You have equality in your hearts as well as in your minds."

This evaluation of the spirit of the Wayne State campus is not made only by foreign visitors. A member of your faculty, a relative newcomer to this state, who occupies a joint position with our sister universities, recently said to me: "I don't know another campus where integration is more complete, where there seem to be no barriers between people, where individuals are recognized for their own value." These events and these statements are merely the latest in a long series that are an integral part of your heritage and which you should be very proud indeed to own—and quick to defend.

Like the College of Medicine, the Colleges of Nursing, and Education, and Social Work have exerted powerful influences in this community toward the full recognition of human rights. Their work has come from dozens of men and women speaking out of deep conviction, over many years. It is their sorrow, in which we all share, that so much still remains to be done.

What continues to be important, however, is that the graduates of these colleges will march tonight before us to receive their diplomas. They will be joined by the engineers, lawyers, pharmacists, business men, and scientists. Each of you, as you move into the vital professional life of this metropolitan area and this state, has been exposed to the arts and sciences whose function it is to liberalize our lives—to make us rich because they make us whole men. You will carry with you into our broader life our convictions about human dignity and human rights.

The members of the class of 1963—like all the classes that have preceded them—will be a cross-section of our people. You are an elite group only in your individual accomplishments. This university proudly recognizes that the men and women of this graduating class are here only because of their native ability, their strong motivation, the devotion of their families, and the dedication of the citizens of our state. This is what your university means by social democracy. The academic procession here tonight is our Walk for Freedom, and we shall continue it twice a year into the distant future.

When the peoples of the world think about Detroit—and everyone in the world who can read and many who cannot have heard about our city—they remember us for two major achievements. The first is the technological revolution which created mass production. The development of the assembly line was an astonishing achievement.

After the first assembly line was put together, Mr. Ford took another simple step—a step as simple as Mr. Lincoln's and as radical in its shaping of history. He introduced the five-dollar day, because he understood that mass production had to have a mass-consuming public. As simply as that Detroit set about creating a society in which desperate want would disappear and in which men would be freed from economic slavery—we set out to create an economy of abundance.

In those days, Wayne State was not yet even organized as a university. The role we played was small, but it was significant. We offered a higher education to the sons and daughters of the men who were creating this new society. Many of them were your fathers and grandfathers; some are in this room. They were immigrants from every corner of the world, drawn to this dynamic city by a new dream. One of the important minority groups were the Ukranians (who came here to escape the Russian Revolution) and many central European Jews. They were a different kind of minority. They suffered from economic and social discrimination when they first arrived, but they were not culturally disadvantaged.

In the 1920's, the students of this university represented all the major races, religions, and nationalities. They studied side by side in the classrooms of Old Main, worked in the library and the laboratories, competed with one another for the top place in the class, put pressure on the faculty to give them more and more and more.

By the 1930's Wayne State was playing a larger role. During this decade, the conception of industrial democracy emerged clearly enough for men to test it. Sometimes the test meant slugging it out with fists; sometimes it meant sit-down strikes. But the idea was never lost; and as Wayne's graduates entered the labor force through the ranks of management, or labor, or the professions, the concept of human rights grew stronger. Two of your fellow alumni: Louis Seaton, a representative of the world's largest corporation, and Walter Reuther, a representative of our greatest union, have done as much as any two individuals to shape the ideas and understandings and agreements under which American industry operates today. These were not just economic agreements; they involved basic human rights. Their achievements are social science in action, and they are achievements of which each of you can be proud.

Since all this is a natural part of your heritage, I can speak to you specifically about the moral crisis that is immediately before us. No matter how well we have done, American universities, including Wayne State, have not done nearly well enough in helping the Negro achieve his full share of human rights. We have accepted the talented Negro who has found his way to the admissions office, but we have done too little actively to seek him out. We must find new ways to seek him out,—with scholarships, because he is still the most economically disadvantaged of our people. We must give him personal encouragement to seek a higher education because he is still of the culturally deprived group in this country.

Wayne State University has been working closely with President Kennedy's Committee on Equal Employment Opportunities, especially since Vice-President Johnson launched the Centennial celebration in Detroit in January. We have examined our own personnel practices to see if we can make the opportunities for employment at the University known to a wider number of people. As a result of the proved ability of this university to deal with such matters, Mr. Hobart Taylor, who directly represents Vice-President Johnson, has organized regional conferences on our campus. There have been three of them this spring, and in addition members of the faculty have been working in Washington with President Kennedy's Committee on Equal Employment Opportunities. At the June meeting, the Board of Governors approved the university's entering into an agreement with the federal government for a carefully conceived plan for progress in the area of human rights where we might be most helpful. We are now prepared to make an extraordinary effort to meet the extraordinary conditions of today.

The pressure of Negro Americans for full recognition now is wholly justified. It goes beyond the conditions of humanity for the rest of us to expect them to be patient any longer. As the graduates pass across this platform, you will see that our Negro citizens are freely welcomed into some professions, and that forces which are beyond their control as individuals limit their participation in others. That some of these forces are purely educational does not lessen or alter the need for sharp change. You will see that as Americans we have much to do. Even if we get about it with dispatch it will take many years.

Some individuals in America appear to believe that greatness of mind and greatness of spirit are related to the color of our skins. Those of us who have come out of the tradition of this university, however, know that greatness of mind and spirit are related only to membership in the human family. It is in this knowledge that we must work together at Wayne State University in this metropolitan community, in this state, and in this nation for human liberty and human rights.

THE EMANCIPATION PROCLAMATION*

BY THE PRESIDENT OF THE UNITED STATES OF AMERICA.

A PROCLAMATION

———————

Whereas on the 22d day of September, A.D. 1862, a proclamation was issued by the President of the United States, containing, among other things, the following, to wit:

That on the 1st day of January, A.D. 1863, all persons held as slaves within any State or designated part of a State, the people whereof shall then be in rebellion against the United States, shall be then, thenceforward, and forever free; and the executive government of the United States, including the military and naval authority thereof, will recognize and maintain the freedom of such persons, and will do no act or acts to repress such persons, or any of them, in any efforts they may make for their actual freedom.

*James D. Richardson, *A Compilation of the Messages and Papers of the Presidents, 1789-1897*, published by Authority of Congress, 1900, VI, 157-59.

That the Executive will, on the 1st day of January a-foresaid, by proclamation, designate the States and parts of States, if any, in which the people thereof, respectively, shall then be in rebellion against the United States; and the fact that any State or the people thereof shall on that day be in good faith represented in the Congress of the United States by members chosen thereto at elections wherein a majority of the qualified voters of such State shall have participated shall, in the absence of strong countervailing testimony, be deemed conclusive evidence that such State and the people thereof are not then in rebellion against the United States.

Now, therefore, I, Abraham Lincoln, President of the United States, by virtue of the power in me vested as Commander in Chief of the Army and Navy of the United States in time of actual armed rebellion against the authority and Government of the United States, and as a fit and necessary war measure for suppressing said rebellion, do, on this 1st day of January, A.D. 1863, and in accordance with my purpose so to do, publicly proclaimed for the full period of one hundred days from the day first above mentioned, order and designate as the States, and parts of States wherein the people thereof, respectively, are this day in rebellion against the United States the following, to wit:

Arkansas, Texas, Louisiana (except the parishes of St. Bernard, Plaquemines, Jefferson, St. John, St. Charles, St. James, Ascension, Assumption, Terrebonne, Lafourche, St. Mary, St. Martin, and Orleans, including the city of New Orleans), Mississippi, Alabama, Florida, Georgia, South Carolina, North Carolina, and Virginia (except the forty-eight counties designated as West Virginia, and also the counties of Berkeley, Accomac, Northampton, Elizabeth City, York, Princess Anne and Norfolk, including the cities of Norfolk and Portsmouth), and which excepted parts are for the present left precisely as if this proclamation were not issued.

And by virtue of the power and for the purpose aforesaid, I do order and declare that all persons held as slaves within said designated States and parts of States are and henceforward shall be free; and that the executive government of the United States, including the military and naval authorities thereof, will recognize and maintain the freedom of said persons.

And I hereby enjoin upon the people so declared to be free to abstain from all violence, unless in necessary self-defense; and I recommend to them that in all cases when allowed they labor faithfully for reasonable wages.

And I further declare and make known that such persons of suitable condition will be received into the armed service of the United States to garrison forts, positions, stations, and other places and to man vessels of all sorts in said service.

And upon this act, sincerely believed to be an act of justice, warranted by the Constitution upon military necessity, I invoke the considerate judgment of mankind and the gracious favor of Almighty God.

In witness whereof I have hereunto set my hand and caused the seal of the United States to be affixed.

Done at the City of Washington, this 1st day of January A.D. 1863, and of the Independence of the United States of America the eighty-seventh [year].

[SEAL]   ABRAHAM LINCOLN

By the President:

WILLIAM H. SEWARD, *Secretary of State*

NOTES ON
THE CONTRIBUTORS

Arnold M. Rose holds B.A. (1938), M.A. (1940), and
Ph.D. (1946) degrees from the University of Chicago. He
has served as research associate for the Carnegie Corporation, statistician for the United States War Department,
and professor of sociology at Bennington College, Washington University, and the University of Minnesota.

He collaborated with Gunnar Myrdal and Richard
Sterner in the research and writing of *An American Dilem-
ma*, published in 1944. His other writings include *The
Negro in America* (1948); *The Negro's Morale: Group
Identification and Protest* (1949); *Union Solidarity: In-
ternal Cohesion in a Labor Union* (1952); *Theory and
Method in the Social Sciences* (1954); and *Sociology: The
Study of Human Relations* (1956). He edited *Institutions
of Advanced Societies* (1958) and *Human Behavior and
Social Processes* (1962).

Professor Rose has served as president, Society for the

Study of Social Problems, 1955-56; president, Midwest Sociological Society, 1961-62; and chairman, International Group for Psychiatric Sociology, since 1956.

The HONORABLE LYNDON B. JOHNSON, President of the United States, is a graduate of Southwest State Teachers' College and the Law School of Georgetown University. From 1928 to 1931 he was a teacher and principal in the public schools of Texas. He served as secretary to Texas Congressman Kleberg from 1931 to 1935 and as Texas Director of the National Youth Administration from 1936 to 1937.

A member of the United States House of Representatives from 1937 to 1948 and of the Senate from 1949 to 1960, he served as the Senate Democratic Leader during his last seven years in the Senate.

During the Second World War, he served in the South Pacific as a Lt. Commander in the U.S. Navy and was awarded the Silver Star for gallantry under fire. From 1961 to 1963 he was Vice-President of the United States. Among his varied responsibilities in this position is the chairmanship of the President's Committee on Equal Employment Opportunities. He became President on November 22, 1963.

JOHN HOPE FRANKLIN received his A.B. degree from Fisk University in 1935, his A.M. and Ph.D. degrees from Harvard University in 1936 and 1941, respectively.

He has taught at Fisk University, St. Augustine's College, North Carolina College at Durham, and Howard University. In 1956, he became professor and chairman of the Department of History at Brooklyn College. He has served as visiting professor at Harvard University, University of Wisconsin, Cornell University, the University of California at Berkeley, and the University of Hawaii. In Europe he has twice served as professor at the Salzburg Seminar in American Studies and at Cambridge University. He has accepted an appointment as professor of American history at the University of Chicago, beginning in 1964.

His published works include *The Free Negro in North Carolina: 1790-1860*; *The Civil War Diary of James T. Ayers*; *From Slavery to Freedom: A History of American Negroes*; *The Militant South*; and an edition of Tourgee's *A Fool's Errand*. His most recent book is *Reconstruction after the Civil War*, published in 1961.

Professor Franklin has served on the U.S. National Commission for UNESCO, is a member of the Fisk University Board of Trustees and the Board of Directors of the Salzburg Seminar in American Studies.

CARLETON L. LEE was graduated A.B. from Talladega College in 1933, and received his A.M. degree from the University of Chicago (1935), his D.B. from Chicago Theological Seminary (1937), and his Ph.D. from the University of Chicago (1953).

Combining an interest in theology, teaching, and social work, he was a case aide for the Chicago Relief Administration, 1938-39; chaplain of Tuskegee Institute, 1947-53; and a fraternal worker for the World Council of Churches at Mainz, Kastel am Rhein, West Germany, 1953-55.

During 1944-45 he was professor of philosophy and acting dean of Turner Theological Seminary; and from 1955 to 1957, professor and chairman of the Department of Philosophy and Religion, Tougaloo Southern Christian College. Since 1957 he has been director of religious activities, professor of philosophy and religion, and chairman of the Humanities Division, Central State College, Ohio.

Professor Lee is the author of articles in the field of religious thought and human relations.

BROADUS N. BUTLER was born in Alabama. He received his A.B. degree from Talladega College in 1941; his A.M. (1947) and Ph.D. (1952) degrees from the University of Michigan.

From 1951 to 1953 he served as a staff member of the Church Youth Service, Wayne County Juvenile Court. After a year of teaching at St. Augustine College, he was dean of guidance and assistant professor of humanities at Talladega College until 1956. For the past seven years he has been a member of the Wayne State University faculty. In 1956 he was academic adviser and instructor in English. He has been assistant to the dean, College of Liberal Arts, since 1957 and graduate officer, College of Liberal Arts, since 1959.

He has written articles on philosophy, education, politics, and human relations for both scholarly and popular publications, and since 1962 has contributed a weekly editorial column to the *Michigan Chronicle.*

Active in local and national professional and philanthropic organizations, he is a board member of the Association for Study of Negro Life and History; the School of Theology, Episcopal Diocese of Michigan; the Greater Detroit Fair Housing Committee; the United Community Services of Metropolitan Detroit. He is a member of the Mayor's Task Force for Manpower Retraining Program Committee.

Born in Dalecarlia region, Sweden, in 1898, GUNNAR MYRDAL studied law at the University of Stockholm and was graduated in 1923. He received a doctorate of laws in economics in 1927 and was appointed docent in political economy at the same university.

During 1929-30 he traveled in the United States on a Rockefeller fellowship, and in 1930-31 he was in Switzerland as associate professor in the Post-Graduate Institute of International Studies at Geneva. In 1933 he was appointed to the Lars Hierta chair of political economy and public finance at the University of Stockholm.

Active in public affairs in Sweden, he was advisor to the Swedish government on social, economic, and fiscal affairs, 1933 to 1938, and secretary of commerce for Sweden from 1945 to 1947. From 1947 to 1957 he was executive secretary of the United Nations Economic Commission in Europe.

In 1938 Professor Myrdal gave the Godkin lectures at Harvard University, later collected in the volume *Population: a Problem for Democracy* (1940). In 1937 the Carnegie Corporation chose Professor Myrdal to direct a study of the American Negro, and published his report and conclusions as *An American Dilemma* (1944).

His many publications in the field of political economy include *The Political Element in the Development of Economic Theory* (1953); *Development and Under-Development: The Mechanism of National and International Inequality* (1956); *An International Economy: Problems and Prospects* (1956); *Economic Theory and Underdeveloped Regions* (1957); and *Beyond the Welfare State* (1960).

Professor Myrdal is a member of the Royal Academy of Sweden and a fellow of the Econometric Society. He is an honorary member of the American Economic Association.

Born in Charleston, South Carolina, G. FRANKLIN EDWARDS received his B.A. degree from Fisk University in 1936 and his Ph.D. from the University of Chicago in 1952. During 1941-42 and 1946-47 he was Rosenwald Fellow at the University of Chicago.

From 1937 to 1939, he was instructor in social studies at Fessenden Academy, and was assistant professor of sociology at Fisk from 1937 to 1939. Now professor of sociology at Howard University, he has been a member of the faculty since 1941.

He is the author of many articles and several books in the field of sociology, including *The Negro Professional Class* (1959).

ROBERT C. WEAVER holds a Ph.D. degree from Harvard University and has lectured and taught at Northwestern University, Columbia University, and New York University.

Interested in housing and urban problems, to which he has devoted the past twenty-five years, he has been executive director of the Mayor's Committee on Race Relations for the city of Chicago, deputy commissioner of housing for the state of New York, and vice-chairman of the Housing and Redevelopment Board of the city of New York.

He is the author of two books and numerous articles on minority problems, housing, and urban affairs.

DONALD B. KING was graduated from Washington State University Law School in 1954; received his LL.B. degree from Harvard Law School in 1957; and his LL.M. degree from New York University School of Law. In the summers of 1960, 1961, and 1962, he received a Ford Foundation grant for the Summer Program for Teachers of Law.

During 1957-58 he was instructor of law, University of Washington Law School. In 1959 he went to Dickinson Law School as visiting assistant professor of law, and was assistant professor of law at the same university 1960-62. Since 1962 he has been associate professor of law at Wayne State University.

Professor King is the author of numerous articles in legal periodicals and journals primarily in the areas of civil liberties, legal education, international law, and criminal law. He was associate editor of the *Foreign Exchange Bulletin* in 1962 and editor in 1963.

He is a member of the Washington State and American Bar Associations.

Born in Macon, Georgia, CHARLES W. QUICK was graduated A.B. from Talladega College in 1935; LL.B. from Harvard Law School in 1938, and LL.M. from New York University School of Law. Returning to Harvard Law

School in 1939 for research and writing, he later practiced law in Cleveland until his appointment to the Office of Price Administration as assistant general counsel in charge of rationing for the United States.

He was instructor at North Carolina Law School, 1940-41, and at Howard University Law School, 1948-59. During a year of graduate work at New York University School of Law, he received a Kenneson research fellowship. In 1957-58, while on leave from Howard University, he was appointed senior research fellow in law and the behavioral sciences at the University of Chicago Law School. He was a visiting professor at Wayne State University Law School, 1958-59, and was appointed professor of law in 1959.

Professor Quick has published articles on various aspects of the law of evidence, constitutional law, bankruptcy, and legal education. He is associate director of the Regional Delinquency Control Training Center at Wayne State University.

He has lectured widely at American colleges and universities, including Emory University, University of Cincinnati, Monteith College, and Morgan State College. In 1954 he was one of the counsel in the school segregation cases before the United States Supreme Court, and is now one of the legal consultants of the Legal Defense Fund of the National Office of the NAACP.

He is a member of the Ohio, Federal, and United States Supreme Court Bars.

JAMES Q. WILSON holds an A.B. degree from the University of Redlands (1952), and received his A.M. (1957) and Ph.D. (1959) degrees from the University of Chicago.

He taught at the University of Chicago during 1960-61. Since 1961 he has been a lecturer on government at Harvard University and a member of the Joint Center for Urban Studies at Harvard and the Massachusetts Institute of Technology.

He is the author of *The Amateur Democrat: Club Poli-*

tics in Three Cities, and co-author (with Edward C. Banfield) of a forthcoming book, *City Politics.*

RAYFORD W. LOGAN has been chairman of the Department
of History at Howard University since 1942. A graduate
of Williams College (A.B., 1917; A.M., 1929) and Harvard
University (A.M., 1932; Ph.D., 1936), he has taught at
Virginia Union University and Atlanta University. He has
also served as acting dean of the Graduate School at
Howard (1942-44) and as a member of the program of
African Studies since 1954.

He is the author of *The Diplomatic Relations of the
U.S. with Haiti, 1776-1891; The Negro and the Postwar
World: A Primer* (1945); *The African Mandates in World
Politics* (1948); *The Negro in American Life and Thought:
The Nadir, 1877-1901* (1957); and *The Negro in the United
States* (1957). Edited works include *What the Negro
Wants* (1944) and *Memoirs of a Monticello Slave* (1951).

Professor Logan was a member of the Board of Editors
of *Hispanic American History,* 1949-50, and was editor of
Journal of Negro History and *Negro History Bulletin,*
1950-51.

A graduate of Kentucky State College, WHITNEY M.
YOUNG, JR., did graduate work at Massachusetts Institute
of Technology and at the University of Minnesota, where
he received a master's degree in social work.

From 1954 to 1961 he was dean of the Atlanta University
School of Social Work, and he has taught at St. Catherine's
College, the University of Nebraska, and Creighton Uni-
versity. During 1960-61 he was a visiting scholar at Har-
vard University under a special grant from the Rockefeller
Foundation.

He is currently a member of the President's Committee
on Youth Employment, and of the President's Committee
on Equal Opportunity in the Armed Forces; he is vice-

president of the National Association of Social Workers.

In 1960 he received the Outstanding Alumni Award from the University of Minnesota; North Carolina A. & T. College honored him with the LL.D. degree in June 1961.

C. ERIC LINCOLN is a graduate of Le Moyne College (A.B., 1947); Fisk University (M.A., 1954); University of Chicago (D.B., 1956); and Boston University (M.Ed., 1960; Ph.D., 1960).

An ordained minister of the Methodist Church, he is now professor of social relations and administrative assistant to the president of Clark College, Atlanta. He has been guest lecturer at Colby College, Emory University, Boston University, Massachusetts Institute of Technology, Harvard University, and Dartmouth College.

He is the author of *The Black Muslims in America* (1961), and of many articles on American Negro protest movements.

CLARENCE B. HILBERRY was named the fourth president of Wayne State University July 1, 1953, having served as acting president since the preceding September. He came to Wayne in 1930 as a member of the faculty of the Department of English, and later became head of the department. Subsequently, he was appointed dean of administration and served in that position until his appointment to the presidency. Prior to coming to Detroit, he had taught English at Albion College and at the Y.M.C.A. College in Chicago.

President Hilberry earned his A.B. and A.M. degrees from Oberlin and his Ph.D. from the University of Chicago, in the field of English literature. Albion College honored him with the LL.D. degree in 1954. In 1957 he received three honorary degrees: LL.D., Michigan State University; LL.D., Oberlin College; Sc.D. in business administration, Cleary College. He received an honorary

LL.D. degree from Hillsdale College in 1962 and from Detroit Institute of Technology in 1963.

President Hilberry has been active in the work of the North Central Association of Colleges and Secondary Schools. He has served on the NCA Commission on Colleges and Universities whose function is to evaluate for purposes of accreditation the institutions of higher education in the nineteen-state North Central region. He is now a member and, at its inception, served as chairman of the Committee on NCA Leadership Training and Studies, developing a program underwritten by the Carnegie Corporation and designed to provide guided field experiences and conferences for young men who show promise of becoming leaders in higher education. His contributions were recognized by his recent election as an honorary member of the North Central Association, an honor equivalent to an earned degree in educational statesmanship. Recently, President Hilberry served as president of the Association of Urban Universities and is currently a representative of the AUU on the Board of Commissioners of the National Commission on Accrediting.

President Hilberry also serves on the boards of many local cultural and social agencies among which are the Detroit Institute of Cancer Research, the Detroit Symphony Orchestra, the Economic Club of Detroit, Cranbrook School, the Young Men's Christian Association, and the United Foundation.

INDEX

Index

American Council on Human Rights, 259
American creed, 219, 237, 239; precepts and idealism of, 46; religion and the development of, 48; defined, 238; Negro commitment to, 240
American Dilemma, 183, 265, 273, 277
American Economic Association, 277
American Mercury, 193
American Revolution, 1-2, 49
Amos and Andy, 193, 194
Anderson, Archibald W., 199-200
Ann Arbor, Mich., 37
Anthropology, 201
Anti-Negro organization and Civil War sentiment, 92-93
Anti-lynching legislation, 61
Anti-slavery: societies, 73; Quakers, 79; candidates, 85; organization, 88
Anti-Slavery Society, 79
"The Apartment," 195
Appomattox (Battle of), 12
Apprenticeship training programs, 131, 218
Aptheker, Herbert, 50
Arabic, 231
Area Redevelopment Administration, 132
Argentina, 201
Arkansas, 217; national guard, 196
Armageddon, 228, 231, 233; Battle of, 228, 232; complex, 236
Arnett, B. W., 189
Aruba, 203
Asia, 96, 220
Assembly line, 266
Association for the Study of Negro Life and History, 187, 201, 276
Association of Urban Universities, 282

Athens, Ga., 194
Atlanta, Ga., 24, 173, 188, 216, 250; riots of 1906, 57; University, 280
"Atlanta Compromise Speech," 188, 191
Atlanta Conference, eighth, 48
Atlanta Negro Voters League, 173
Atlantic, 192
Attorney General, U.S., 70
Automation, 132, 136, 181, 200, 216, 217

Baker v. Carr, 197
Baldwin, James, 260
Baldwin, Mrs. Ruth Standish, 211
Banfield, Edward C., 280
Banneker, Benjamin, 246
Baptists, 48
Baptist Association of Savannah, 49
Barnett, Ross R., 211
Barton, Rebecca, 65
Battle Creek, Mich., 73, 80
Beard, Charles: pseudo-objectivity of, 41
"Before You Migrate—Investigate," 217
Belgian Congo, 102, 115, 198
Bennington College, 273
Benton, Thomas H., 86
Berlin, West. *See* West Berlin
Bethel African Methodist Episcopal Church, 82, 85
Beyond the Welfare State, 277
Bibb, Henry, 73, 85
"Big Boy Leaves Home," 68
Bilbo, Theodore G., 211
Birmingham, Ala., 196
"The Birth of a Nation," 195
Blackburn, Thornton and Mrs., 79
Blackburn Riot of 1833, 79, 81
"Black Codes," 36
Black Islam, 223, 228
"Black Laws," 189

284

The manuscript was prepared for publication by Mrs. Barbara Woodward. The book is designed by Richard Kinney. The text type face is Linotype Caledonia designed by W. A. Dwiggins in 1940. The display face is American Type founders' Caslon 540, a modern cutting based on designs by William Caslon in the 18th Century.

The book is printed on Glatfelter, P. & S. Wove and bound in Bancrofts Linen finished cloth over boards. Manufactured in the United States of America.